Professional Standards for Teachers and School Leaders

A key to school improvement

Edited by Howard Green

RoutledgeFalmer
Taylor & Francis Group

LONDON AND NEW YORK

First published 2004
by RoutledgeFalmer
2 Park Square, Milton Park, Abingdon, Oxfordshire, OX14 4RN
1004608455
Simultaneously published in the USA and Canada
by RoutledgeFalmer
29 West 35th Street, New York, NY 10001

RoutledgeFalmer is an imprint of the Taylor & Francis Group

Typeset in Sabon by Wearset Ltd, Boldon, Tyne and Wear
Printed and bound in Great Britain by Antony Rowe Ltd,
Chippenham, Wiltshire

British Library Cataloguing in Publication Data
A catalogue record for this book is available from the British
Library

Library of Congress Cataloging in Publication Data
A catalog record for this book has been requested

ISBN 0-415-33528-0

Contents

Figures

Tables

Contributors

David Barnard is a Director with Hay Group, an international management consultancy that focuses on helping organisations to get the best out of their people. In 1998 and 2000, he led research programmes into headteacher and teacher effectiveness for the TTA and DfES. David works in the fields of leadership development, leadership team effectiveness and emotional intelligence. He is a Sloan Fellow of the London Business School.

David Brunton is a Senior Consultant with Serco Learning. Prior to this, he worked for many years in higher education. David is particularly interested in human resources issues and policy analysis in educational settings. He is a Fast Track Assessor, and has been involved in the design of the FT selection and recruitment process.

Pauline Buzzing has extensive experience of teaching in primary and secondary schools of all types. She is Head of a Professional Centre in West Sussex. In 1986, she started the first LEA scheme for returners to teaching. Pauline was awarded the OBE in 1994. Since 1993, she has been a freelance consultant, and a primary and secondary registered inspector for Ofsted, working all over the country.

Kit Field is Head of the Department of Professional Development, in the Faculty of Education at Canterbury Christ Church University College. Kit has a background in modern foreign languages, and was a Head of Department in Derbyshire before embarking upon a higher education career. Kit has published widely in the fields of modern foreign languages, mentoring, inspections, subject leadership and middle management, and continuing professional development.

Howard Green has held two secondary headships, in Oxfordshire (1983–1990) and in Plymouth (1992–1998). He has also established two national leadership development programmes at the National Educational Assessment Centre (1990–1992) and the Teacher Training Agency (1998–1999), where he was responsible for setting up the

Leadership Programme for Serving Headteachers. He has worked as an adviser at the Department for Education and Skills, and is now a Consultant with the National College for School Leadership. He has been directly involved with the development of the National Standards for Headteachers, Threshold and Fast Track.

Lorraine Harrison is a Principal Lecturer in the School of Education, University of Brighton. She is the course leader of the PGCE (Primary) course, and is also involved in the planning for and implementation of a range of diverse 'routes' into teaching. Lorraine has recently led development programmes for flexible (or modular) PGCE provision, and also the DfES Fast Track Programme. She is currently involved in the development of a foundation degree that will provide career opportunities for practitioners working in Early Years settings.

Phil Holden is an experienced educationalist, organisational development consultant, training strategist, writer and deliverer of a diverse range of training and development programmes, including: national programmes, e.g. LPSH, NPQH (former South East Centre Manager), Investment in Excellence; Master Writer and Trainer for Threshold Assessors and External Advisers; leadership and management programmes in higher education (up to Masters level); Investors in People, Managing Change; programmes on leading and developing creativity, teambuilding and improving professional relationships; and courses for leadership teams and subject leaders. He has published various training manuals, and most recently co-authored *Effective Subject Leadership* with Kit Field and Hugh Lawlor (Routledge, 2000).

Hugh Lawlor is Professor of Education at Canterbury Christ Church University College, and Director of the AstraZeneca Science Teaching Trust. He was previously the Director of Continuing Professional Development and Research at the Teacher Training Agency, and Senior Inspector in the Kent Local Education Authority. He has published extensively on leadership and management, continuing professional development, and development planning.

Maureen Lee worked for five years as a Senior Adviser and LEA Induction Co-ordinator in a large LEA. She is now an education consultant, which involves her in working with many teachers, schools and LEAs across England. Maureen has also worked as a consultant to the Teacher Training Agency Induction Team, and has written articles on effective professional development for teachers early in their careers. She has developed training programmes and portfolios for NQTs, induction tutors, Advanced Skills Teachers, and teachers in their second and third years of teaching.

Janet Tod is a Reader in Education at Canterbury Christ Church University College. Her work involves teacher training at undergraduate and postgraduate levels in the area of Special Educational Needs. Publications linked to her funded research include a series of books on IEPs, and articles and books on SEN policy and dyslexia.

Harry Tomlinson was, until 2002, Centre Manager for the NCSL for the Yorkshire and Humber Region for the NPQH, and Contract Manager for the DfES for the same region for Performance Management. He was also Project Director for the NCSL for one of the seven consortia delivering the LPSH. He is now a Visiting Professor at Leeds Metropolitan University and Chief External Examiner at Aberdeen and Dundee Universities. In 2000 he was awarded an individual National Training Award (DfES); in 2001 an MBA; and in 2002 a Diploma in Performance Coaching. He is Treasurer of the British Educational Leadership Management and Administration Society (BELMAS), and a Consultant for the Lithuanian Government. He has published over 30 articles in the last three years, including in China, Hong Kong and the USA. The two most recent books he has co-authored are *Performance Management in Education: Improving Practice*, and *Living Headship: Voices, Values and Vision*.

Emma Westcott is a Policy Adviser to the General Teaching Council for England, with responsibility for initial teacher training and induction. She is writing here in a personal capacity. She has previously held educational policy posts with the Local Government Association and the Association of University Teachers.

Trevor Yates is currently the Professional Leader for School Improvement at Cambridge Education Associates. His responsibilities have included Project Director of the administration of employment-based routes into teaching; quality assurance, and threshold assessment. Prior to joining CEA Trevor was Principal at Paignton Community College, and Centre Manager for NPQH.

Introduction

Howard Green

The national context for educational reform

The current Labour Government in England has committed itself to invest-ment in reform across the public sector, including education, based on four principles:

- standards and accountability – the importance of a national frame-work of standards and accountability;
- devolution and delegation – the need for greater freedom and innova-tion at the front line;
- flexibility and incentives – the role of greater flexibility and less demar-cation;
- expanding choice – the assurance for parents that poor provision will be tackled quickly and effectively, and that for pupils the curriculum will allow them to develop in the best way.

(DfES 2003)

In education, this reform has been a continuous process which started under Conservative governments in the mid- and late 1980s. Early policy changes included more funding going directly to school budgets, with a move towards greater self-management for schools, and the development of the framework for the National Curriculum. These were followed during the 1990s by the establishment of the Office for Standards in Edu-cation (Ofsted), a much more frequent cycle of school inspections, and the publication of national test and public examination results as league tables, all resulting in much higher levels of accountability for schools and the teaching profession. Alongside these initiatives came others, like the National Literacy and Numeracy Strategies in primary schools, the Key Stage 3 Strategy in secondary schools, target-setting for pupils related to national benchmarks, and performance management for teachers.

The first decade of the twenty-first century is likely to be characterised by a greater balance between the drive from central government to see standards in schools rise further, and more devolution, flexibility and choice for parents and pupils. Schools are being given more control over the nature of the curriculum and patterns of organisation. The current Labour Government now has key advisers who talk regularly about the shift from the 'informed prescription' of the 1990s to the 'informed professionalism' of the 2000s.

The National Standards for teachers and school leaders

An important development during the late 1990s was the drawing up of seven sets of National Standards for teachers and school leaders that defined role expectations and set benchmarks for performance. Five of these Standards (for Qualified Teacher Status, Induction, Subject Leader, Special Educational Needs Co-ordinator and Headteacher) describe basic levels for performance, whereas two (for Threshold and Advanced Skills Teacher) are aspirational, describing highly effective performance. Table I.1 lists the National Standards, notes whether they are statutory or advisory, and indicates whether they were developed by the DfES or the Teacher Training Agency (TTA).

The National Standards are now widely used for initial teacher training, induction, continuing professional development and performance management. The Standards for Subject Leaders underpin the national programme for middle managers, 'Leading from the Middle', and the Standards for Headteachers are used as the framework for the National Professional Qualification for Headship (NPQH), which will become a requirement for headship from 2004. Both these leadership development programmes are now the responsibility of the National College for School Leadership (NCSL).

The main elements in each of the Standards can be described under the following ten dimensions of teaching and leadership:

- knowledge and understanding;
- planning and setting expectations;
- teaching and managing pupil learning;
- assessment and evaluation;
- pupil achievement;
- relations with parents and the wider community;
- managing one's own performance and development;
- managing and developing staff and other adults;
- managing resources;
- strategic leadership.

Despite these common threads through the Standards, they differ in significant ways because they were developed at different times by different government bodies. Chapter 13 addresses this issue in more detail.

Table I.1 National Standards for teachers and school leadership

Standard title	Advisory/statutory	Developed by:
Qualified Teacher Status (QTS)	Statutory	TTA
Induction	Statutory	TTA
Threshold	Statutory	DfES
Advanced Skills Teacher (AST)	Statutory	DfES
Subject Leader	Advisory	TTA
Special Educational Needs Co-ordinator (SENCO)*	Advisory	TTA
Headteacher	Advisory	TTA (updated by DfES)

Source: Adapted from: *Teachers' Standards Framework*, DfES 2001

Note
*There are also Standards for Special Educational Needs Specialists

In addition to the seven sets of Standards listed in Table I.1, the DfES has developed a set of criteria that are used as the final stage of the selection process for the Fast Track into teaching and towards leadership. The Fast Track competencies and values are also aspirational, and are particularly interesting as they have been designed to identify potential for teaching and leadership. Within this context, the Fast Track selection process is looking for transferable skills and attributes in the applicants.

Related national developments

Alongside the development of the National Standards by the TTA and the DfES, there have been two other important and related initiatives in English education. First, the school inspection process, implemented by Ofsted, has helped to extend understanding of teacher effectiveness and the quality of school leadership and management. Second, the international management consultants, the Hay Group (formerly Hay McBer), have carried out two major studies for the TTA and the DfES on highly effective teachers and headteachers. These studies have been used to inform the development of the Threshold Standards and the Leadership Programme for Serving Headteachers (LPSH) respectively. The LPSH is another programme run by the National College for School Leadership, and is now the largest senior management development programme in Europe, accessed by over 10 000 headteachers at the time of publication.

The establishment of the General Teaching Council for England (GTCE) has created another agency that has a legitimate interest in the further development of the National Standards for the teaching profession. In the future, the DfES is likely to be working with the TTA, NCSL, GTCE and Ofsted at various stages in this process of review and revision.

Outline of the book

This book has drawn together a group of experienced practitioners to write about the origin of the National Standards and related developments in English education, the application of the Standards in specific contexts, and issues for the future. They are all committed to the national imperative for the continuous improvement of the quality of learning in our schools and the professional development of teachers.

In Part 1, Professor Hugh Lawlor describes the origin of the 'rainbow pack' at the TTA, the first brightly coloured collection of four sets of National Standards for QTS, Subject Leader, SENCO and Headteacher. Then Pauline Buzzing writes about teacher and headteacher effectiveness from the viewpoint of an Ofsted registered inspector, and David Barnard provides an account of the Hay Group's studies of highly effective teaching and school leadership.

In Parts 2 and 3, there are detailed case studies of the application of each set of standards in practice. For teachers, Lorraine Harrison writes about QTS Standards; Maureen Lee about Induction and Advanced Skills Teacher Standards; Trevor Yates about Threshold Standards, and David Brunton about the competencies and values for Fast Track teachers. For school leaders, Janet Tod writes about SENCO Standards (also making reference to the SEN Specialist Standards), Kit Field and Phil Holden about Subject Leader Standards, and Professor Harry Tomlinson about Headteacher Standards.

The chapters by David Brunton (Chapter 8) and Janet Tod (Chapter 9) are longer than most for particular reasons. The Standards for Fast Track are rather different, as they describe the potential for teaching and leadership. Also, the assessment of these Standards depends, unusually for education in England, on a formal assessment centre process. The SEN Specialist Teacher and SENCO Standards raise important questions about the nature of inclusion in English schools and the extent to which all teachers and subject leaders should possess relevant knowledge and skills.

Finally, in a look to the future, Emma Westcott considers a possible role for the GTCE in the further development of the National Standards, and Howard Green draws together the issues emerging throughout the book. The National Standards for teachers and school leaders have been one of the keys to school improvement and rising standards in English education. They have been widely used to help fulfil the statutory requirements of teacher and headteacher training and performance management, and to inform an increasing range of continuing professional development (CPD). The challenge now is to ensure that they are reviewed and, if necessary, adapted to meet the changing needs of schools in the future.

Critical issues

There remain more fundamental questions about the nature of 'Standards' as a means of defining and developing professional roles in education and the disparate origins of the standards for teachers and school leaders in England. Although the main part of this book describes the origin and application of these standards, Chapters 12 and 13 set them in a more critical context. Whether readers of this book are based in England or in other countries, our intention is that you will understand something of the journey to establish professional standards as a key to school improvement in England and then be encouraged to contribute to similar developments in your own environment.

The first three chapters illustrate the main tensions still to be resolved in developing a coherent understanding about the nature of professional standards. The TTA developed the first set of competence–based standards, which focused on the knowledge, understanding and skills required to be effective: the 'why?' and the 'what?' for teaching, management and leadership. Ofsted supported and challenged this work through the rapidly expanding evidence base derived from school inspections. Then the Hay Group, working under contract to the Government, helped to shift the emphasis towards high performance and a broader range of personal and professional characteristics: 'the how?' of good teaching and school leadership. We shall return to these critical issues in Chapters 12 and 13.

Latest information on the National Standards

Work on the development of the National Standards in England continues, and therefore a book like this risks being out of date almost as soon as it is published. Readers can find the latest information from the following websites.

1   General information on the development of the Standards Framework: www.teachernet.gov.uk/professionaldevelopment/standardsframework
2   Specific information on the Qualifying to Teach Standards, the Induction Standards, the Career Entry and Development Profile, and the Standards for Higher Level Teaching Assistants: www.tta.gov.uk
3   Specific information on the application of the Subject Leader Standards and the Headteacher Standards to national leadership development programmes like Leading from the Middle and the National Professional Qualification for Headship: www.ncsl.org.uk
4   Specific information on the professional standards developed by the General Teaching Council for England: www.gtce.org.uk

References

DfES (2001) *Teachers' Standards Framework*, London: DfES.
DfES (2003) *Raising Standards and Tackling Workload: A National Agreement*, London: DfES.

Part 1

The national context

Chapter 1

The role of the Teacher Training Agency: the first set of National Standards

Hugh Lawlor

Introduction

The Teacher Training Agency (TTA) was established as a non-governmental agency sponsored by the Department for Education (DfE) in 1994. The Agency's statutory objectives are set out in the Education Act 1994 as:

- to contribute to raising the standards of teaching;
- to promote teaching as a career;
- to improve the quality and efficiency of all routes into the teaching profession; and
- to secure the involvement of schools in all courses for the initial training of school teachers.

(DfE 1994)

The TTA's functions were previously carried out by the Higher Education Funding Council for England (HEFCE), Teaching as a Second Career (TASC), the Council for the Accreditation of Teacher Education (CATE) and the Department for Education (DfE). The Agency had no remit in Scotland or Northern Ireland, but a Unit was established in Wales in 1996. In 1994, the Agency's main functions were:

- the funding of teacher training;
- the accreditation of providers of initial training for school teachers;
- providing information and advice about teacher training and teaching as a career; and
- carrying out or commissioning research with a view to improving the standards of teaching and teacher training.

(DfE 1994)

At this stage strategic thinking about continuing professional development was embryonic, but by the *Corporate Plan 1995* (TTA 1995a) had been translated into an aim to promote well-targeted, effective and co-ordinated continuing professional development. Indeed, the Agency was committed to promoting a coherent approach across initial teacher training, induction and in-service training. Objectives in the *Corporate Plan 1995* included:

- to co-ordinate the identification of national priorities and targeting strategies for continuing professional development in order to inform funding decisions and aid planning;
- to improve the management and leadership skills and abilities of newly appointed headteachers (with the implementation of the HEAD-LAMP scheme by September, 1995);
- to disseminate information about effective continuing professional development practices;
- to carry out or commission investigations in order to inform the Teacher Training Agency's work.

(TTA 1995a)

The strategic role for continuing professional development in the agency was influenced by the results of an extensive survey of headteachers' and teachers' views on continuing professional development carried out by Mori early in 1994/1995. One of the most significant and influential findings expressed by a large proportion of those surveyed was the absence of a personal/professional/career framework for teachers and those in leadership roles in schools. This view was held by a large proportion of newly qualified teachers, and indeed was quoted by many of them as a likely reason for leaving teaching after a few years.

By the end of 1995 the TTA was in a position to send a letter setting out its 'Initial Advice to the Secretary of State on Continuing Professional Development of Teachers' (TTA 1995b). The letter proposed the development of National Standards, which would help to set targets for teachers' development and career progression and would establish clear and explicit expectations of teachers in different key roles. At this point, the four key points in the profession were identified as:

- Newly Qualified Teachers;
- Expert Teachers;
- Experts in Subject Leadership; and
- Experts in School Leadership.

The initial advice was to set the agenda for continuing professional development at the TTA for the next six years until responsibility for CPD was transferred to the General Teaching Council (GTC), and for leadership development to the National College for School Leadership. In both cases, however, the Department for Education and Skills remained the 'sponsoring' authority, and for CPD it retained a strategic role. The term 'expert teachers' caused considerable debate and some amusement within and outside the TTA. Although draft National Standards were prepared for 'expert teachers', they were never implemented. Later, however, these Standards helped to inform the criteria for Advanced Skills Teachers. National Standards for Special Educational Needs Co-ordinators were added at a later date, and replaced 'expert teachers' as a key point in the profession.

Back in 1995 there was no blueprint for a continuing professional development framework other than a consensus within the Agency that any pathway for development should begin with newly qualified teachers and cater for a range of different career roles, with an emphasis on leadership and management responsibilities and functions. One major announcement, in October 1995, was to act as a catalyst to the work on National Standards and the framework. Gillian Shepherd, as Secretary of State for Education, announced at the Conservative Party Conference that there would be a professional qualification for headteachers. Such a qualification would be different from courses and awards in higher education, mainly because of the clear and explicit focus on the professional needs and capabilities of aspiring headteachers.

By the *Corporate Plan 1996* (Promoting Excellence in Teaching), National Standards were to be established in four key roles in the profession. The Plan also identified September 1997 as the implementation date for the National Professional Qualification for Headteachers (later changed to Headship). Priorities identified in the 1996 Plan included:

- improving school leadership and management;
- improving subject leadership;
- increasing Key Stage 2 teachers' subject knowledge, particularly in literacy, mathematics, science, and design and technology;
- increasing the effectiveness of special educational needs co-ordinators.

(TTA 1996)

Early preparatory work on national standards

Prior to wide consultation on the National Standards, considerable preparatory work was taking place in respect of standards for qualified teacher status and standards for headteachers. Changes in terminology reflected the debate in the TTA at advisory group and Board levels. At one stage discussion on the standards for school leaders encompassed the concept of shared or distributive leadership, at least at the senior level in schools. However, it was the strong view of the DfE (and presumably the Secretary of State) that the qualification should be for headteachers and not other school leaders, and that the National Standards should reflect this specific focus.

In the case of the Standards for Headteachers, a small group of TTA officers, higher education staff and two deputy headteachers looked first at the current provision for training and developing headteachers. This provision included diploma and higher degree courses, local education authority and Diocesan Board programmes, professional association programmes, business management models, and the management standards from The Management Charter Initiative (MCI). The latter organisation was responsible for developing National Standards of Performance for managers and supervisors, with the standards forming the basis of National Vocational Qualifications (NVQs). Management standards are based on the concept of competence, which is the ability of a manager to perform to the standards required in employment.

The Standards set out in detail what managers should be able to do in a particular role, as well as the personal competences to perform effectively. Personal competences are those individual skills or behavioural traits which managers use to perform effectively. There was strong support within the DfE for a professional qualification for headteachers that was based on a National Vocational Qualification model, and hence on the management standards. The preparatory group resisted this approach, and decided instead to take the best practices from the MCI competence model and from what was generally viewed as the more intellectually demanding and divergent approach of the higher education provision. The overriding influence was the need to focus on the professional preparation of aspiring headteachers in a way that was relevant and contemporary. Clearly influenced by the management standards, the group defined the National Standards in terms of the skills, knowledge, understanding and attributes required to perform specific tasks and functions according to a given role (identifying key outcomes for headship would come later).

The National Standards would not define the levels of performance of tasks, but the sum of all the components would define the expertise required in a specific role – be it as a newly qualified teacher, subject leader, headteacher or, later, as a special educational needs co-ordinator. Indeed, for the first time the purposes, professional knowledge and understanding, skills, attributes, and key areas for specific roles would be defined. In effect, this group established the template for the National Standards, which would greatly influence the work to follow and the preparation for the National Professional Qualification for Headship.

This group would report to the recently established NPQH Advisory Group (later to become the Headship Training Advisory Group), composed of representatives of higher education, LEAs, industry, professional associations, business schools, two headteachers, two deputy headteachers, governors and Ofsted.

The work of 'expert' groups

As part of the preparation for consultation, the TTA established four 'expert' groups in 1996 to prepare detailed sets of draft National Standards (to be known as the 'rainbow pack' in 1998). 'Expert' groups were established for:

- Newly Qualified Teachers – national standards for Qualified Teacher Status;
- Subject Leadership – national standards for subject leaders;
- School Leadership – national standards for headteachers; and
- a co-ordinating group to ensure consistency and coherence.

Work on developing draft Standards for Special Educational Needs Co-ordinators was undertaken by consultants later in 1996.

Each group was chaired by a senior TTA officer, with membership from LEAs, higher education, governors, industry and newly qualified teachers, subject leaders or headteachers as appropriate. The co-ordinating group included the chairman of each group and a member of the TTA Board. Each group met regularly to draft and redraft the Standards prior to the TTA Board's approval to proceed to wide consultation. It was becoming clear that the main aims of the National Standards were to:

a set out clear expectations for teachers at key points in the profession;
b help teachers at different points in the profession to plan and monitor their development, training and performance effectively, and to set clear, relevant targets for improving their effectiveness;
c ensure that the focus at every point is on improving the achievement of pupils and the quality of their education;
d provide a basis for the professional recognition of teachers' expertise and achievements; and
e help providers of professional development to plan and provide high quality, relevant training which meets the needs of individual teachers and headteachers, makes good use of their time and has the maximum benefit for pupils.

(TTA 1998: 1)

Newly Qualified Teachers – National Standards for the award of Qualified Teacher Status

The Standards would apply to all trainees seeking Qualified Teacher Status (QTS), and would come into effect from May 1998. Trainees would have to meet all the standards, although it was not intended that each standard would require a separate assessment, but rather that groups of standards would be assessed.

The Standards for Qualified Teacher Status were arranged in a different format to the other Standards, but only because of the different professional requirements of a newly qualified teacher. The standards were divided into:

- knowledge and understanding;
- planning, teaching and class management;
- monitoring, assessment, recording, reporting and accountability;
- other professional requirements (e.g. knowledge and understanding of certain legal liabilities, have developed effective working relationships on teaching practice, are aware of the role and purpose of school governing bodies, etc.).

The draft Standards developed by the 'expert' group were quite specific, and replaced the more general 'competences' set out in DfE Circulars 9/92 and 14/93 and the DfEE Teacher Training Circular Letter 1/96. The Standards for Qualified Teacher Status would also have to comply with the DfEE Circular 10/97.

At a later stage the National Standards for Qualified Teacher Status would be used to underpin the Career Entry Profile, which would be completed by all newly qualified teachers. This would be the beginning of the professional development framework and the means by which each teacher could plan developments, keep up to date with research and developments in pedagogy and in particular subjects, and continue to grow as a professional.

Subject Leadership – National Standards for Subject Leaders

Early discussion in the group centred on the relationship between subject knowledge and subject leadership, and on the sharp differences between primary, secondary and special school contexts. It was accepted that subject leaders would require a good knowledge of the subject, but that the Standards would focus mainly on expertise in the leadership and management of a subject (at a later date several subject associations were to prepare subject-specific annexes to complement the generic leadership and management focuses in the Standards, e.g. physical education and science).

It was recognised by the group that the draft Standards were based on how experienced and effective subject leaders would work. One area of concern expressed by some members of the group related to the perceived bias towards the secondary school context. Consultations reinforced this concern, but it was generally felt that any training and development activities would be sufficiently context-specific to overcome any difficulties. It was, however, recognised that other middle–level leadership and management roles (e.g. pastoral, key stage, assessment) were not addressed by the Standards (but might be added at a later stage).

The Standards were divided into:

- core purpose of the subject leader;
- key outcomes of subject leadership (added later);
- professional knowledge and understanding;
- skills and attitudes;
- key areas of subject leadership (i.e. strategic direction and development of the subject; teaching and learning; leading and managing staff; and efficient and effective deployment of staff and resources).

Unlike the National Standards for Headteachers, there was no government support for translating the National Standards for Subject Leaders into a national professional qualification. There were various discussions at one stage about the benefits of introducing a National Professional Qualification for Subject Leadership (NPQSL), but it was probable that the cost and the number of teachers likely to be involved proved too daunting. It was anticipated, however, that LEAs and higher education institutions would adopt the Standards as the basis for training and development activities.

School Leadership – National Standards for headteachers

The timetable for producing draft National Standards for Headteachers was particularly tight, not least because of the Secretary of State's instruction to introduce the National Professional Qualification for Headship (NPQH) in September 1997 (with a short trial period earlier in the year). The group adhered to the remit to focus on the headteacher as leader, and not on emerging ideas about shared or distributive leadership or on devising standards for senior leadership and management (as proposed by some at the TTA).

Once agreed, the National Standards would underpin the NPQH, HEADLAMP and, at a later date, the Leadership Programme for Serving Headteachers (LPSH). Because of this the group reported regularly to the NPQH Advisory Group and, through the TTA officers, to the Board. Two issues were debated at length by the group – how to prevent the Standards being perceived as a checklist, and how to accurately represent the relationship of headteachers to governors and the governing body. The Standards were divided into:

- core purpose of the headteacher;
- key outcomes of headship (added later);
- professional knowledge and understanding;
- skills and attributes;

- key areas of headship (i.e. strategic direction and development of the school; teaching and learning; leading and managing staff, efficient and effective deployment of staff and resources; and accountability).

The group felt that the Standards would need to be regularly updated, not least to capture research evidence and inspection findings about leadership and management, but also to ensure that they reflect the constantly changing national priorities in education from the government.

National Standards for Special Educational Needs Co-ordinators

The National Standards for Special Educational Needs Co-ordinators (SENCOs) were not developed within the 'expert' groups structure, but were still subject to wide and extensive consultation. The TTA commissioned two consultants to prepare the draft Standards, based on the format and parameters defined by the other Standards, and to work closely with a small advisory group of SENCOs, headteachers, higher education SEN tutors and an LEA SEN adviser. This was a small subgroup of the main SEN Advisory Group set up to advise on a training strategy for SEN.

Although it was agreed that SENCOs must have a good knowledge of special educational needs, the Standards focus primarily on expertise in leadership and management. The standards emphasise that the SENCO should support the headteacher in ensuring that all staff recognise the importance of planning their lessons in ways that will encourage the participation and learning of all pupils. The Advisory Group was keen to reinforce this support, to establish SENCOs as senior staff in the school (and members of senior management teams – later leadership groups), and to underline their key role in supporting, guiding and motivating colleagues.

The consultants and advisory groups felt that headteachers and governing bodies must make their expectations of the postholders clear and explicit in terms of the level of responsibility, time available, and the resources dedicated for the work. At a later date the consultants produced guidance for SENCOs. The Standards were divided into:

- core purpose of the SENCO;
- key outcomes of SEN co-ordination;
- professional knowledge and understanding;
- skills and attributes;
- key areas of SEN co-ordination.

There was considerable discussion about whether there should be a National Professional Qualification for SENCOs, but ministerial support was limited. However, it was anticipated that LEAs, higher education institutions and other providers would adopt the Standards as the basis for training and development activities.

Further specialist SEN Standards were developed to support teachers working with pupils with specific learning difficulties (e.g. autism). This work was initiated and overseen by the TTA SEN Advisory Group, set up in 1997.

All the Standards were subjected to extensive consultation and some redrafting. Revised versions of the above four National Standards were published in 1998 in the 'rainbow pack'.

Some early challenges to the National Standards

From higher education

Much of the early criticism from higher education was directed at the NPQH, but some was also aimed at the National Standards. Many in higher education opposed the competency approach to training and development, which was seen as narrow, atomistic and bureaucratic (Glatter 1997). Some also felt that little attention had been paid to earlier and current research and development in leadership career preparation (Ribbins 1998).

The TTA felt that considerable attention had been given to developments within and outside education, and that the National Standards would be updated and modified in the light of contemporary research and inspection findings (in fact, few changes were made to the Standards over the years). More critically, the National Standards were not designed as a list of competences or elements of competences (as in the MCI standards), but rather as skills, attributes and knowledge that would require integrating according to specific contexts or situations (as defined in the key areas). The ability to integrate the relevant aspects of the Standards was seen as distinctly different from checking separate competences, and was more akin to professional capability than professional competence.

There was also some concern that the Standards and the NPQH might not be sufficiently intellectually demanding or promote creativity in new school leaders. Whilst it is true that greater emphasis could have been placed on intellectual and creative aspects in the Standards, it was always intended that the demands of contexts and situations would promote and develop intellectual and creative responses.

Discussions with higher education representatives about giving candidates credit for prior experience and achievements in the NPQH and the relationship of the NPQH to higher education awards made some progress, but there was no general agreement at the time of implementing the NPQH in September 1997.

From faith groups

At the stage when draft Standards were available, and at the end of the consultation process, discussions took place at the Agency with representatives from faith groups. Regular meetings with representatives from the Church of England and Roman Catholic faiths and occasional meetings with representatives from other faiths looked at ways of ensuring that the National Standards for Headteachers and the NPQH took account of specific beliefs, values and doctrines. However, the TTA was keen to promote the NPQH as a unitary qualification without designation according to phase, size of school or religious affiliation.

Lengthy discussions centred on the ways of incorporating faith dimensions in the Standards, and in the end it was agreed that faith groups would prepare their own supplementary materials that linked to and were signposted to relevant standards. Candidates for the NPQH would decide whether or not to use the materials. Some supplementary materials were prepared, but the TTA did not keep a record of the extent to which they were used. By the end of 1997, regular consultations with faith groups were seen as mutually beneficial and served as valuable feedback on the early implementation of the NPQH.

Other developments at the TTA

The TTA had developed a Career Entry Profile, and this was to be an important instrument with the introduction of a statutory induction year for all those qualifying after May 1999. An extensive consultation exercise identified induction standards, monitoring procedures, the support needed, and the assessment arrangements for this year. By the summer of 1999, a revised version of the Career Entry Profile was also published.

The TTA had been working with Ofsted to review the appraisal of headteachers and teachers, and in 1999 was asked to produce guidance on the use of the National Standards in appraisal. However, a revised appraisal scheme was delayed and was eventually replaced with the introduction of threshold assessment and performance management.

From 1999 the National Lottery (New Opportunities Fund) made resources available to ensure greater ICT competence and confidence across the teaching profession. The TTA was commissioned to develop and implement the training arrangements, including the development of needs assessment materials. The TTA established the criteria for training quality and advised on the selection of training providers. It was also involved in planning for the Virtual Teachers Centre, the National Grid for Learning and the University for Industry.

Although responsibility for policy on funding of award-bearing INSET was transferred to the DfES from April 2002, the TTA continued to manage the funds and the bidding process.

Throughout its work, the TTA recognised the need to include a clear and explicit dimension on special educational needs. Earlier work focused on developing the National Standards for Special Educational Needs Co-ordinators, and by 1997 the TTA was asked to develop a training strategy for special educational needs. A highly committed and powerful SEN Advisory Group was established to advise on and steer developments in this work. Activities included the development of National Standards for SEN Specialists, and advising Ministers on developing a new qualification based on the Standards to replace the mandatory (for teachers of the visually and hearing impaired) and other SEN qualifications.

The TTA continued to develop the NPQH as a mandatory qualification for all first-time headteachers and, since transfer of this programme to the National College for School Leadership, the decision has been taken to make the NPQH mandatory from April 2004. The Headteacher Leadership and Management Programme (HEADLAMP) for newly appointed headteachers has now been reviewed, and the revised Headteacher Induction Programme (HIP) was launched in September 2003.

The Leadership Programme for Serving Headteachers (LPSH) was initially designed and regulated by the TTA working with the Hay Group. It aimed to link the personal effectiveness of experienced headteachers and school improvement. The programme consists of pre-workshop activities – analysis of personal and school performance; a four-day workshop – feedback on personal performance, leadership styles, school performance, and preparation of an action plan for personal goals and school improvement targets; post-workshop activities – regular contact with a leader from the business sector, use of ICT, use of a Development Guide; and a follow-up day.

Leadership Development Activities (NPQH, HEADLAMP and LPSH) continued at the TTA (and by late 2000 at the DfES) until they were transferred to the National College for School Leadership (NCSL) in April 2001. Responsibility for promoting continuing professional development policies and practices was transferred to the DfES at a strategic level, with support from government agencies, including the NCSL and GTCE.

Later reviews of the QTS and headteacher standards resulted in a few minor amendments to the latter, but more substantial changes to the QTS standards. There were fewer QTS standards, and their greater generic focus gave more flexibility for providers and students. In 2003 the NCSL commenced a more substantial review of the Standards for Headteachers. More detailed information about these Standards and the National Programmes for Headteachers can be found in Chapter 11.

The TTA has actively promoted teaching as an evidence- and research-based profession. Research activities include supporting research consortia of schools, LEAs and higher education institutions (and, in previous years, teacher-research grants); creating a Teachers' Panel to contribute to the national debate on research; and sponsoring conferences to illustrate how research can enhance teaching and learning.

References and further reading

DfE (1994) Remit Letter. From the Rt Hon Gillian Shepherd, Secretary of State for Education to Geoffrey Parker, Chairman of the Teacher Training Agency, 5 October, London: DfE.

DfEE (1999) *Quinquennial Review of the Teacher Training Agency*, London: DfEE.

Glatter, R. (1997) 'Context and capability in education management,' *Educational Management and Administration* 25: 2.

MCI (1993) *The MCI Effective Manager*, London: The National Forum for Management Education and Development.

Ribbins, P. (1998) 'Some thoughts on the careers and continuing professional development of headteachers in England and Wales and principals in Cyprus,' Keynote paper given at a Seminar on Current School Leader Preparation: The Way to the Future, Cyprus.

TTA (1995a) *Corporate Plan 1995: Promoting High Quality Teaching and Teacher Education*, London: TTA.

TTA (1995b) 'Initial Advice to the Secretary of State on the Continuing Professional Development of Teachers,' London: TTA.

TTA (1996) *Corporate Plan 1996: Promoting Excellence in Teaching*, London: TTA.

TTA (1998) *Corporate Plan 1998–2001*, London: TTA.

TTA (1998) *National Standards for Headteachers*, London: TTA.

TTA (1998) *National Standards for Qualified Teacher Status, Subject Leaders, Special Educational Needs Co-ordinators, and Headteachers* ('rainbow pack'), London: TTA.

TTA (1999) *Corporate Plan 1999–2002*, London: TTA.

TTA (2000) *Corporate Plan 2000–2003*, London: TTA.

Chapter 2

The framework for school inspection: a perspective on the effectiveness of teachers and school leaders

Pauline Buzzing

The Office for Standards in Education (Ofsted): introduction and impact

The introduction of school inspections (Table 2.1) by the Office for Standards in Education (Ofsted) has been one of the most significant changes in English education over the past decade. It reflects wider changes that are evident for other people in the working world, for professionals are now accountable for their performance in a way that was previously unknown.

In the decade from 1993, the process of inspection, based on the Ofsted Framework, underpinned the work of many schools in their effort to drive up standards. Some would argue that inspection is the biggest lever in getting, and enabling, schools to focus on particular issues. The search for constant improvement results in a permanent commitment to finding better ways of enhancing all aspects of a school's work to raise standards and make better provision for our children.

Teachers and headteachers now work within the Ofsted Framework, but radical challenges demand fundamental and imaginative change and, though some see the Framework as exactly that – a framework that they can use creatively and imaginatively – others think it is too restrictive because:

Table 2.1 Ofsted inspection history

1992	Education Act established Ofsted inspection – four-year cycle
1993	First batch of secondary schools inspected
1994	First batch of primary schools inspected
1996	Framework revised
1997	Second round of secondary inspections begins
1998	Second round of primary inspections begins
1999	Short inspections begin for some schools
2000	Revised Framework introduced
2001	Consultation on further revisions for round three
2003	Third round of inspections began.

- it has been dictated by others;
- the answers are already known;
- creativity is not required;
- all that is needed is to carry out prescribed actions.

Preparation for the inspection and the inspection week

During the first inspection cycle, the lead-time for an inspection was very long. Now it is much shorter: self-evaluation is in the culture of most schools as part of Performance Management and through the work of LEA consultants and advisers. The most recent (2003) Ofsted Framework takes account of this, and the school's own self-evaluation (S4) form is a vital part of the inspection team's preparation for their work in the school.

First-hand evidence of the school's work with its pupils and students forms the bulk of an inspector's time in the school. Observation of teaching and learning, discussions with pupils and students, and scrutinising their work all contribute to an emerging picture of the school, underpinned by discussions with teachers, other adults working in the school, parents, and governors.

Closer to the time of the inspection, many registered inspectors offer to be available to answer teachers' questions before the inspection. These rarely seem to relate to the criteria for judging teaching: on the whole teachers usually want information about the process of the inspection, and welcome the reassurance that particular teaching styles are not 'right' or 'wrong' – the criterion is 'Do the pupils and students at their various attainment levels make progress in the lesson?'

By the time every school had been inspected for the first time, the report of Her Majesty's Chief Inspector (HMCI) had isolated two major factors in the drive for improvement.

The keys to raising standards in schools where achievement is currently too low are first to improve the quality of teaching and, second, to strengthen the leadership provided by the headteacher. Every school in England has now been inspected and there is a strong base of evidence about what makes a good teacher and headteacher.

Teaching and learning as the key to raising standards

The way forward was clear: the quality of teaching is more significant than any other factor in raising standards. First-rate accommodation, excellent resources, brilliant schemes of work: all are of limited value if the actual teaching, the point of delivery, the interaction between teacher and pupil are not of high quality. HMCI's statement emphasised the centrality of teaching in the learning process:

There is no doubt that if standards of pupils' attainment are to be raised, then the quality of teaching must be the focus of everyone's efforts.

This extract is a reminder of a shift of emphasis to stress that encouraging children to achieve high standards is an important part of a school's (and a teacher's) work. For the first time, the framework set down a list of factors that would be evident in effective teaching. These criteria offered a national perspective, and were rooted in national research findings.

This made the kind of feedback teachers received on their teaching doubly important, and, as part of the second round of inspections, inspectors were encouraged to be more open in the way they fed judgements back to teachers after a lesson. Prior to the introduction of Ofsted inspections, it was not unusual for teachers to go through the whole of their careers without encountering inspection, observation of their teaching, or feedback of any kind.

Feedback about teaching, and a changing culture

It is hard, now, to appreciate fully the change in culture that this represented. Of course, some teachers did observe each other's lessons, were mutually supportive, and talked openly about what went on in their classrooms. Many tried constantly to improve their practice: the network of Teachers' and Professional Centres that flourished up and down the country in the 1970s and 1980s is testimony to that. Primary schools, especially, took advantage of twilight INSET sessions, and teachers gave up their own time to attend, since little supply cover was available in some authorities to allow them out of school during the day.

Yet a significant minority steadfastly refused to become involved. It was one headteacher's proud boast that he had never attended an INSET session at his local Centre in 30 years. Others found it frustrating that when they tried to move things on, some colleagues, suspicious of change, would refuse to look at different ways of doing things. Change might be possible within a teacher's classroom, but whole-school change faltered unless all could agree, voluntarily.

During personal experience of running a Teachers' Centre in the 1980s, a course on Classroom Management could not run because of lack of takers. An adviser explained: 'You can't professionalise failure. Nobody is going to admit they need to improve their classroom practice.'

Twenty years on, how odd that sounds! No-one's classroom is sacred now; we all know we must improve, and all teachers must accept that being observed is part of the process of accountability. This has been particularly difficult for some teachers, who had been left to drift, perhaps for decades. Most teachers have welcomed the feeling of support that comes from developing professional dialogue with colleagues, which often began in the preparation for an Ofsted inspection. Nine years on, observation of classroom practice is now a normal part of the life of all schools.

The strength of a developing, open dialogue removes uncertainty and clarifies teachers' understanding of their own effectiveness. A programme shown on national television, documenting an early Ofsted inspection, contained an interview with a Head of Department who was very anxious about the quality of her teaching. 'If they say I'm no good, I'll give up,' she said. She was anxious and distressed. The programme then gave extracts from the lesson, and showed the Ofsted inspector's feedback – a very good lesson. She burst into tears. How could she be so uncertain about her own competence? It was an interesting cameo, with a familiar scenario.

A newly qualified teacher spent an unhappy year in a very difficult school, where there was little support. Staff struggled with discipline, and there were few resources. At the end of the year the young teacher left, and the headteacher, an experienced woman close to retirement, gave a speech describing the young teacher as 'the best probationer I've seen in the whole of my career'. It was the first judgement that teacher had heard of her teaching in the whole year.

These two examples reflect what many teachers experienced – they had no idea of what the management in the school thought of their teaching. Now, we have all learned the language of feedback: its value, how to give it, and how to take it. Ofsted tells its inspectors that teachers should be in no doubt as to the strengths and weaknesses of their teaching as observed during the inspection.

Feedback works best when observer and the observed focus on the main purpose of their work – to improve the provision in the classroom for the pupils, thus improving how they learn, how much progress they make and, ultimately, raising the standards they reach. It is at its most threatening where the teacher takes it as direct, personal criticism. It is feedback on 'what you do', not on 'what you are'.

Feedback that focuses on the teacher (Figure 2.1a) can leave the teacher's self-esteem and confidence very exposed. It is better to focus on the common aim these two professionals share (Figure 2.1b) – to improve provision for the pupils, and hence raise standards.

Feedback on 'what you do' can be constructively expressed, since we can change much of what we do, and most of us change the way we do things anyway. We do what we do because of what we know; when we know more, we do it differently.

When time allows (and this is difficult in the pressured few days of an Ofsted inspection), feedback develops into dialogue, and this ongoing debate between inspectors and those who are inspected has resulted in a refining of the criteria in the various Frameworks. The first operated from 1993 until the spring of 1996, then there were some changes in 1997/1998 for the

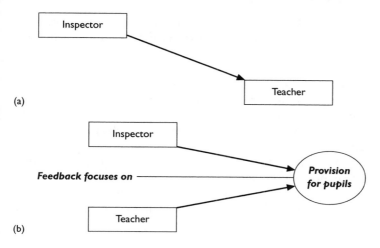

Figure 2.1 Feedback: (a) focusing on the teacher; (b) focusing on provision for the pupils.

second cycle of inspections; a third Framework began in January 2000, and a fourth for the third round of inspections in the autumn of 2003.

Renewed focus on learning

Throughout this time the weight given to learning has increased, so that teaching as a 'performance' during the inspection has become much less important than the impact of teaching as the major influence, over time, on the pupils' learning. Evidence from the scrutiny of the pupils' work is crucial here. Inspectors are encouraged to study this evidence carefully, since it represents work produced over time, and can indicate progress over time – what Ofsted now defines as 'achievement'.

Schools are asked to produce a sample of the work of higher, average and lower attaining pupils for scrutiny early on in the inspection. This gives inspectors a good picture of the standards pupils attain, and of the progress they make. It also gives information about teaching (Table 2.2).

Table 2.2 Information gained from work samples

Range of work set
Marking:

- Does it encourage pupils?
- Does it give credit for what has been done well?
- Does it diagnose what needs to be done?
- Does it tell the pupil what to do to improve?

Evidence of improving standards

The HMCI report of 1998 lists improvements in teaching that were already evident at the start of the second cycle. For example, in primary teaching:

- There was more challenging, direct teaching, often to the whole class, so that the attention of all pupils could be engaged more effectively.
- Primary schools were moving away from reliance on a single class teacher, so that pupils gained from the subject knowledge and enthusiasm of individual teachers.
- Setting was becoming more common, so that the pupils' learning needs could be more closely matched to the tasks they were set.
- More systematic attention was paid to the teaching of literacy and numeracy to give pupils the basic skills that underpin all their learning.

Each year, HMCI's report publishes the percentages of teaching in the categories of good and better, satisfactory and unsatisfactory or poor (Table 2.3).

The most dramatic drop in primary schools in unsatisfactory teaching occurred by the end of the first cycle of Ofsted inspections: in the academic year of 1993/1994 the unsatisfactory teaching was running at 25 per cent in Key Stage 1, and 30 per cent in Key Stage 2. The highest percentages of good and very good teaching were with the youngest children. The percentage of

Table 2.3 Percentages of teaching in various categories, primary level

Under fives	Good or better	Satisfactory	Less than satisfactory
1996/1997	63	30	7
1997/1998	67	28	5
1998/1999	70	27	3
1999/2000	76	22	2
2000/2001	77	20	2
Key Stage 1 (Years 1–2)	Good/very good	Satisfactory	Unsatisfactory
1996/1997	41	50	9
1997/1998	50	44	6
1998/1999	56	40	4
1999/2000	67	27	6
2000/2001	69	27	4
Key Stage 2 (Years 3–6)	Good/very good	Satisfactory	Unsatisfactory
1996/1997	43	47	10
1997/1998	53	39	7
1998/1999	60	35	5
1999/2000	72	23	5
2000/2001	75	22	4

Table 2.4 Percentages of teaching in various categories, secondary level

Key Stage 3	Good/very good	Satisfactory	Unsatisfactory
1996/1997	55	37	8
1997/1998	61	32	7
1998/1999	67	29	5
1999/2000	71	18	11
2000/2001	75	20	5
Key Stage 4	Good/very good	Satisfactory	Unsatisfactory
1996/1997	61	35	4
1997/1998	66	30	4
1998/1999	71	26	3
1999/2000	75	19	6
2000/2001	82	14	3
Post-16	Good/very good	Satisfactory	Unsatisfactory
1996/1997	81	19	1
1997/1998	82	18	0
1998/1999	89	11	0
1999/2000	92	8	1
2000/2001	92	8	0

good and very good teaching observed was roughly similar in Key Stages 1 and 2, but improvements in teaching in Key Stage 2 have moved ahead faster than in Key Stage 1. In the Foundation Stage and in both key stages, the smallest improvement was in the most recent year: the first full academic year in which teaching has been more closely matched with its impact on learning.

A similar pattern is evident in the figures for secondary teaching (Table 2.4).

In 1993/1994, the percentage of unsatisfactory teaching was 19 per cent in Key Stage 3 and 17 per cent in Key Stage 4. Within four years, the good or better teaching was running at more than 50 per cent in each key stage, and teachers were said by the Chief Inspector to be 'planning and preparing more effectively and teaching in a more challenging, direct way'.

In the secondary sector, percentages were initially higher in Key Stage 4 than in Key Stage 3, and Post-16 teaching began with a huge 20 per cent lead over the teaching in Key Stage 4. By the most recent figures, the gap was halved.

Defining the quality of teaching

Underpinning all this is an assumption that judgements can be made on the quality of teaching, and that satisfactory teaching, good teaching and the rest can be reduced to a checklist. Some would undoubtedly dispute this, but the Ofsted list works surprisingly well through a wide age range, encompassing nursery and reception lessons as well as those post-16.

The following list of criteria for effective teaching has been added to in more recent editions of the Framework for Inspection, but in 1997/1998 the categories within teaching were defined as follows:

- Teachers' knowledge and understanding
- Teachers' expectations
- Teachers' planning
- Methods and organisation
- Management of pupils
- Use of time and resources
- Quality and use of day-to-day assessment.

Reports were specific in their highlighting of how and why teaching was unsatisfactory. Take this example from a 1998 report:

> Unsatisfactory teaching, for example, in mathematics and modern languages, results from low expectations and a slow pace. In modern languages, use of the target language is too variable, and poorly planned lessons provide too few challenges for pupils. In science, the use of prescriptive worksheets limits opportunities for pupils to learn in different ways.

By the time the third Framework was introduced in January 2000, the use of homework had been included, together with judgements on the teaching of basic skills. The use of support staff had been added to the use of time and resources, reflecting the increasingly important part they are playing in the teaching process. 'Day-to-day assessment' had become 'ongoing assessment'.

Additional emphasis on impact is evident in the 2000 list (see Appendix to this chapter) – it is no longer just 'Teachers' planning', but the *'effectiveness* of the planning'; no longer 'Methods and organisation', but the *'effectiveness* of teaching methods'. The language is deliberate, and the Chief Inspector commented:

> I wrote last year that 'we have a new and rigorous focus on what actually works'. We do . . . The agenda is, or ought to be, obvious.

The impact of teaching on learning is what matters

This emphasis on outcomes was further strengthened by a new section on learning, including:

- Acquisition of skills, knowledge and understanding
- Pupils' intellectual, physical or creative effort
- Productivity and pace of working

- Pupils' interest, concentration and independence
- Pupils' knowledge of their learning
- How well pupils with special educational needs learn
- How well pupils with English as an additional language learn.

In a sense, the acquisition of skills, knowledge and understanding is not new, since what else is this category but a judgement on the progress pupils are making? How could pupils make progress if they did not acquire knowledge, skills and understanding? It could also be argued that the degree of effort pupils make, their productivity and pace of working, their interest and concentration are subsets of their attitudes and enthusiasm for what they are doing.

However, the concentration of this list and the rephrasing of the section's heading to encompass 'Teaching and learning' sends a strong message about the importance of impact. Whereas discussions with teachers highlight intentions, those with pupils show impact. Successful teaching is to be judged by how well the pupils learn, and the teacher's task is to gauge the needs of the learners and to match all the aspects of teaching to those needs. There has to be something of the actor in every teacher, but teaching is not a performance, and misses the point if it does not meet the needs of the pupils.

This emphasis on learning, on 'letting the pupils in to the learning process', has paid handsome dividends for many teachers. Setting clear learning objectives for pupils of different attainment levels, sharing them with the learners, referring to them during the lesson, and evaluating progress towards them has added purpose and streamlining to many lessons. It harnesses the energy of the pupils in helping to achieve objectives, so that learning can really move forward, and build steadily on what has gone before.

In one inspection report, in a school where the very good or excellent teaching accounted for 40 per cent of the lessons seen, a summary of missed opportunities gives a useful blueprint for raising the 27 per cent of teaching and learning that was satisfactory to a higher level. The list gives a very clear picture of the learning:

These weaknesses included:

- Missing opportunities to challenge higher attainers by, for example, using follow-up questions during question and answer sessions;
- Insufficient opportunities for pupils to think and learn for themselves;
- Not drawing the lesson to a close by reviewing what had been learnt and checking this against the lesson's learning objectives;
- Slow pace with, for example, no time limits for a task;

- Not ensuring that all pupils are actively involved in the lessons;
- Marking that does not include comments which show pupils how they can improve their work;
- Whole-class teaching which does not use any visual material, and is dull for the pupils; ineffective classroom management when, for example, pupils talk while the teacher is talking or pupils make too much noise when they are working;
- A lack of awareness of the pupils' response during whole-class teaching.

(Secondary report, 2001)

The link between teaching and learning

The framework for teaching and learning applies right across the age range, and the list of teaching and learning criteria applies in the Foundation Stage as well as to Post-16 classrooms. The following extract, regarding the reception class of a primary school, shows how the criteria apply to young children:

> Teaching is now good, sometimes very good, and this means that the children learn well and standards are rising, Particular strengths in the teaching include a carefully planned practical curriculum where children are made aware of what they are learning. Additionally, there are high expectations for the children's independence and good strategies to develop this. This allows the teacher to focus very well on the teaching of basic skills of reading, writing and mathematics to small groups of children, enabling them to learn very well at these times.

Teaching and learning; cause and effect, have become inextricably linked in inspection reports:

> There is very good teaching in every class. As a result, pupils are learning very well and making very good progress over time so that standards are rising at a faster rate than in other schools.
> (Community nursery and primary school, 2001 inspection)

Outcomes are clearly visible:

> Year 4 attainment reflects the good teaching pupils now receive, which shows high expectations and promotes positive pupil efforts and behaviour, leading to generally good achievement.

Whereas outcomes had been implicit in some reports – such as in one that stated 'Most lessons are marked by crisp pace and rely on good standards of discipline' – the most recent reports have been much more direct in showing the cause and the benefit:

> Successful lessons also contain a suitable variety of tasks and methods: this keeps interest alive and results in a good pace of learning, particularly when time deadlines are set for tasks.
>
> (Secondary school inspection, 2000)

This is an important lesson for departments who might wonder why their own experience is different from others in the school, and the only way to find out is by tracking pupils through the day and seeing what their learning experiences are like. If variety, pace, challenge and all the elements of good and very good lessons are what they experience elsewhere, satisfactory teaching is likely to result in pedestrian learning, and will not raise attainment.

Despite the change in the teaching criteria to encompass learning, and despite the inclusion of five-year-olds in the Foundation Stage, thereby incorporating the reception year (and becoming under sixes), the trend of steady improvement has remained upwards.

Parents' views on the quality of teaching

One significant fact is that parents are now asked to comment on the quality of teaching (Table 2.5). Most parents have a view on this: it is not a question that elicits high percentages in the 'don't know' column. They, after all, have the experience of listening to their children day after day, and of observing the progress they are making. The assumption behind this is that good teaching can be judged from its outcomes, and a lay person does not need professional training to be able to make a judgement. Occasionally parents are wrong, but more often than not they can pinpoint problems, and have a pretty good idea of where the good teaching is in the school, regardless of its style. They want their children to make progress, after all. The example, of the 2000–2003 questionnaire shows the questions **that relate overtly to teaching, leadership and management** (see Appendix).

Pre-inspection commentary

Every registered inspector produces a pre-inspection commentary, based on the documents received from the school, the initial visits, and the meeting with parents. The commentary consists of relevant data and information, plus comments and evaluations on it, and hypotheses and issues to address during the inspection. Even at this early stage, hypotheses about teaching and learning are formed. In a primary school where, for

Table 2.5 Ofsted parents' questionnaire

1 My child likes school
2 My child is making good progress in school*
3 Behaviour in the school is good*
4 My child gets the right amount of work to do at home*
5 **The teaching is good***
6 I am kept well informed about how my child is getting on*
7 I would feel comfortable about approaching the school with questions or a problem*
8 The school expects my child to work hard and achieve his or her best*
9 The school works closely with parents*
10 **The school is well led and managed***
11 The school is helping my child become mature and responsible*
12 The school provides an interesting range of activities outside lessons*

Note
Asterisked points give parents a chance to comment on the outcomes of systems set up by and monitored by the school's management to move the school towards the vision created by the leadership.

Points 3, 4, 6, 12 ask, indirectly, for comments on the systems set up (behaviour, activities outside lessons, reporting on progress, and homework).

Points 8, 11 ask for comments on the impact of the school's ethos in helping their child to become mature and setting expectations of hard work.

Points 6, 7, 8, 9 ask for comments on the organisation's relationship with parents as partners in the education of their children: whether they are kept well informed; feel that the school works closely with them, and whether they feel they can approach the school with questions or a problem.

example, the English results were consistently below those of mathematics and science, the question has to be asked 'Does this mean that the teaching in English is not as good?' or, conversely, 'Is there something about the mathematics and science teaching that raises standards to a high level?' Where the analysis of data shows that the girls are performing less well or better than the boys, or the higher attainers do less well in value added terms than do lower attainers, there are questions that must be asked about the quality of the teaching they are receiving.

From September 2001, it became a requirement for the commentary to be shared with the headteacher: most recently, it has become clear that governing bodies and senior staff may also have access to this document. This is useful in that it enables the school to show its own awareness of these issues and to indicate how the teaching has tried to address them. The new S4 (self-evaluation) form is crucial in clarifying the school's view of its own work and the strategies it has adopted.

Ofsted's analysis of the quantitative and qualitative data gathered in the first round of inspections

The challenges facing schools at the end of the first cycle of inspections in 1998 were summed up in HMCI's report as threefold:

1 The gap in achievement between schools serving similar communities was too wide
2 Education was still too much of a lottery
3 The two basic challenges were still there:

- Teaching needed to be further improved
- Leadership needed to be improved also.

The report commented: 'It is upon these two imperatives that the policy agenda should focus.'

By the start of the second cycle, it became clear that schools ignored the key issues at their peril. The first report was to be the baseline from which the second was judged, with new categories to enter into the report, grading the school for its rate of improvement since the previous report. The responsibility for overseeing that improvement lay with the management, in the shape of the governing body, whose responsibility it is to report progress on improvements to the parents, and which relies on the leadership of the school – mainly the headteacher – to drive improvement forward through the management systems in the school.

Leadership and management

Leadership and management are closely related – in fact so closely related that some of the earlier reports treated them as a single entity. It was not uncommon to hear inspectors say 'Leadership and management is . . .', but now the wording is clearly 'leadership and management are . . .' – in other words, they are quite separate, distinct elements in the inspection process. Early reports often focused on the headteacher, with mention of the governing body, but few references to other managers in the school.

Even in secondary schools, in 1993, 'leadership and management' really had the emphasis on the latter and dealt with meetings, administration and communication. The 1996 framework moved the focus towards planning, monitoring and evaluation: middle administration really did begin to become middle management. Ofsted was refining its own process.

In schools up to Key Stage 2, every teacher is often a manager of a subject or area (such as assessment or special educational needs) and has a role to play in the management structure. In the current climate of constant change, the role of the school's managers is crucial in creating a context within which people can view change, initiate it and cope with it.

The constantly changing scenario, coupled with the normal disruptions of school life, means that it is doubly essential for the school's leadership to provide a secure direction. It means stepping out of a scenario in which the rules and the script are known, and into the unknown. Whereas management has an annual cycle, leadership is forever pressing forwards.

Table 2.6 A vision of the future

- Is there a clear vision?
- Does it agree with the context?
- Is it expressed, understood and shared?
- Is there a written statement of aims that reflects the vision?
- Will it guide strategic thinking?
- Are decisions taken based on it?

Underpinning it is a vision of the future, created by shaping and reshaping ideas into a coherent whole (Table 2.6). Reflection is a key skill for head-teachers, since abstract concepts rarely work out exactly as expected.

Of the list of tasks for the future, the headteacher will take personal responsibility for some. Some of the tasks will require strengths that the headteacher already has; others will need to be developed. Leadership pre-supposes that profound learning and development will be practised by all members of the school community, and not just the pupils. This in turn has implications for the organisational structure of the school, which must be appropriate for a learning community, and it must be expressed in terms of aims or goals – those promises that the school makes to each individual child.

It also has implications for retention; for leadership that cannot inspire, express a vision or take the workforce with it; may simply create antagonism and a feeling of being bullied. Where headteachers develop strategies to improve the overall quality of teaching, they take into account the total experience of the pupils, and create programmes with supply and temporary teachers in mind. This vision has to be based on core purposes and values that permeate every aspect of school life: development planning, appraisal, appointment procedures, budget allocations and the rest. Current recruitment problems and teacher shortages have serious implications for schools that are trying to implement a coherent vision.

Collecting evidence for leadership and management

Evidence collected includes documentary evidence about the headteacher's formal role, observation of how the headteacher goes about his or her work; discussions with the headteacher about what is being done and why; and discussion with others about what the headteacher is doing and why.

Leadership is crucial: even a well-managed school will not raise standards and bring about improvements without it. The National Commission on Education in 1995 reported that 'no evidence of effectiveness in a school with weak leadership has emerged from any of the reviews of research'. There is no official or correct definition of leadership, and it is difficult to reduce leadership to a check-list analysis, but it is clear that leadership of any complex organisation is too much for any one person. There must be a vision, but it must be shared, and its impact must be evident in the school's daily life, as well as in its long-term goals and planning.

Even in short inspections, inspectors had to make judgements on aspects of leadership and management (see Appendix), including:

- the leadership and management of the headteacher and key staff;
- the effectiveness of the governing body in fulfilling its responsibilities;
- monitoring and evaluation of the school's performance and taking effective action
- strategic use of resources, including specific grant and other funding;
- the extent to which the principles of best value are applied.

So the 'key staff' and the governing body were now included in the overall judgements about leadership and management, and the word 'team' appeared frequently in reports. An effective primary school, inspected in March 2000, was commended for the headteacher's 'very good leadership of a strong staff team, committed to school improvement'.

The HMCI report of February 1998 stated

> Schools have now recognised the need to delegate responsibilities to co-ordinators, but many have been unable to provide adequate amounts of time for the key staff who are leading developments to oversee and evaluate work across the school.

In the years since then, even the very smallest schools have made time available for their middle managers to monitor and evaluate work in their subjects or areas. The 1992 Education Act that established Ofsted and set up the cycle of inspections also meant that schools had to produce documentation on how the organisation was managed. Looking at the roles of the managers is an important part of the Ofsted week. Inspectors interview subject co-ordinators or heads of department, the SENCO, the foundation stage and key stage co-ordinators, year heads, deputies, governors and headteachers. They study job descriptions, and expect the managers' roles to be clearly spelt out. They investigate the management structure in the school, and expect senior managers to be monitoring middle managers, for middle managers to be monitoring others, and for the whole process of monitoring and evaluation to be threaded throughout the school at every level.

For many teachers, anticipation of these interviews generates as much anxiety as being observed in the classroom – perhaps more, since classroom observation happens more frequently than being interviewed on their management role. Yet the questions inspectors are likely to ask are very straightforward (see Figure 2.2).

Questionnaire for co-ordinators   **Subject:**

You may wonder what kind of questions the inspection team will ask about your work as a co-ordinator. The questions below will help you to clarify your thoughts and show you the kind of information we need. You can use the questions as triggers to your thinking.

1. Your role
- How long have you been co-ordinator for this subject?
- Do you have any particular qualifications and experience that help you?
- What opportunities have you had to attend INSET related to the subject?
- Do you have a job description? What are your key responsibilities in this post?
- Have you audited or evaluated your resources recently?

2. Finance
- Do you have a budget for your subject?
- How much is it?
- How do you decide on the priorities for expenditure?

3. The subject
- What is the current status of the subject policy?

No policy	In draft	Recently accepted
Due for revision	Recently revised	Date

- Are there associated guidelines or schemes of work?
  What do these include?
  How were the policy and guidelines (schemes of work) produced?
  Who was involved?
- How is the subject planned and organised? Classes? Sets?
  What time is given to it each week?
  What provision do you make in the subject for pupils with special educational needs?
  What provision do you make in the subject for pupils who have English as an additional language?
- How do you develop the pupils' skills in literacy?
- How do you develop the pupils' skills in numeracy?
- How do you develop the pupils' skills in ICT?

4. Monitoring and evaluation
- In what ways do you work with colleagues to influence the quality of teaching and learning?
- Do you have any non-contact time for this work?

5. Assessment, recording and reporting
- How do you assess the pupils' progress in the subject?
- What records do you keep? (Mark books/portfolios/RoA etc.)
- Is an annual written report sent to parents?
- How else do you keep parents informed of their children's progress?

6. Staffing, accommodation and learning resources
- **Staffing:**
  Who teaches the subject?
  Are INSET days and staff meetings used to support work in this subject?
- **Accommodation:**
  Is it adequate for the needs of the subject?
  Is it suitable for practical work?
- **Resources:**
  Are they adequate and of good quality?
  Where are they kept?

7. Future developments planned for the subject

Figure 2.2 Questionnaire for co-ordinators.

The improving evidence base

At the whole-school level, leadership and management need a strong grasp on the direction of the school in order to take it forward, but there is no prescribed way of doing this. The 2000 framework represented a marked change, a formalisation of what works well, and draws on Ofsted's own experience of the past nine years, as well as developments from elsewhere in the education world. Setting targets and monitoring and evaluating progress towards them are much sharper processes now than in the past, and they are more closely related to the outcomes for pupils. Inspectors stand back now and use data, an audit of weaknesses, look at the targets and express them as relating to the pupils in different target groups. Value added analysis has allowed us to do that.

Inspectors and schools have very detailed data about individual groups, individual subjects and individual teachers, informed by rigorous analysis against national benchmarks and individual pupil performances. Earlier data were less statistically reliable.

To start with, inspectors and schools looked at attainment against national standards and in relation to the pupil's ability. Attainment is still matched against the national standards, and there are more accurate data to allow that to be done. Now, however, information about achievement can be worked out, giving a measure of the value added, assessing from the pupil's prior attainment, so that it is possible to talk about some aspects of how well the pupils learn.

There is now a second source of evidence with which to compare its current performance and direction, so that judgements can be made on improvement. From the PANDA, the DfES have produced value added information, which is useful to people outside the school but is also invaluable to managers inside the school to enable them to set realistic and relevant targets.

The performance data show that specialist schools and colleges are adding more value than other schools. The reason being that, from the start, their managers have been required to focus on the outcomes in terms of the pupils, and targets have been refined or rejected according to this yardstick. After all, what else is there but defining what we want the children to be able to know, understand and be able to do?

Ofsted has drawn on this, as well as on parallel work on standards for headteachers, subject leaders and classroom teachers. A 1999 secondary school report clearly showed the influence of Technology College status:

> The governors and the headteacher provide very good leadership, setting a clear direction for the school. An example of this is the successful application for the school to become a Technology College as a way of addressing weaknesses identified at the last inspection ... The

school is now more sharply focused on the outcomes that pupils achieve in terms of academic attainments and personal development.

For some schools, those outcomes at the time of the first inspection may have meant that it was placed in special measures. As the end of the first cycle of inspections approached in 1996/1997, it was possible to identify some common factors that such schools faced. The leadership and management were usually weak, resulting in a lack of strategic planning to take the school forward, and there was a high proportion of unsatisfactory teaching. The outcome of this was poor examination and national test results.

Studying the schools that managed to move forward from a special measures judgement, HMCI reported that:

> improvement for most schools has followed a pattern of strengthening of leadership and management, development of planning, policies and procedures, monitoring and evaluation of the impact of changes and finally, significant rises in the quality of teaching and pupils' standards of attainment.

Underpinning it all, 'Strong leadership . . . is a key feature of all the schools that have made substantial improvement'.

However, leadership on its own is not enough to ensure the smooth running of an institution as complex as a school. The management cycles that operate ensure that the vision will become reality, and will be reflected in the daily life of the school at all levels.

Management systems are responsible for ensuring that the school is:

- using a wide range of evidence to evaluate how well the school is doing, drawn from a wide range of stakeholders – parents, pupils, staff, the wider community, as well as through analyses of data;
- being honest about strengths and, especially, weaknesses in auditing present provisions;
- involving a range of people, including governors, in drafting development planning priorities for the whole school;
- ensuring that department/area plans link closely into the whole school plans;
- ensuring that targets set are expressed in terms of the expected outcomes from the pupils;
- identifying clearly who is responsible for what, by when, and how success will be determined.

The 2003 edition of the Ofsted Framework places even greater emphasis on leadership at all levels, on governance and on management. It places on schools the duty of self-evaluation and focuses on the effectiveness of teachers' skills in meeting the needs of individual pupils.

Various official publications have supported the move to underline the importance of leadership: HMI papers on subject leadership, for example.

Looking ahead

At the time of writing, the future shape of Ofsted is unclear. The move to self-evaluation in S4 asks 'How well is the school doing ...?' in various aspects of its work, and is underpinned by the crunch question 'How do you know?' which demands evidence of one kind or antoher. This development is sure to inform and modify the inspection process.

Information about all Ofsted publications and current developments may be found on the Ofsted website: www.ofsted.gov.uk

Appendix

From the Ofsted Framework 2000 – criteria for judging teaching and learning

3 How well are pupils and students taught?   Teaching and learning

What is the quality of teaching and what is its impact?

	Grades 1–7 for	U5s	KS1	KS2	KS3	KS4	Post-16	School
3A	Teaching							
3.1	Teachers' knowledge and understanding							
3.2	Teaching of basic skills							
3.3	Effectiveness of teachers' planning							
3.4	Teachers' expectations							
3.5	Effectiveness of teaching methods							
3.6	Management of pupils							
3.7	Use of time, support staff and resources							
3.8	Quality and use of ongoing assessment							
3.9	Use of homework							

3B Learning							
3.10 Acquisition of skills, knowledge and understanding							
3.11 Pupils' intellectual, physical or creative effort							
3.12 Productivity and pace of working							
3.13 Pupils' interest, concentration and independence							
3.14 Pupils' own knowledge of their learning							
3.15 How well pupils with SEN learn							
3.16 How well pupils with EAL learn							

From the Ofsted Framework 2000 – criteria for judging leadership and management

Grades 1–7 for	School
7A The leadership and management of the headteacher and key staff	
7B The effectiveness of the governing body in fulfilling its responsibilities	
7C Monitoring and evaluation of the school's performance and taking effective action	
7D Strategic use of resources, including specific grant and other funding	
7E The extent to which the principles of best value are applied	
7F Adequacy of staffing, accommodation and learning resources	
7.1 Leadership ensures clear educational direction	
7.2 Reflection of the school's aims and values in its work	
7.3 Delegation and the contribution of staff with management responsibilities	
7.4 Effectiveness of governing body in fulfilling statutory duties	
7.5 Governors' role in shaping the direction of the school	

7.6   *Governors' understanding of the strengths and weaknesses of the school*

7.7   *The monitoring, evaluation and development of teaching*

7.8   *The school's strategy for appraisal and performance management*

7.9   *The appropriateness of the school's priorities for development*

7.10 *The action taken to meet the school's targets*

7.11 *Shared commitment to improvement and capacity to succeed*

7.12 *Induction of staff new to the school and effectiveness of provision, or potential, for training of new teachers*

7.13 *Educational priorities are supported through the school's financial planning*

7.14 *Effectiveness of the school's use of new technology*

7.15 *Specific grant is used effectively for its designated purpose(s)*

7.16 *Match of teachers and support staff to the demands of the curriculum*

7.17 *Adequacy of accommodation*

7.18 *Adequacy of learning resources*

Chapter 3

Research by the Hay Group into highly effective teachers and school leaders

David Barnard

The Hay Group is a professional services firm that helps organisations worldwide get the most from their people. It has undertaken two major research and development projects for the TTA and the DfES since 1998.

The argument of this chapter is that Hay Group's research adds a dimension to the understanding of professional effectiveness in schools. The National Standards provide one aspect of *what* teachers and head-teachers need to do at work; Hay's research provides a picture of *how* they can be effective. More importantly, perhaps, Hay has developed ways in which professionals can assess the impact of what they do on the colleagues or students they lead. We believe that this is an invaluable addition to the ways in which individuals can plan their personal development so as to focus developmental effort and maximise the benefits for pupil progress. In the final analysis, however, professional standards and the various elements of Hay Group research are mutually supportive in helping to provide a route map for the continuing development of the teaching profession.

Introduction

It's not what you do, it's the way that you do it

Think of a really good waiter. What makes him good at his job? The chances are that it would not take long to come up with a list of words like warm, sociable, responsive, attentive and, perhaps, co-ordinated or dexterous. But what about things like good at food hygiene, thorough knowledge of health and safety standards, or cellar management? The last three are, of course, very important, if you do not want to poison your customers or give them corked wine – but would they spring to mind first? Given a set of basic skills, it is the waiter who really *wants* to do the job well that strikes you as more effective. The waiter with perfect technical skills but an icy disregard for diners' enjoyment is less likely to entice you back into the restaurant.

This relatively trivial example points up the essential difference between Hay's work in education and the overarching standards agenda. To be sure, the standards established for a variety of roles in education do include aspects of *how* people should do their jobs, but their main focus is on *what* people have to do: the tasks, duties and responsibilities required to be effective in role. Hay, on the other hand, unambiguously examines *how* people do their jobs and the impact that has on others.

No cloning – a flexible approach

There is another key difference between Hay's approach and the approach taken by the National Standards and the Ofsted Inspection Framework. The Standards set out what is expected from all jobholders, irrespective of any specific situation or detailed context. Hay looks for different patterns of behaviour that enable different people in different circumstances to deliver successful outcomes in different ways. So, thinking again of our waiter, there are fine gradations of behaviour expected in different kinds of contexts. For example, the way a waiter demonstrates courtesy at the Dorchester is different, at a detailed level, from the way a waiter demonstrates courtesy in Pizza Express. This is not to say that one context is more important than another, but simply that, whilst the absolute standards of food hygiene remain the same, the relative standards of social interaction need to be finely attuned to the situation and the people involved.

There is perhaps no more complex social interaction than that in the classroom, the playground, the sports hall, or the school canteen. This is why so many headteachers and teachers have found Hay's flexible approach to the way they think about performing their job well so attractive, valid and useful, complementing the National Standards and the Ofsted Framework.

What accounts for our behaviour?

Before going on to describe Hay's research for the TTA and DfES, it may be helpful to outline Hay Group's heritage in competency research. The notion of behavioural competencies, indeed the coinage 'competency', was Professor David McClelland's. McClelland was Professor of Psychology at Harvard University. He set out to discover why it was that people who, on the face of it, have the same skills, knowledge and experience could have such widely divergent performance outcomes when they were doing the same sorts of jobs. He came to the conclusion that it was not raw capability that mattered, but how a person used it.

Our own experience confirms this: the brilliant student who left school at sixteen, the outstanding musician who never practised her instrument, the athlete who did not want to give up his Saturday mornings to compete for the school. All may have been highly capable people. However, something was missing, and the missing link, in McClelland's view, was motivation. We do the things we do because we like the feeling we get when we have done them. This is the source of energy for people who do difficult and stretching jobs. It accounts for the resilience we see in the teaching profession when some of the tasks associated with the job may be unappealing – the outcomes from the achievement of these tasks fulfil the teachers' needs and concerns about education, or about children, or about social justice.

The problem is that these behavioural drivers, which McClelland called social motives, are non-conscious. They are very hard to measure, and they are hard to change. So the *practical* way to help people think about doing their job with more energy, commitment and focus is to look at the level of behavioural competencies – i.e. those things that highly effective people do more often, or with greater intensity, than average performers.

The research

Researching behavioural competencies in the teaching profession

Interview approach

Hay's approach to the research projects for the TTA and for the DfES (then the DfEE) was the same as McClelland's, and it was the same for headteachers and teachers. It did not involve, for the most part, asking people to speculate on what made a good headteacher or a good teacher. Teachers and headteachers spent between two-and-a-half and three hours describing in detail what they had actually done in their own jobs to be successful. The format was a structured interview called a Behavioural Event Interview. Teachers and heads talked about what they did, what they said, what they thought, and how they felt, not in retrospect but *at the time of the event*. The research also focused on how they behaved at times when they were frustrated and things were not going well, because, as we all know, outstanding people often display a different and powerful set of behaviours when times are tough. These are the situations where highly effective people learn and grow most.

Choosing the sample and establishing their performance levels

Of course, the choice of the samples of headteachers, deputy headteachers, heads of department and teachers was also critical. Hay's researchers not only needed a truly representative group spread geographically, by sex, by race, by urban or rural area, by subject (in the case of teachers) and by phase; they also needed to know how good the participants were at their jobs using some reliable measure or measures of performance.

In the case of headteachers, the choice was based on the quality of Ofsted reports as well as on the opinions of LEAs, professional associations and so on. In the case of teachers it was much harder, because Hay needed to know how much pupils had progressed when they were being taught by each sample teacher. This was an area in which Hay had limited experience. Therefore, Professor David Reynolds and his team worked with Hay to gather start-of-year and end-of-year pupil performance data for the classes taught by the teachers in the sample. In this way it was possible to establish a robust added-value measure that would enable teachers to be sorted into those who were outstanding and those who were average. An additional criterion for inclusion in the sample was that the teacher should be fully effective in the view of his or her headteacher.

This ability to sort the sample is important to the way in which Hay conducts its competency research. It is not so interesting, or so useful, to be able to say: 'This is what the outstanding people are doing'. Nor is it very interesting to say: 'This is what very poor teachers are doing'. It is exciting and potentially much more useful to be able to paint a picture of how the majority of teachers delivering sound performance can plan their own development so as to move towards the outstanding, thereby 'raising the bar' for the whole profession (see Figure 3.1).

In order to do this, Hay's analysis of the behavioural data collected during the interviews focused on the question: 'What is the difference

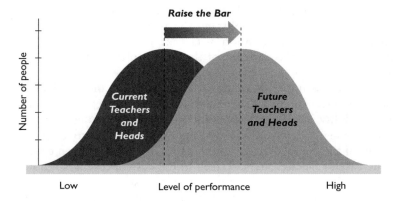

Figure 3.1 Change in level of performance.

between what outstanding teachers do and what average teachers do?' Telling that story in a clear way, using the language of the profession, helps very many people to identify and focus on the specific things that might enable them to make a step-change in their performance. Moreover, if the teacher's performance is measured by pupil progress, personal development based on this research could result also in a step-change in the learning opportunities and eventual attainments of their pupils, or, in the case of headteachers, in the learning opportunities provided by their schools.

Creating models of excellence

Over the course of a number of research projects between 1998 and 2000, 160 heads and 180 teachers were interviewed and then sorted into groups that the data suggested were outstanding, and groups that the data indicated were average. Of course there were others about whom the researchers could not be certain, and their data were not used. As a result, Hay could investigate the difference between average and outstanding teachers and headteachers, using a statistical analysis of behaviours evident in their interview scripts, to establish what it was that people who were outstanding did at a higher degree of complexity or sophistication (or more often) than those who were average. The hurdle for statistical significance in this analysis was that the outstanding could be sorted from the average with better than 80 per cent accuracy.

Social statisticians will know that this could easily result in a statistical artefact rather than something useful, so the research team also looked at the *themes* in the stories the interviewers had heard. What sorts of concerns were in the minds of those who were really good at their jobs? This thematic analysis enabled the behavioural data to be organised in a way that made intuitive sense to jobholders. These arrangements of competency data were called 'Models of Excellence', and they are important in simplifying the way in which the research is used in practice. Hay's intention was that teachers and headteachers should be able to see the patterns of their jobs in the way findings were presented.

This clustering is not only an aid to understanding and a valuable way of promoting face validity. The 'clustering' of competencies highlights areas of capability in which all jobholders need some strengths, helping to focus development actions. Nobody can possibly hope to display high levels of all of the competencies represented in a model – fifteen competencies in the case of headteachers, sixteen in the case of teachers – but every teacher or headteacher needs strengths in each cluster.

Figure 3.2 shows the way in which the teacher competencies are arranged as sixteen competencies in five clusters. (Both the TTA and the

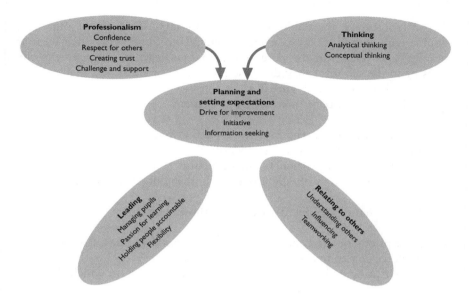

Figure 3.2 Teacher competencies.

DfES prefer to refer to the competencies as 'professional characteristics'. The terms are, for all practical purposes, interchangeable.)

Using the competency models – current applications

The way in which these competencies have been used differs between headteachers and teachers. For headteachers, the Models of Excellence have been an integral part of the Leadership Programme for Serving Headteachers (LPSH). Over 10 000 headteachers have now had feedback during the programme on their competencies as seen by colleagues in schools. This competency feedback is based on a 360 degree questionnaire administered to colleagues in schools in advance of the workshop part of the programme.

The use of the teacher model was different. The teacher competency research was commissioned by the DfEE in the run up to the introduction of threshold assessments. It provides the framework in which teachers can express their personal views about *how* they do the job as an adjunct to the evidence of personal development and achievement in the classroom. Hay's experience of working with teachers in schools suggests that much more value can be realised from this research by more frequent use of the competency model in the context of continuing professional development and performance management.

Structure of the dictionaries of professional characteristics

The competencies are published in a 'dictionary'. Each is set out on a double-page spread so as to enable individuals to think about their current practice and reflect on the potential impact on learning outcomes in the class or in the school if they do something more often or at a higher level. An example is shown in Figure 3.3.

On the left-hand page there are three elements:

- the name of the competency with its definition;
- a core question that helps to identify whether or not the behaviour is underpinned by a particular intention; and
- a brief explanation of why it matters in the context of the job.

On the right-hand page there are another three elements:

- descriptions of the competency in action that are organised into levels of increasing complexity or sophistication;
- a description of how these levels work (i.e. the way in which development can be seen); and
- a summary of other competencies with which this one often combines.

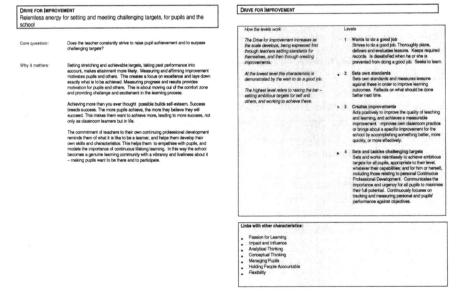

Figure 3.3 Dictionary of competencies.

Those who want more detail on the teacher competencies and the statistical basis for our work can find the complete model and report on the DfES website at http://www.dfes.gov.uk, and those who wish to explore the headteacher competency model can find it on the NCSL website at http://www.ncsl.org.uk/

Measuring my impact

The world is full of good advice, and it is all too easy to provide a picture of excellence and leave it at that. A natural response would be: 'Yes, but what does that mean for me?' This is where the second, and perhaps most exciting, part of Hay's research is so valuable. As a result of the work we have done, headteachers, middle managers and teachers can ask for and receive upward feedback on the impact that their behaviour has on the staff or students they lead.

How leaders unleash the discretionary effort of their staff

The headteacher work in this regard is relatively easily dealt with because Hay did validating rather than original research into the impact of head-teachers on their staff. The reason for this is that the relevant aspects of the experience an adult has when being led by another adult are the same whether you work in a bank, a school, or a manufacturing company. As an employee, I want to know what my job is, how I have to do it, where I am going, what authority I have, and what flexibility I have to do the job. I also want to know the kind of support I can get from colleagues to achieve results, and I would like to feel that I am rewarded appropriately for my efforts. Table 3.1 describes these climate dimensions in more detail.

Hay's research over many years has shown that if these conditions are met, then people will be more engaged in their work. They will actually contribute more, not by more effort or longer hours, but through 'discretionary effort': the intensity with which they do the job and the excitement they have when the job is well done.

School climate – how it feels to work here

In the LPSH these dimensions of the way staff feel when they are led by the headteacher are called the 'school climate'. In most other situations this measure is called organisational climate. It is a very well tried and tested measure of the impact that leaders are having on an organisation.

Figure 3.4 shows the sort of feedback that a headteacher might get from staff as part of the measure of school climate. The value of this measure is

Table 3.1 Climate dimensions

Flexibility	The feeling employees have about constraints in the workplace; the degree to which they feel there are no unnecessary rules, procedures, policies and practices that interfere with task accomplishment; and the feeling that new ideas are easy to get accepted
Responsibility	The feeling that employees have a lot of authority delegated to them; the degree to which they can run their jobs without having to check everything with their boss and feel fully accountable for the outcome
Standards	The emphasis that employees feel management puts on improving performance and doing one's best; this includes the degree to which people feel that challenging but attainable goals are set for both the organisation and its employees
Rewards	The degree to which employees feel that they are being recognised and rewarded for good work; the sense that such recognition is directly and differentially related to levels of performance
Clarity	The feeling that everyone knows what is expected of them and that they understand how those expectations relate to the larger goals and objectives of the organisation
Team commitment	The feeling that people are proud to belong to the organisation; the degree to which they will provide extra effort when needed; the trust that everyone is working toward a common objective

that it provides a gap analysis; it expresses the felt need of the team. Heads can therefore think about aspects of their behaviour that may have an impact on each of these dimensions. This is valuable, because our research consistently shows that climate can predict future performance of a work group, and it can account for around 30 per cent of the variability in output (e.g. pupil progress outcomes).

A headteacher receiving the feedback shown in Figure 3.4 would need to consider gaps between the climate staff experience now (Actual) and the climate they would wish to experience (Ideal), where those gaps are over 20 percentile points. In this case, the head might first wish to understand more about why staff do not have a feeling of responsibility in their roles, and feel that the systems around them are inflexible. In this way, the feedback is the springboard for a process of enquiry that can involve all staff.

Classroom climate

The Hay Group researchers were nervous, however, of applying this concept and these six dimensions – so well tested in the adult world of public service, commerce and industry – within the classroom. Research

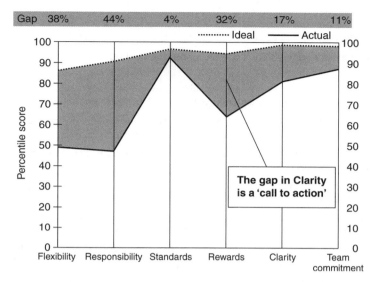

Figure 3.4 Feedback on school climate.

undertaken by Hay Group colleagues in high schools in the USA led us to the idea that original research into the aspects of classroom climate that related most closely to pupil progress would be a valuable addition to the understanding of the role of the outstanding teacher. Hay therefore embarked on a separate strand of research to enquire into how pupils felt when they were being taught by outstanding teachers. In short, the research team sought to understand what truly made a difference to the learning environment for pupils and what factors affected the discretionary effort of pupils, and they sought to relate this understanding to the professional characteristics of outstanding teachers in their ability to create the appropriate conditions for pupil progress. The upshot of this research – which, incidentally, has been universally accepted by teachers Hay works with – is that there are nine dimensions of classroom climate to which teachers should pay careful attention if they wish to enhance the learning opportunities for their pupils. Table 3.2 gives the definitions of these new classroom climate dimensions.

Figure 3.5 shows these dimensions as they are displayed on Hay Group's Transforming Learning website, which is a personal development service for teachers and heads based on the research described in this chapter. The action-planning modules provided by the service enable headteachers or teachers to ask themselves questions about which particular patterns of behaviour are likely to be necessary in order to make them more successful in their roles. The service helps them get

Table 3.2 Dimensions of classroom climate

Clarity around the purpose of each lesson – how each lesson relates to the broader subject, as well as clarity regarding the aims and objectives of the school

Order within the classroom, where discipline, order and civilised behaviour are maintained

A clear set of *standards* as to how pupils should behave and what each pupil should do and try to achieve, with a clear focus on higher rather than minimum standards

Fairness: the degree to which there is an absence of favouritism, and a consistent link between rewards in the classroom and actual performance

Participation: the opportunity for pupils to participate actively in the class by discussion, questioning, giving out materials, and other similar activities

Support: feeling emotionally supported in the classroom, so that pupils are willing to try new things and learn from mistakes

Safety: the degree to which the classroom is a safe place, where pupils are not at risk from emotional or physical bullying, or other fear-arousing factors

Interest: the feeling that the classroom is an interesting and exciting place to be, where pupils feel stimulated to learn

Environment: the feeling that the classroom is a comfortable, well-organised, clean and attractive physical environment

This chart shows a summary across all classroom climate dimensions. It shows the gap between you own perceptions and your pupils' perceptions of the actual level of each climate dimension.

In reviewing this summary, your key question is: Do I understand and share my pupils' perceptions of the classroom climate?

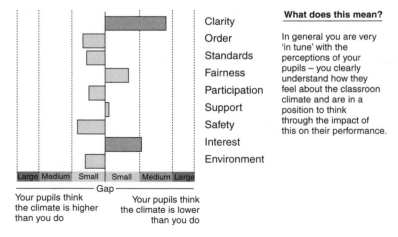

Figure 3.5 Summary of classroom climate dimensions.

beyond the problem of an unattainable ideal – as represented by the national standards or the models of excellence. It is practical, suggesting ways to link the realities of a job to the impact one makes as measured by climate.

Leadership styles

For headteachers or middle managers going through the LPSH or using the Transforming Learning website, there is a third area which they might wish to consider. Leadership styles are those patterns of behaviour that one's direct reports (i.e. members of a workgroup) experience as coercive, authoritative, democratic, affiliative, pacesetting or coaching. Each of these words has a very particular meaning in Hay's approach (see Table 3.3).

These definitions are important because they help leaders of schools or departments to understand how people experience the way they are led. All too often a leader thinks that he or she is coaching but the experience of their direct reports is of coercion. The feedback gained as a leader through the LPSH or through the Transforming Learning website gives food for reflection about how one can adapt one's responses and behaviours to different situations and different people in order to make them feel stronger and more capable.

Observing the classroom teacher

In the classroom, researchers did not attempt to collect data from students on the leadership styles of their classroom teachers. Whereas the classroom climate measure is a measure of students' own *feelings*, leadership styles are clearly a judgement about the teachers themselves. It was felt to be inappropriate for students to be asked to give feedback directly on the style of their own teacher.

The research team did experiment with an attempt to have teachers complete questionnaires about the classroom leadership of their teaching colleagues. On analysis, the internal structure of the questionnaire collapsed. One might just as well have asked a single question: 'Do you consider your colleague to be a good teacher?' This was expected, because all Hay's previous research shows that only the people in a work group (i.e. direct reports) are able to give an accurate picture of the leadership styles of the work group leader.

Hay therefore used established research into teaching skills arranged under Ofsted inspection headings to link pedagogical techniques to classroom climate and performance outcomes. This provided a basis for classroom observation of the teacher research sample. The outcome of this work was a confirmation that sheer pedagogical skill is an important

Table 3.3 Leadership styles

The coercive style Primary objective: immediate compliance. When used effectively, the coercive style draws an immediate and, for the most part, willing response from employees. In cases when employees resist directions, despite the effective use of the coercive style, employee termination is the next logical step. When not used effectively, over the long term the coercive style draws passive resistance, rebellion, resignation and, in the worst instances, physical damage to an organisation or strategic damage to major objectives.	**The authoritative style** Primary objective: providing long-term direction and vision for employees. When used effectively, the authoritative style motivates employees, particularly new ones, by focusing their attention on the long-term goals of the organisation or work group and the way in which day-to-day efforts support these goals. When not used effectively, this style fails to take full advantage of the natural talents and ideas of knowledgeable employees.
The affiliative style Primary objective: creating harmony among employees and between manager and employees. When used effectively, the affiliative style motivates employees by supporting them during either highly routine or stressful times. By strategically and explicitly focusing on the human element of a situation, this style often succeeds in getting the job done. When not used effectively, the affiliative style leads to low standards, a sense of favouritism, lack of clarity, and frustration for many employees.	**The democratic style** Primary objective: building commitment among employees and generating new ideas. When used effectively, the democratic style motivates employees by empowering them to make decisions about their own work processes and goals. It is designed to create teamwork and team commitment to achieve those goals. When used ineffectively, the democratic style produces confusion, delays and conflict among employees or between employees and the manager due to a lack of focus and direction.
The pacesetting style Primary objective: accomplishing tasks to high standards of excellence. When used effectively, the pacesetting style works for employees who are completely self-motivated and understand their objectives. It is also important for demonstrating that a manager can 'pitch in with the troops' when necessary. This style is less effective in times of organisational change, when an explicit discussion of the mission and employees' roles is warranted. It can also produce extreme stress as the manager takes on more of the work of his or her subordinates.	**The coaching style** Primary objective: long-term professional development of employees. When used effectively, the coaching style motivates employees by linking their daily work to personal long-term objectives. It helps employees develop sound thinking strategies that build their confidence in functioning more autonomously. When not used effectively, the coaching style leaves employees unsure about what they should be doing next, and can result in diminished standards and procrastination in solving problems.

element in pupil progress – necessary, but not sufficient. Once again, details are available in the full report on the DfES website.

Continuing professional development

Putting Hay's work in context

The Literacy and Numeracy Strategies have had a significant effect on the quality of teaching and learning in classrooms up and down the country. The implementation of the strategies has done much to make the experience of children more consistent. However, this more standardised approach, by its very nature, is less amenable to adaptation in the light of the specific circumstances of a school, a teacher or a class (though many teachers are now more comfortable in making such adaptations).

Hay is philosophically more concerned about how jobholders can be helped to do their job better – whatever their starting point. The crucial consideration in using Hay Group work is the context of the school, the head or the teacher. This contextual link allows an individual to work out where to focus his or her development effort. Rather than spending a lot of time and effort on weaknesses that may not really matter very much, the professional takes responsibility for considering the areas of personal development that will make the biggest difference to pupil progress or learning opportunities.

The picture that Hay uses to help leaders think about the relationship between competencies or characteristics, leadership styles and context for school improvement (or climate) has four 'circles'. Figure 3.6 shows the four-circle diagram for a headteacher. (There is a slightly different variant for classroom teachers owing to the lack of a leadership style measure for classroom teachers – see above.)

Figure 3.6 shows causal links. It enables heads to think about how the way they behave and the leadership styles they adopt affects the feeling of the work group – the staff – they lead. The usefulness of this approach to leaders' personal development is very well established. It is not the only way of thinking about how I, as a leader, affect the output of the staff I lead, but Hay has found it to be intuitively helpful and capable of rigorous measurement. The percentage impact numbers in Figure 3.6 are conservative values from Hay's work in contexts outside schools. Hay researchers are now working with colleagues at the University of Newcastle to establish the strength of causality in the context of school leadership.

As you can see, the place of the National Standards is in the first circle, which describes what the role of headteacher is. Another part of this circle is Hay's description of the behaviours that lead to success as a head

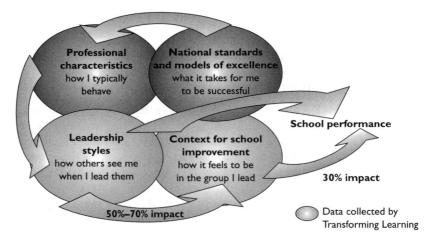

Figure 3.6 How headteachers deliver performance.

(the Models of Excellence). The final part of the first circle is the unique job each head holds as a result of the context of the school and the demands placed upon him or her by the governing body. By placing due emphasis on the realities of a head's particular job, and by focusing on both the final performance outputs and the intermediate output of school climate, a head can think fruitfully about the relative merits of taking personal developmental action in any area of professional skill or characteristic.

Here we come once again to a differentiator between the professional standards as articulated in the documentation guiding the profession, and the research that Hay has done. The standards provide a framework within which people can think about their professional development, but they are voluminous and relatively complex. Policy-makers have clearly recognised this, and have worked hard to reduce the complexity of the frameworks into simpler and more attractive formats. However, for all that, their thrust is towards quality standards, and in this respect they represent static targets or minimal levels rather than dynamic developmental approaches.

Hay Group's approach depends on the standards of the framework, but also focuses on the job holders and how they can create excitement for themselves and others about the improvements they can make in the job that they have chosen to do. Professional characteristics represent the artist's palette for the professional in the classroom or the school. They have their tones, deep or light, and choices must be made that may not be easily measured or easily accounted for. These choices arise from the particular concerns and the particular situation of the people involved in the class or the school. None of these choices can be legislated for; none of these choices can be set out in standards.

Self-directed change

How are people helped to make the right choice? The answer is not by prescription. The only person who can direct his or her own change and development is the teacher or the headteacher involved. No one can force an adult to change; no one can force an adult to learn something they do not wish to learn. This may be true of children too, but that is not the province of Hay Group.

Hay's concern with the professional standards agenda is that, on its own, it smacks of exhortation. It has more of the stick than the carrot about it. What Hay has gathered from work with public sector and private sector organisations around the world is that when people choose to change on their own account, the effect is orders-of-magnitude greater than when change is imposed upon them. It is for this reason that the Transforming Learning website is designed using the self-directed change model first developed by David Kolb and Richard Boyatzis (1970).

There is a bizarre disconnection between the disciplined and patient way that people learn to play an instrument, or become an artist, or represent a client in a court of law, compared with intolerance and impatience about friends' or colleagues' unpreparedness to change their day-to-day behaviour. It is as hard to learn to deploy or change the palette of professional characteristics one uses as it is to learn to paint a picture. It is as hard to learn to change behaviour as it is to play the flute. Great artists, great craftsmen, great teachers seem to achieve truly outstanding outcomes with barely conscious effort, but for the majority these have to be worked for. Such an effort needs to be sustained over time, which is very hard in the context of a stressful job.

Kolb and Boyatzis have therefore developed a four-stage approach to the way in which people can learn to change. The four stages are:

- the motivation to change;
- readiness to change;
- deciding to act; and
- metamorphosis, or change over time (see Figure 3.7).

The first stage is the one that is so often left out of any personal development planning. The danger of a professional standards approach to change is that one might simply apply a tick-box approach to gaps in one's capability. However, the truth is that people find it very difficult to look at

> **Step I**
> **The motivation to change**
> Realising who I am and who I want to be
> Gathering data on my real self and imagining my ideal self

> **Step II**
> **Readiness to change**
> The balance of change and continuity
> Reflecting on felt needs and strengths on which to build

> **Step III**
> **Deciding to act**
> Creating mindfulness and attention
> Establishing my goal and creating a practical plan

> **Step IV**
> **Metamorphosis**
> Changes in the real or ideal self
> Experimenting and practising in a safe and supported environment

Figure 3.7 The four steps to embed change.

that list of gaps and find the energy to take the effort to make the necessary changes.

Experience shows that it is only when teachers and headteachers reconnect with the passion that took them into the profession they love that they can find the resilience to make lasting changes over time in the way they do their job. Teachers and heads want so much for their students and schools. Hay's research has shown that the gifts each teacher brings to the classroom make a real difference to the progress children make, irrespective of the social context for the school.

Embarking on a journey of professional development is rewarding in its own terms, but especially so when one knows that the results can be so important for pupils. This is the message of hope that lies at the heart of Hay's work. Though they are burdened by bureaucracy and regulation, though they may be measured in inappropriate ways, though they may feel that creative approaches to teaching and learning are not valued, professionals can break through these external obstacles by paying more attention to releasing their own full potential.

References and further reading

Barnard, D. and Lees, A. (1999) *Highly Effective Headteachers: An Analysis of a Sample of Diagnostic Data from the Leadership Programme for Serving Head-teachers*, London: Hay Group.

Boyatzis, R.E., Leonard, D., Rhee, K. and Wheeler, J.V. (1996) 'Competencies can be developed, but not the way we thought,' *Capability* 2(2): 25–41.

Goleman, D. (2000) 'Leadership that gets results,' *Harvard Business Review* 78–92.

Hay Group (2000) *Research into Teacher Effectiveness: A Model of Teacher Effectiveness.* Report by Hay Group to the UK Department for Education and Employment. Available at: www.dfee.gov.uk/teachingreforms/mcber.

Hay Group (2002) Transforming Learning. Website service to enable headteachers, middle managers and classroom teachers to collect upward feedback from direct reports and pupils. Available at: www.transforminglearning.co.uk/

Kolb, D.A. and Boyatzis, R.E. (1970), 'Goal-setting and self-directed behavior change,' *Human Relations* 23: 439–457.

Leonard, D. (1996) 'The Impact of Learning Goals on Self-Directed Change in Management Development and Education,' Unpublished doctoral dissertation, Case Western Reserve University, Cleveland.

Litwin, G.H. and Stringer, R.A. Jr. (1968) *Motivation and Organisational Climate,* Boston: Harvard Business School Division of Research.

McClelland, D.C. (1985) *Human Motivation,* Glenview, IL: Scott, Foresman.

McClelland, D.C. and Boyatzis, R.E. (1982) 'Leadership motive-pattern and long-term success in management,' *Journal of Applied Psychology* 67: 737–743.

Spencer, L.M. and Morrow, C.C. (1996) 'The Economic Value of Competence: Measuring ROI,' Paper presented at the Conference on Using Competency-Based Tools and Applications to Enhance Organizational Performance, Boston.

Part 2

National Standards for teachers

Chapter 4

Qualified Teacher Status

Lorraine Harrison

> Teaching is one of the most influential professions in society. In their day to day work, teachers can and do make huge differences to children's lives . . .
>
> (DfES 2002:2)

Introduction

This chapter provides a case study of how the original Standards for Qualified Teacher Status were applied on a training programme for primary teachers at the University of Brighton. Although there is now a new set of QTS Standards, the principles in applying these Standards remain the same, as does their application to training programmes for teachers in secondary schools.

The 1994 Education Act established the Teacher Training Agency (TTA), an executive, non – departmental public body. The purpose of this organisation is to 'raise standards in schools by attracting able and committed people to teaching and by improving the quality of teacher training' (DfES 2002). One aspect of the TTA's original remit for Initial Teacher Training (ITT) was to review the structure and content of courses in order to establish Standards for the Award of Qualified Teacher Status (QTS). Key DfEE circulars on these developments were 14/93, 10/97 and 4/98 (DfE 1993; DfEE 1997; DfEE 1998). Circulars 10/97 and 4/98 signified the development of a more focused agenda that identified:

- course requirements;
- Standards for the Award of QTS;
- primary English, mathematics, science and ICT curricula;
- secondary English, mathematics, science and ICT curricula.

Circular 4/98 identified clear and precise expectations for all beginner teachers, and signified a policy linking institutional funding and judgements about quality (Carroll and Harrison 2000) as evidenced through

Ofsted inspections of ITT. These Standards therefore provided institutions with clear professional expectations that were required to be embedded within all courses.

This chapter provides an overview of the ways in which the Standards for the Award of QTS have been incorporated within the Post Graduate Certificate of Education (PGCE) (Primary Years) course in the School of Education at the University of Brighton. It illustrates how the course has interpreted these Standards in relation to:

1   Course development
2   Course structure and content
3   Partnerships with schools and school-based training
4   Professional development.

Course development

At the University of Brighton, policies and initiatives within course development have been shaped by national developments as well as university quality assurance mechanisms and School of Education monitoring, evaluation and review. Course changes have been implemented on an annual basis in order to ensure that the school of Education's ITT provision matched DfEE (DfES), TTA and Ofsted requirements. In the case of the PGCE (Primary Years) course, developments have arisen from clear principles that underpin current DfES requirements. These principles are as follows.

Principle one – A commitment to shared aims and clear vision of the model of the teacher.
The current aims of the course embrace the School of Education's commitment to prepare graduates to:

• become effective teachers with a capacity for critical and creative thought;
• have the ability to exercise independent judgement in on-going curriculum development;
• acquire the skills, knowledge and understanding consonant with the role of the teacher as a professional practitioner;
• be prepared to respond to the demands of the school and wider community.

The model of the teacher suggests that successful students will:

• be effective practitioners across the primary age phase (5–11 years);
• make a significant contribution to the work of a school in a particular subject area;

- be versatile and resourceful;
- have high levels of professional competence and a secure grasp of principles underlying good practice;
- demonstrate a positive attitude towards their own professional development.

Principle two – A recognition of the need to broaden existing provision to accommodate a wide range of students with different experiences and /or circumstances.

Principle three – A commitment to the continued refinement of provision through critical review of course evaluations and the annual review of academic health.

Principle four – The recognition of and need to sustain the characteristics of high quality provision as endorsed by external moderation procedures (including Ofsted).

Course development therefore takes into account the requirements of the TTA as well as the philosophy of the course and the School of Education's own quality assurance mechanisms. This means that the School of Education can provide students with a rigorous, distinctive experience, whilst at the same time ensuring that course provision will enable them to meet the Standards for QTS.

Course structure and content

DfEE Circular 4/98 contained requirements that were intended to 'equip all new teachers with the knowledge, understanding and skills needed to play their part in raising pupil performance across the education system' (DfEE 1998: 3). This publication contained details of the Initial Teacher Training National Curricula for primary and secondary teachers, and acknowledged that effective implementation of these requirements 'may require considerable changes for some providers' (DfEE 1998: 3). The Initial Teacher Training Curricula represented a 'key element in the government's plans for raising attainment in literacy and numeracy and making progress towards the national targets' and specified what students 'must be taught and be able to use in relation to' English, mathematics, science and ICT (DfEE 1998: 5).

The Standards were written to be 'specific, explicit and assessable ... designed to provide a clear basis for the reliable and consistent award of QTS regardless of the training route or type of training leading to QTS' (DfEE 1998: 8). Those Standards that relate specifically to students intending to teach in a primary setting (within the 5–11 age range) are set out in six separate annexes as shown in Figure 4.1.

Annex A: Standards for the Award of Qualified Teacher Status

A KNOWLEDGE AND UNDERSTANDING
    2. Standards for primary subjects

B PLANNING, TEACHING AND CLASS MANAGEMENT
    1 Standards for primary English, mathematics and science
    2 Standards for primary and secondary specialist subjects
    4 Standards for primary and secondary for all subjects:
      a. planning
      b. teaching and class management

C MONITORING, ASSESSMENT, RECORDING, REPORTING AND ACCOUNTABILITY

D OTHER PROFESSIONAL REQUIREMENTS

Annex B: Initial Teacher Training National Curriculum for the use of Information and Communications Technology in Subject Teaching

A EFFECTIVE TEACHING AND ASSESSMENT METHODS

B TRAINEES' KNOWLEDGE AND UNDERSTANDING OF, AND COMPETENCE WITH, INFORMATION AND COMMUNICATIONS TECHNOLOGY

Annex C: Initial Teacher Training National Curriculum for Primary English

A PEDAGOGICAL KNOWLEDGE AND UNDERSTANDING REQUIRED BY TRAINEES TO SECURE PUPILS' PROGRESS IN ENGLISH

B EFFECTIVE TEACHING AND ASSESSMENT METHODS

C TRAINEES' KNOWLEDGE AND UNDERSTANDING OF ENGLISH

Annex D: Initial Teacher Training National Curriculum for Primary Mathematics

A PEDAGOGICAL KNOWLEDGE AND UNDERSTANDING REQUIRED BY TRAINEES TO SECURE PUPILS' PROGRESS IN MATHEMATICS

B EFFECTIVE TEACHING AND ASSESSMENT METHODS

C TRAINEES' KNOWLEDGE AND UNDERSTANDING OF MATHEMATICS

Annex E: Initial Teacher Training National Curriculum for Primary Science

A PEDAGOGICAL KNOWLEDGE AND UNDERSTANDING REQUIRED BY TRAINEES TO SECURE PUPILS' PROGRESS IN SCIENCE

B EFFECTIVE TEACHING AND ASSESSMENT METHODS

C TRAINEES' KNOWLEDGE AND UNDERSTANDING OF SCIENCE

Annex I: Requirements for all Courses of Initial Teacher Training

A TRAINEE ENTRY AND SELECTION REQUIREMENTS

B COURSE LENGTH AND COVERAGE

C PARTNERSHIP REQUIREMENTS

D QUALITY ASSURANCE REQUIREMENTS

Figure 4.1 Standards for QTS – standards relating specifically to the primary setting.

It was essential that the content of the PGCE (Primary Years) course demonstrated that it met the Standards contained within Circular 4/98, and that this content also reflected the principles outlined under 'Course development' above. It was also necessary to develop a range of learning outcomes that would provide an indication of the overall achievements expected of all students by the end of the course, and to demonstrate how these learning outcomes linked to the Standards. Table 4.1 provides details of the PGCE learning outcomes and their relationship to the Standards.

Table 4.1 PGCE (Primary Years) learning outcomes and their relationship to the DfEE Standards for QTS

PGCE (Primary Years) learning outcomes	DfEE Standards for QTS
A good understanding of the purposes, scope, structure and balance of Curriculum 2000 as a whole and within them, the place and scope of the primary phase, the key stages (including the Early Learning Goals), the primary core and foundation subjects and religious education	Annex A, section 2 (a & b)
A secure knowledge and understanding of and the ability to apply, the teaching and assessment methods specified in current DfEE requirements	Annex B, section A Annex C, section B Annex D, section B Annex E, section B
A secure knowledge and understanding of their subject specialism in academic and professional contexts and a preparedness for the role of the specialist	Annex A, section 2 (d & f)
Competence in planning, teaching, evaluating and assessing the core subjects, ICT and the subject specialism across the primary age range	Annex A, sections B & C Annex B, section B Annex C, sections A & C Annex D, sections A & C Annex E, sections A & C
A working knowledge and understanding of their current professional and legal responsibilities in relation to school policies and practices	Annex A, section D
The capacity to form and sustain effective professional relationships with pupils, colleagues, parents/carers	Annex A, section B
The capacity to apply to the process of education throughout the primary years, the graduate skills of critical awareness, independent judgment, clarity of communication and commitment to continued professional development	Annex A, section D

The content of the university-based element of the course is made up of the following strands:

1   Core curriculum provision and ICT
2   Foundation subjects, religious education and subject specialism
3   Professional studies.

Within the core curriculum and ICT strand, students are prepared to teach these subjects with competence, confidence and enthusiasm. They are required to develop their personal understanding of the subjects to a depth and quality suitable for teaching them across the primary age phase, and are also required to practise teaching these subjects during school place-ments and periods of school-based training. For each core subject, students are provided with the following experiences:

• a series of taught sessions;
• completion of a subject audit;
• participation in a school-based training week.

Mapping course provision against the Standards

The content of the Science element of the course is an example of how the philosophy of the university tutors is reflected and reference is made to appropriate Standards. Table 4.2 is taken from the PGCE (Primary Years) student handbook, and provides an impression of how the range of student experiences is organised in order to develop effective teachers of science.

Table 4.2 reveals the wide range of Standards linked to the university-based provision. This supports the DfEE suggestion that the Standards should not be used in a 'mechanistic, tick-list approach or entail each Stan-dard being supported by its own evidence base' (DfEE 1998: 8). The Standards, therefore, have been interpreted from an holistic, rather than atomistic, perspective.

Using formal assignments as evidence for achievement against the Standards

Competence against the Standards is also evidenced through formal assessments. The core subjects, ICT, specialist subjects and professional studies are all assessed formally. These assessments have been designed so that they provide opportunities for students to demonstrate their know-ledge and understanding of the subject in question as well as their ability to apply this knowledge and understanding within a professional context. The professional studies element of the course, for example, links closely

Table 4.2 Student experience in Science and its relationship to the DfEE Standards for QTS

Content	Description	Standards
Taught sessions	The science sessions provide an introduction to the subject in terms of its value as a discipline and its centrality as a core subject within the National Curriculum. They acknowledge the different starting points of students in terms of their own understanding and seek to promote in them the confidence and competence to involve children in practical, investigative scientific experiences as well as the conjecture that constitutes scientific thinking. Sessions begin with an examination of scientific ideas and the development of science in the primary curriculum. Students' procedural and conceptual understanding is developed alongside pedagogical knowledge and understanding, and acknowledgement is given to the role that subject knowledge plays in effective classroom practice. Throughout the sessions, emphasis is placed on the use of ICT in subject teaching	Annex E Sections A & C
Subject audit	All students are required to complete an audit of their competence in science at the beginning of the course and identify action plans to develop their capability through experiences in school and at the university. Subject knowledge is assessed during the final stages of the course	Annex C Section C
School-based training	Students will work collaboratively in school to develop models of good practice. Working with pupils across the primary phase, they will explore: the role of assessment; progression, continuity and differentiation; and classroom management issues relating to health and safety	Annex A Sections A, B1, B4 (a & b), C, D

to the professional standards laid down in Circular 4/98 (Annex A, section D). The assignment requires the student to produce an annotated lesson plan (associated with a core curriculum subject) with supporting rationale that demonstrates their ability to identify the key teaching and learning processes and the centrality of formative assessment within each phase of the lesson. This piece of work is assessed against the student's ability to:

• Produce a coherent, well-structured lesson plan which:

> has clear, appropriate learning intentions;
> identifies appropriate teaching strategies relevant to the task and the children;

identifies assessment techniques and opportunities to enhance teaching and learning;

demonstrates the ability to make judgements about future teaching based on assessment of pupils learning

- Relate taught theory to practice, indicating how background reading has informed thinking and extended understanding
- Identify key elements of DfEE Circular 4/98 within the plan, with reference to planning, teaching, and class management, monitoring, assessment, recording, reporting and accountability
- Write coherently and accurately, referencing their work using the Harvard Convention.

The assignment requires the student to select and interpret a specific range of standards in order to support their written work. This is a necessary skill that relates to an individual's ability to take responsibility for his or her own professional judgement, both throughout the course and during the induction year and beyond.

Partnerships with schools and school-based training

A significant part of the PGCE (Primary Years) course is undertaken in school settings. Students are required to spend a minimum of eighteen weeks in school and experience two significant school placements (in two different schools). They also undertake three school-based training weeks, where they teach aspects of English, mathematics and science in a range of settings and age groups. The school-based elements of the course provide the context where students are able to demonstrate all aspects of their professional competence. Consequently, the School of Education has established a strong (and continually developing) partnership with schools in the region in order to ensure that appropriate procedures are put in place that enable students to develop appropriate expertise as teachers.

Circular 4/98 emphasised the importance of partnership requirements, and stated that:

in the case of all courses of ITT, higher education institutions and other non-school trainers must work in partnership with schools ensuring that: schools are fully and actively involved in the planning and delivery of ITT, as well as in the selection and final assessment of trainees.

(DfEE 1998: 137)

The School of Education had worked within an established formal partnership scheme since 1990. This scheme was developed by a group of representative headteachers and university tutors, who agreed that:

- the training, support, supervision and assessment of students would be a shared responsibility between the school and the university;
- the assessment of students would be undertaken jointly, by tutors and mentors, the summative report being agreed by both parties;
- schools would appoint mentors to undertake an agreed part of the formal supervision of students;
- a training programme for mentors would be set up.

These principles have formed the basis for subsequent developments, and mean that the School of Education has continued to develop appropriate mechanisms that have refined partnership arrangements in response to DfEE requirements. In order that new initiatives and refinements are fully understood and implemented by all those involved in the partnership, the university organises partnership training on an annual basis. Representatives from partnership schools: are invited to contribute to new initiatives; are kept informed of changes; disseminate the agreed roles and responsibilities of the partnership; explore new ways in which school experience can be embedded in ITT; and help to ensure comparability of experience for all students.

Following the publication of DfEE Circular 14/93, the university created a working group (of headteachers and university tutors) to shape the competence statements into a set of expectations for students on their final school placement. Expectations were then established for the first and interim placements, to ensure focus, continuity and progression. These expectations allowed school mentors and university tutors to record the range, quality and evidence of student achievements. The expectations were then modified to accommodate the new Standards following the publication of Circular 4/98.

Current expectations for each school placement are subdivided into general expectations and expectations relating to each core subject, ICT and subject specialisms. These expectations provide explicit guidelines to students about the requirements for their teaching, and enable school and university staff to make links between university and school-based elements of the course. The general expectations have been subdivided into the following headings and reflect those headings:

- knowledge and understanding;
- planning;
- teaching and class management;
- monitoring, assessment, recording and reporting;
- other professional requirements.

Table 4.3 provides an example of the expectations for teaching and class management for the initial and final school placements. The expectations

Table 4.3 Student expectations for teaching and class management for the initial and final school placements.

Expectations for teaching and class management

Initial school placement	*Final school placement*
By the end of the placement, students must be able to:	By the end of the placement, students must be able to:
• Establish and maintain a purposeful working atmosphere	• Establish and maintain a purposeful working atmosphere for effective learning
• Ensure effective teaching of whole class, groups and individuals	• Show appropriate use of whole class, group and individual teaching to make effective use of time whilst meeting individual needs
	• Indicate high expectations of behaviour through appropriate intervention, a good standard of discipline, well-focused teaching and positive and productive relationships
	• Use critical evaluation to improve teaching effectiveness
	• Operate procedures under the Code of Practice on the identification and assessment of special educational needs (with guidance)
	• Manage the work of other adults in the classroom with guidance
• Provide opportunities for pupils to consolidate knowledge	• Understand the development of pupils' acquisition and consolidation of knowledge, understanding and skills
• Select engaging teaching methods to stimulate intellectual curiosity, communicate enthusiasm for the subject, and maintain motivation	• Use teaching methods which sustain the momentum of pupils' learning and keep all children engaged through stimulating intellectual curiosity, communicating and fostering enthusiasm, and maintaining motivation;
• Structure lessons: outline content and aims; present content around key ideas; use appropriate vocabulary; use good examples as illustration; provide accurate, well-paced explanations; use effective questioning; listen and respond to children constructively	• Set high expectations of all pupils
	• Provide well-structured information, outlining content and aims, signalling transitions and summarising key points (including work-related examples)
• Match teaching approaches to the subject matter and the pupils being taught	• Use clear presentation of content around key ideas, and clear instructions and demonstrations (well-paced, appropriate vocabulary and examples)
• Provide opportunities for pupils to consolidate knowledge	• Use effective questioning with attention to pupils' errors and misconceptions (involving all pupils), and provide constructive responses to pupils (taking pupils' learning forward)
• Select and make good use of learning resources	• Provide opportunities for consolidation (setting work/homework to reinforce and develop learning)
	• Select and use resources well

for the final placement are closely matched to the DfEE Standards, whilst the expectations for the initial placement take into account the nature and scope of university sessions experienced by students thus far.

Following the publication of Circular 4/98, the TTA has produced a range of exemplification materials including video extracts to assist ITT providers when making judgements about student achievement against the Standards. The materials are designed to 'support the reliable and consistent assessment of trainee teachers' and 'provide a training resource that will help to prepare colleagues in schools and Higher Education Institutions (HEIs) to make such rounded, confident and sound judgements in relation to the Standards' (TTA 2000: 4). The School of Education has incorporated these materials within its partnership training programmes so that expertise can continue to be developed, thus exemplifying improved practice to students, university tutors and school partners.

The TTA resource entitled *Supporting Assessment for the Award of Qualified Teacher Status. Video and Text Material Relating to Planning, Teaching, Class Management, Assessment and Monitoring from the Year 3 Classroom* (TTA 2000) was used as the basis for a series of partnership training sessions during 2002. School mentors and university tutors were invited to attend these sessions, the aims of which were for participants to:

- identify (through observations and evaluation) a student teacher's strengths and areas for development;
- select and justify evidence to support judgements made;
- evaluate achievement against the expectations for the final school placement;
- identify appropriate professional targets;
- compare judgements with an agreed (TTA) perspective.

These training sessions enabled participants to observe an episode of teaching, make judgements about the quality of this teaching, and compare these judgements within the group and with those published in the TTA booklet. Participants became more confident about their judgements and were better equipped to provide constructive feedback and suggest appropriate targets for development when subsequent observations of students were carried out.

A significant outcome of this training was an agreement to set up a working group to develop an example of how the Standards could be interpreted so that differentiated judgements about the quality of teaching could be made. These interpretations of the Standards were compiled, piloted, evaluated and refined, and are now used by mentors and tutors to assess the quality of teaching during the final placement. They have resulted in a refined understanding of the standards for QTS among all partnership schools. An example of these can be found in (Table 4.4). The

Table 4.4 Interpretations of the DfEE Standards for QTS in relation to teaching and class management

Teaching and class management

Very good	Good	Satisfactory	Unsatisfactory
All pupils focused, motivated, thoroughly engaged in tasks	All pupils focused, motivated and engaged in tasks	Most pupils focused, motivated and engaged in tasks	A significant number of pupils not focused, motivated or engaged in tasks
Precise match of differentiated activities	Well-matched, differentiated activities	Reasonable match of task to ability	Poor match of task to ability
Stimulating (occasionally inspirational), well-structured and well-paced presentation	Clear, well-structured, well-paced presentation	Satisfactory presentations with some structure, pace and clarity	Presentations lack structure, pace and clarity
Variety of engaging teaching strategies, judiciously chosen	Variety of effective teaching strategies	Variety of teaching strategies	Some evidence of varied teaching strategies
Consistently effective deployment of other adults in the classroom	Effective deployment of other adults in the classroom	Developing capacity to use other adults in the classroom	Ineffective use of available adults in the classroom
Imaginative and effective use of a wide range of resources	Effective use of a wide range of resources	Use of a range of appropriate resources	Inappropriate use of resources
Classroom activity and behaviour is sensitively managed and adapted to accommodate pupil needs	Classroom activity and behaviour is well managed and adapted to accommodate pupil needs	Classroom activity and behaviour is generally well managed and adapted to accommodate pupil needs	Classroom activity and behaviour is poorly managed and not adapted to accommodate pupil needs
Consistently able to use assessment of pupil learning to inform teaching	Generally able to use assessment of pupil learning to inform teaching	Developing ability to use assessment of pupil learning to inform teaching	Little evidence of the ability to use assessment of pupil learning to inform teaching
Insightful use of a wide range of effective questioning techniques	Effective use of a range of effective questioning techniques	Effective use of some questioning techniques	Reliance on a limited range of questioning techniques

section relating to teaching and class management has been reproduced, and can be compared to the expectations for the final placement as illustrated in Table 4.3.

Professional development

The existence of a course structure and partnership scheme that makes explicit references to the Standards for QTS is fundamentally important. However, it is also essential that the design of the course can provide opportunities for individual students to track their progress and achievements against the Standards. An individual's account of progress and subsequent collection of evidence must also be endorsed by a university course tutor so that the university can be confident about its recommendation to the DfES that the Standards have been met.

The course team has developed a professional development profile that is used by the student throughout the course. This document provides the basis for the completion of the Career Entry and Development Profile; a document that identifies professional strengths and areas for further development and is used to create a programme of professional development activities throughout the induction year and beyond. The professional development profile is set out under the following sections:

- *Section 1* *Course overview.* This section contains details about the course.
- *Section 2* *School experience.* This section allows the student to record details of school placements and school-based training. Individuals are invited to identify significant teaching experiences.
- *Section 3* *Standards for the Award of Qualified Teacher Status.* This section contains details of the Standards for the Award of QTS. Individuals are required to keep track of their progress towards these Standards in order to identify areas of strength and areas for further development. This information is used explicitly when completing section 6 of the profile.
- *Section 4* *Audits.* Students are required to keep copies of subject audits in this section. Students record their levels of understanding and take appropriate action to develop their subject knowledge. Satisfactory knowledge and understanding is confirmed through the successful completion of subject-based tasks at the end of the course.
- *Section 5* *Assessed work.* This section contains copies of all course assignments and feedback sheets.
- *Section 6* *School placement feedback and reports.* This section

contains copies of feedback from school placements and school-based training weeks. It provides an overview of an individual's development throughout the school-based elements of the course.

- *Section 7* *Profile of professional development and action plan.* Information contained in all previous sections is used to develop this section. Students are required to identify areas of competence and priorities for development at regular intervals throughout the course. They are also required to complete an action plan where they identify a number of pertinent action points in relation to progress. Each target generates points for action, dates for review and the identification of criteria for success.

The professional development profile provides the student and university tutor with a comprehensive account of progress throughout the course together with a range of evidence linked explicitly to the Standards. This information is updated continually by the student and endorsed by the university tutor to confirm that the Standards have been achieved.

Recent developments

The Standards for the Award of QTS have been incorporated into every aspect of PGCE (Primary Years) course provision. Whilst they have not significantly changed the philosophy of the course or the team's view about the model of a teacher, they have provided explicit guidance about the range of subject knowledge and breadth of professional expertise that should be expected of a student who is recommended for QTS. As such, a shared understanding about the professional knowledge, understanding and skills of beginner teachers is understood and has become transparent. This common understanding is now shared with all those involved in ITT – especially partnership schools. As this understanding has grown, so has the responsibility for involvement in making judgements against the Standards and the contribution, to the training process, of serving teachers and headteachers within the partnership.

Students now have greater opportunities to take responsibility for their own learning, and can use previous knowledge and experience to contribute to their audits of knowledge. The professional profile enables them, with agreement from university tutors, to identify strengths and create action plans to prioritise development in specific areas of need. This process has emphasised the importance of professional development and created a meaningful link to continuing professional development throughout the induction year and beyond.

The implementation of Circular 4/98, however, has created a number of challenges. It has meant a demanding and rigorous period of course review, both in terms of university provision and the training role of school-based partners. The Circular itself is immensely detailed, and it is a huge task for students to gather sufficient evidence across such a wide range of expectations. The TTA has recognised this and, following a lengthy and comprehensive period of consultation, has recently published a new set of expectations entitled *Qualifying to Teach, Professional Standards for Qualified Teacher Status and Requirements for Initial Teacher Training* (DfES 2002). This publication contains the revised Standards for the Award of QTS, which are organised in the following three sections:

1   *Professional values and practice.* These Standards outline the attitudes and commitment to be expected of anyone qualifying to be a teacher, and are derived from the Professional Code of the General Teaching Council for England.
2   *Knowledge and understanding.* These Standards require newly qualified teachers to be confident and authoritative in the subjects they teach and to have a clear understanding of how all pupils should progress and what teachers should expect them to achieve.
3   *Teaching.* These Standards relate to the skills of planning, monitoring and assessment, and teaching and class management. They are underpinned by the values and knowledge covered in the first two sections.

(DfES 2002: 6–12)

This publication emphasises the complex nature of the profession and describes teaching as:

involving more than care, mutual respect and well-placed optimism. It demands knowledge and practical skills, the ability to make informed judgements, and to balance pressures and challenges, practice and creativity, interest and effort, as well as an understanding of how children learn and develop. It recognises the important part other people play in pupils' learning: in the classroom, the home and the local community.

(DfES 2002: 2)

The refinements to the Standards and the view of the teacher represent a shift in emphasis that will be interpreted in ITT courses from September 2002.

Alongside these refinements come opportunities for providers to enjoy 'autonomy' in deciding how best to organise their training. This, in turn, allows institutions to develop ways of recognising and acknowledging students' individual needs. Most importantly, perhaps, is the suggestion from the TTA that courses may develop specialist areas of study (e.g. the teaching of children with special educational needs) or an aspect of training relevant to the particular needs of a region. Thus, the processes outlined in this chapter will be put in operation in order to ensure that the PGCE (Primary Years) course continues to meet current DfES requirements, whilst continuing to develop provision that benefits from distinctive characteristics. Therefore, the process of course development, both as a result of internal and external evaluation, is (and should be) a continuous process in order that capable, committed teachers continue to be educated.

References and further reading

Carroll, M. and Harrison, L. (2000) 'Developing a model of partnership in primary ITT,' in Watson, D. (ed.) *New Directions in Professional Higher Education*, Buckingham: Open University Press, pp. 43–51.

Department for Education (1993) *Circular 14/93: The Initial Training of Primary School Teachers: New Criteria for Courses*, London: DfE.

Department for Education and Employment (1997) *Circular 10/97: Teaching; High Status, High Standards. Requirements for Courses of Initial Teacher Training*, London: DfEE.

Department for Education and Employment (1998) *Circular 4/98: Teaching; High Status, High Standards. Requirements for Courses of Initial Teacher Training*, London: DfEE.

Department for Education and Skills (2002) *Qualifying to Teach. Professional Standards and Requirements for Initial Teacher Training*, London: TTA.

Teacher Training Agency (2000) *Supporting Assessment for the Award of Qualified Teacher Status. Video and Text Material relating to Planning, Teaching, Class Management, Assessment and Monitoring from the Year 3 Classroom*, London: TTA.

Teacher Training Agency (accessed on 3 March 2002) About the Teacher Training Agency. Available at: http://www.canteach.gov.uk/about/index.htm.

Teacher Training Agency (accessed on 3 March 2002) Flexibility is Key to High Quality Teacher Training. Available at: http://www.canteach.gov.uk/about/press/2002/02013.htm.

Teacher Training Agency (accessed on 3 March 2002) National Standards. Available at: http://www.canteach.gov.uk/info/standards/index.htm.

Chapter 5

Induction

Maureen Lee

Introduction

Achieving qualified teacher status is an important milestone in a teacher's career – the culmination of intensive study, practical classroom experience and rigorous reflection on experience and learning. Meeting the QTS standards by the end of initial teacher training requires commitment and determination, and is characterised by the blending of newly acquired knowledge, skills and understanding about teaching with personal strengths and qualities drawn from previous experience.

As initial training comes to an end, new teachers look ahead to their first posts with eager anticipation but also trepidation. For the first time they will be the class teacher, the form tutor, the new team member, a fully fledged member of the teaching staff – with all the excitement, opportunity and accountability which accompanies each of those new roles. However long ago their first year of teaching, most teachers will agree that being a newly qualified teacher is a unique experience, often the sharpest of learning curves and a period of time when access to high quality support structures can make the difference between success and failure.

Statutory induction arrangements

It was in recognition of the special demands and challenges of the first year of teaching and a parallel recognition of the need for high quality support for new teachers that statutory induction arrangements were introduced in England in 1999. All newly qualified teachers (NQTs) who have qualified since May 1999 are now required satisfactorily to complete a period of three terms' statutory induction in order to remain eligible to teach in a maintained school or non-maintained special school. Within the statutory arrangements every attempt is made to ensure that NQTs are given a fair chance to succeed; for example, headteachers must ensure that their new teachers:

- have a reduced teaching load, equivalent to 90 per cent of the normal average timetable of other teachers in the school;
- are enabled to use their release time to further individualised development needs;
- are allocated an induction tutor who will work closely with them throughout their induction period.

NQTs should also be allocated teaching timetables or groups which do not place unreasonable demands upon them, and receive additional support if they do not teach the subject(s) and key stages for which they have been trained.

The Induction Standards feature very strongly in the shape and structure of the statutory induction period, setting out with clarity what must be achieved so that all those involved in the process can work positively and progressively towards a successful induction period which builds on the foundations of initial training and also supports subsequent career progression.

This chapter sets out to identify the links between the Standards for the Award of Qualified Teacher Status and the Induction Standards (DfES 2001). It then goes on to highlight the positive benefits of having a set of standards for the first year of teaching – benefits to NQTs themselves, to schools, to LEAs and to the teaching profession more generally. Ideas for ways of using the Induction Standards to further develop good practice in induction are included, together with comments from colleagues who have worked intensively with the Standards over the past three years.

The structure of the Induction Standards and links to QTS Standards

Since the introduction of statutory induction in September 1999 there have been two sets of Induction Standards, the later set being introduced for those who began as NQTs from September 2003. This review was necessary during 2002 in order to build on the new QTS Standards which were introduced the previous year (see Chapter 4). The final paragraphs of this chapter also refer to the way the new Induction Standards were generated.

In contrast to the more numerous QTS standards, there are far fewer induction standards. This relative brevity prompts many positive comments from both NQTs and their employing schools, who see this set of Standards as both manageable and confidence-building. This is not to say that the Induction Standards are in any way unchallenging; nor that the Standards for the Award of QTS are too detailed. It is precisely because the QTS Standards are so thorough that the Induction Standards can be presented so concisely.

In order to meet requirements for satisfactory completion of induction, NQTs must:

- meet all of the Induction Standards by the end of their induction period;
- continue to meet the requirements of the QTS Standards consistently and with increasing professional competence;
- demonstrate independent performance against those QTS standards where an experienced teacher may have given support during initial training.

Creating a bridge from initial training to induction

The Induction Standards are designed to build upon the QTS Standards in such a way that beginning teachers can progressively develop their expertise and make logical connections between experiences and learning in initial training and the learning opportunities and expectations of the first year of teaching. There is considerable and deliberate cross-over between the two sets of Standards, representing a positive acknowledgement that during induction NQTs should not be faced with a completely new set of expectations. They should be using the opportunities of their first teaching posts to consolidate, develop and extend their existing teaching knowledge, skills and expertise. They should be enabled by the system to take confidence from their earlier successes and to build on them to tackle new challenges. There should be planned opportunities to take forward their own individual areas of practice that require further development. The Induction Standards provide just this structure and, if applied thoroughly and imaginatively, will form the basis of a strong bridge from initial training to first teaching post.

The Career Entry and Development Profile

Since 1998 all newly qualified teachers have moved forward from initial teacher training with a Profile, which details the structure of their training, together with any other relevant experience they may have. The profile also sets out their areas of strength, and areas of practice in which they will benefit from further support during induction. It is important to note that these areas for development are not weaknesses – all NQTs must meet all the QTS Standards before gaining QTS, and weaknesses would mean that they would not satisfactorily complete their training and therefore not gain QTS. In September 2003, this document was revised and renamed the Career Entry and Development Profile.

In order to establish continuity between initial training and induction, NQTs must take their Profile with them to their first posts and share its contents with their induction tutor. Headteachers must ensure that discussion of the profile does indeed take place, and that it is used as the basis for the NQT's induction action plan. The structure for individualised, relevant, continuing professional development for each NQT is therefore in place.

The responsibilities of the NQT

Newly qualified teachers are expected to become increasingly proactive and independent during their induction period. By the end of induction they are expected to be taking responsibility themselves for setting targets, for their pupils and for themselves. They are expected actively and consistently to demonstrate their effectiveness in planning and teaching, monitoring and assessing pupils' progress, and providing informative reports to parents and carers, and at the same time to be seeking to further their knowledge and understanding about effective teaching. They are expected to make an active contribution to the classes they teach, and, as the year progresses, to make an impact more widely within the school, to 'make a real and sustained contribution to school improvement and to raising classroom standards' (DFES Circular 5/99).

So, how specifically do the Induction Standards build upon those for the award of QTS? First, both sets of Induction Standards are organised according to the same structure as the QTS Standards upon which they build (see Table 5.1).

Until September 2003 the Induction Standards were grouped within only the last three subsets (i.e. there were no specific standards for subject knowledge and application). An initial reaction might be to view this as a gap, a negation of the importance of subject knowledge or a missed opportunity for underlining the importance of continuing professional development within subject teaching. However, looked at another way, the absence of a subset of standards for knowledge and understanding can be viewed as placing still greater emphasis on subject development within the induction period. This is because all the Induction Standards were viewed in relation to the subjects taught. Target setting, assessment, behaviour

Table 5.1 Induction Standards

Until September 2003	From September 2003
Knowledge and understanding	Professional values and practice
Planning, teaching and class management	Knowledge and understanding
Monitoring, assessment, recording, reporting and accountability	Teaching
Other professional requirements	

management, reporting to parents, knowing about and acting upon current research – none can be effective without appropriate and improving subject knowledge. A continuing focus on subject knowledge and understanding is therefore embedded within the Induction Standards in a way that is both coherent and practical.

This thread has been carried forward into the new Induction Standards, which specify that NQTs must show commitment to their professional development by identifying areas where their professional knowledge and understanding need to be improved, and then taking steps to address these needs.

The second way in which the Induction Standards and QTS Standards are inter-related is in their shared areas of focus. The same important features of teaching are expected; in some cases the Induction Standards restate QTS expectations and in others they extend their challenges.

The Induction Standards have clear expectations that newly qualified teachers will be:

- proactive;
- increasingly competent;
- independent;
- effective in implementation of school policies;
- establishing effective relationships;
- taking responsibility for their pupils' progress and their own development;
- demonstrating commitment to, and action towards, raising standards and school improvement.

The ways in which the Induction Standards are used

Experience of using the Induction Standards since 1999 has demonstrated their positive impact. In particular, having a clear set of Standards for the induction period has provided particular impetus to developing good practice in induction generally. The Induction Standards have:

- helped to determine the content of NQT induction support programmes;
- contributed to fair and rigorous monitoring and assessment procedures for new teachers;
- established a mechanism for quality assurance;
- encouraged collaboration and disseminating of good practice;
- established good practice in celebrating new teachers' achievements.

Using the Induction Standards to structure NQT support

All newly qualified teachers will set out to teach their first class(es) with their own set of strengths and development needs. They will have different subject specialisms, different pre-teaching experience, different skills and expertise, and of course different personalities. Even those with the same subject specialism will have different strengths and enthusiasms within that subject. They are also all in different schools, with different policies, different staffing profiles and different groups of pupils. In order to make the best possible progress as NQTs, they will therefore need individualised induction programmes.

At the same time there are many common features across schools – in terms of curriculum, organisation and ethos. Most importantly, there is a common set of standards for beginning teachers, focusing on high standards of professionalism and on raising pupil achievement, which all teachers must reach in initial training and during induction.

Individualised programmes of support

Used in conjunction with the Career Entry and Development Profile, the Induction Standards provide the structure whereby NQTs can move forward individually, building on their strengths and working to improve in areas of their practice where they are less confident or have had less experience. Schools or LEAs cannot decide that all NQTs must have exactly the same support programmes, since NQTs must be able to use their entitlement release time to take forward their own individual professional development – i.e. be supported to meet the Induction Standards in the context of their own prior achievements and their own development needs. Schools cannot view induction solely as induction into the policies and practices of the school, important as that is. Some NQTs will need much more support than others to meet particular standards; others will make particularly rapid progress and need challenging opportunities which take them beyond the Induction Standards and into the Standards for Subject Leaders (see Chapter 10). NQTs who have met the Fast Track assessment requirements may come into this category (see Chapter 8).

Learning together during the induction year

The Induction Standards have also enabled those who arrange induction support programmes, whether for individuals or groups of NQTs, to rethink their provision and ensure that they offer appropriately targeted support. NQTs often say that they miss the camaraderie and collaboration of their ITT courses. Once in their first posts they may be the only new teacher in the school, and even where there are several NQTs they may not

---

Box 5.1 Senior LEA Adviser and NQT Induction Co-ordinator

Each year we review the NQT courses that are offered centrally. The information we use to inform the review is now drawn from:

- evaluations of the current year's programme;
- information about NQTs' objectives in their Career Entry and Development Profiles;
- a focus group of NQTs to discuss the Induction Standards – for which particular standards had they needed most support?

This year we made major changes to our programme as a result, ensuring that all the course tutors focused tightly on the Induction Standards, in particular those which the review process had highlighted. For our primary NQTs this was target setting, taking account of ethnic and cultural diversity, and effective deployment of support staff.

---

encounter their peers on a day-to-day basis. There is a definite need for groups of NQTs to come together to look at their common concerns, to celebrate their achievements jointly, and to learn from others in both similar and different situations.

The Induction Standards provide a content structure for such collaborative opportunities. Individual schools, groups of schools, LEAs, ITT providers and other organisations which provide NQT development programmes can use the Standards to ensure appropriate and targeted provision (see Box 5.1).

Evaluating provision for NQT induction

In the Induction Standards, NQTs and their schools also have ready-made evaluation criteria with which they can evaluate the quality of provision. The key question is, how far has this development opportunity assisted an NQT in meeting his or her stated objectives?

The review format in Table 5.2 can be used by induction tutors and NQTs to highlight strengths and weaknesses, and to plan the specific support needed to enable the NQT to meet that standard.

Of course, and as previously mentioned, some NQTs may demonstrate achievement of the Induction Standards well before the end of their induction period, showing the potential to move rapidly ahead in their development, perhaps focusing on selected Subject Leader Standards for the latter part of the year. Because induction programmes must be individualised to an NQT's needs, there is scope for this enhanced progression which will provide opportunities for all new teachers to have suitably challenging opportunities to meet their own particular needs.

Table 5.2 NQTs' review format

Induction Standard	Good	Satisfactory	Development need	Support planned – when, where, who?	Review date

However, for most NQTs for most of the time, and for all NQTs in the early stages of their induction period, the Induction Standards can be seen to have made a very important contribution to the establishment of the principle of an entitlement to a high quality induction support programme designed to meet the particular challenges of the first year of teaching. The introduction of the Standards has been instrumental in establishing a common vocabulary, a shared focus and an open and clear agenda for NQT development programmes (see Box 5.2).

Box 5.2 Induction tutor, primary school

I was an NQT myself five years ago, before statutory induction and the introduction of the Induction Standards. I had very good support from my school at that time, plenty of encouragement to build up my strengths and work on my weaker areas, in just the same way as NQTs do now. What I didn't have was the benefit of the shared vocabulary and shared focus the Induction Standards have helped us to develop. In September, Kate and I looked at all the standards and used them to work out what support she needed, who would provide it, when and how. I then talked to her year group team about the standards we had decided to focus on each half term, and made sure that they were involved in helping Kate to achieve them.

We used a grid format from the LEA's NQT portfolio to record Kate's progress against the standards, and to plan the support she needed to work towards them (see Table 5.3).

Table 5.3 Induction Standards: extract from planned support programme

First/second/third term of induction period (delete as appropriate)

Induction Standard	Good	Satisfactory	Development need	Support planned – How?	When? Where? Who?	Evidence of achievement
Planning, teaching and class management d.Plans effectively where applicable to meet the needs of pupils with special educational needs and, in collaboration with the SENCO, makes an appropriate contribution to the preparation, implementations, monitoring and review of Individual Education Plans				OT – literacy/ numeracy co-ordinators G – SENCO OT – SENCO In – new staff induction session C – meeting individual needs	First two weeks October Fortnightly until November October and December Nov 29, SCITT Training School	

Notes: OT, observe teaching; C, NQT course; In – school-based INSET; D, discussion; G, guidance; R, reporting to parents/carers; P, planning; A, assessment records; O, observation; R, review meeting; PP, pupil progress.

Using the Induction Standards for monitoring and assessment of NQTs

Statutory requirements

By the end of their induction period all NQTs, in whichever school in England they teach, must demonstrate that they have met all the induction standards. Statutory arrangements for induction require that NQTs are allocated an induction tutor who will work closely with them throughout the induction period and who will monitor their progress and plan their support programme with them in the light of the outcomes of the monitoring process (see Box 5.3). All NQTs should have at least six opportunities to be observed in the classroom, and receive oral and written feedback following those observations. They should also have professional review meetings every six to eight weeks to identify their achievements and to set new or revised objectives. At the end of each term an assessment meeting is held, when the evidence of the NQT's progress is drawn together and a proforma is completed and sent to the Appropriate Body (the LEA in which the school is located or, for independent schools, the Independent Schools Council Teacher Induction Panel, ISCTIP).

The Appropriate Body's responsibilities are:

- to assure itself that schools understand and are able to meet their responsibilities for monitoring, support and guidance and for undertaking a rigorous and equitable assessment of the NQT;
- to decide, in the light of headteachers' recommendations, whether an NQT has satisfactorily completed the induction period and to communicate this decision to the NQT, the headteacher and the GTC. It may, in exceptional circumstances, offer an NQT the opportunity of an extension to the induction period.

At the end of the third assessment period, the headteacher makes a recommendation to the Appropriate Body as to whether the NQT has or has not satisfactorily completed induction. The Appropriate Body then makes the decision based on that recommendation.

Formative, continuous process

It is incorrect to describe the induction assessment process as three formal assessments, one at the end of each term. Evidence is gathered continuously, and will be located in the day-to-day work of the NQT – for example, in their marking of pupils' work, their reports to parents and carers, and their planning and assessment records. Assessment of an NQT's progress is therefore continuous, with fixed-point reporting three

Box 5.3 NQT, secondary school

My support programme has been very focused on assisting me to meet the Induction Standards, and my induction tutor has been genuinely involved in that process. The sense of partnership that has developed between us has ensured that I remained positive, even when I was finding it difficult to achieve the level of professional practice required by the Induction Standards. The regular reviews of objectives have enabled me to identify and reflect in a meaningful way upon the progress I have made. These meetings have helped me to consolidate the experience gained during initial teacher training, and to see how the QTS and Induction Standards knit together.

times a year. An important further point is that NQTs themselves have a responsibility for self-review, self-monitoring and self-assessment. Monitoring and assessment should not be a process which is done *to* them but collaboratively *with* them.

Support and training for induction tutors

For induction tutors, assessment against national criteria was the new dimension introduced by statutory induction arrangements in 1999. Prior to that, in many schools NQTs were well supported. In some, but not so many, NQTs' progress was also monitored rigorously through classroom observation and well-focused review meetings. However, post-1999 all induction tutors have been required to ensure that NQTs are monitored with the Induction Standards in mind – whether they undertake the observation and review themselves, or arrange for colleagues to do so. This has thrown up a development and training need for existing mentors (now induction tutors) and for subject leaders who may be contributing to the NQT monitoring and assessment process.

Schools, LEAs, Higher Education Institutions and other training providers across England have taken the Induction Standards as the focus for their support for induction tutors (and other colleagues involved in NQT monitoring) so that they can interpret, use and apply the standards more accurately and confidently. In secondary schools a senior member of staff (an induction manager or professional tutor) may hold regular training and development meetings with the staff who are taking the induction tutor role. In primary schools this may happen within individual schools or, more often, across groups of schools, through induction tutor networks and development groups. Similarly, LEAs and ITT providers are responding to the need to build the expertise of induction tutors in making fair assessment judgements about NQTs' progress, through development programmes which include training in evaluating evidence against the QTS and Induction Standards.

Interpreting the standards

A productive strategy for establishing common interpretations of the Induction Standards is the use of 'key questions' (Simco 2000; Bubb 2001). For example, evidence relating to Induction Standard (a) can be interrogated using the following prompts:

- How do you seek the advice of others and share ideas?
- Have you reflected with a colleague in the classes you both teach?
- Have you made any formal contribution in leading others' development?
- What examples do you have of experimenting with new ideas and reporting their effectiveness to colleagues?

In this way it is possible for induction tutors to move towards clarity about what satisfactory performance against the Induction Standards looks like in practice. This is not to say that further work on achieving consistent interpretation of the standards would not be beneficial. The Ofsted report on the first year of statutory induction called for 'further guidance and training on the interpretation of the Induction Standards and how they relate to the QTS Standards'. It also emphasised that 'all staff involved in assessing NQTs need to do so on the basis of good knowledge and understanding of the Induction Standards'. (Ofsted 2000)

NQTs who do not make satisfactory progress throughout their induction period

In those cases where NQTs do not make satisfactory progress throughout their induction period, consideration of the Induction Standards can make a major contribution to unpicking the exact nature and extent of the problem. The first step is to use the Induction Standards to clarify the concern, if indeed there is one. It may be that overly harsh judgements are being made, based on unrealistic expectations and interpretations of the Standards. On the other hand, if rigorous and extensive consideration of all the evidence reveals that there is a weak area within the NQT's practice, detailed consideration of the Standards will then pinpoint the precise difficulties the NQT is encountering and highlight the improvements that are necessary.

From that point, the conditions have been created for everyone to move forward constructively – induction tutors to review the NQT's induction support programme so that there is access to the right sort of support, NQTs and induction tutors together to set new objectives and decide how and when to monitor progress, headteachers and LEA Induction Co-ordinators to satisfy themselves that the right opportunities are being provided and, if not, to arrange additional support and monitoring (see Box 5.4).

Box 5.4 Induction manager, middle school

Having a clear set of criteria for assessment has provided us with the means to build on our previously comprehensive induction system. We now give much more rigorous and formative feedback to our NQTs about their progress.

If we have concerns about an NQT (which has happened twice over the past three years), the Induction Standards also focus us sharply on what we should be able to see as a minimum expectation. In one case we realised that we were not applying the criteria appropriately, and that our concerns were unfounded. In the other, we conducted joint observations and reviews of evidence, carefully applying the Induction Standards, and it was clear that there were serious weaknesses.

NQTs at risk of failing to complete induction satisfactorily

Although the vast majority of newly qualified teachers satisfactorily complete their induction period, if by the end of the three terms an NQT has not made satisfactory progress and cannot be assessed as having fully met the QTS and Induction Standards, the headteacher must recommend that the NQT does not satisfactorily complete induction. This recommendation is carefully scrutinised by the Appropriate Body in order to confirm that statutory requirements for the NQT's induction programme have been met and that the assessment judgements are fair. Many LEAs have set up scrutiny panels for this purpose, comprising headteachers and LEA officers. The NQT has the right of appeal against the decision to the GTC, but if the appeal is not upheld then he or she will not be able to continue to teach in a maintained school or a non-maintained special school in England. (QTS is retained, since it was awarded at the end of initial training). Appeals are made to the GTC, which may result in the Appropriate Body's decision being upheld, or overturned, or a decision that an extension to induction should be allowed in order to provide further opportunities for the NQT to demonstrate achievement of the required standards.

The Induction Standards and overseas-trained teachers

The Induction Standards are also used in the assessment of overseas-trained teachers in order to determine whether or not they can be exempted from the requirement to undertake statutory induction. Since May 2001, if an overseas-trained teacher has at least two years' teaching experience, regulations (see www.canteach.gov.uk) allow them to apply for 'assessment only' for QTS and exemption from induction (i.e. they are not required to follow a training plan prior to assessment). Trained assessors undertake these assessments, using the QTS Standards and, for exemption from induction, the Induction Standards are used as the criteria for assessment.

Using the Induction Standards for quality assurance

The Induction Standards provide a mechanism by which schools and their Appropriate Bodies (LEAs or the ISCTIP) can assure the quality of their NQTs' induction entitlement.

Equal opportunities to meet the Induction Standards

Statutory induction arrangements require NQTs' teaching posts to enable them to make progress against the Induction Standards. This means that posts should be matched to their training; provide regular contact with the same class(es), and should not present them with especially demanding discipline problems. Sometimes a post will be deemed suitable *only* with the provision of additional support – for example, where the NQT is the only teacher of that subject, when induction is completed in a special school, or where the school requires special measures following an Ofsted inspection but permission to employ an NQT has been granted by HMI (see Box 5.5). The Induction Standards are thus used as a quality assurance mechanism, the key question being, will this NQT be provided with every opportunity to meet the Standards and, if not, what additional support arrangements must we make?

Quality assurance responsibilities

Responsibilities for quality assurance of induction rest with both schools and their Appropriate Bodies (LEAs and ISCTIP.) The Teacher Training Agency plays a significant role in quality assurance by developing and providing support materials, advice and guidance to LEAs and schools. The GTCE appeals procedure is also an important part of the process for NQTs who feel they have not been fairly treated. In practice, the Induction Standards are central to all the procedures which are established to monitor entitlement and assure quality.

Tables 5.4 and 5.5 identify two key responsibilities for quality assurance, and demonstrate how they are linked to the Induction Standards. In order to help ensure that quality assurance requirements are met, there are different levels of support. The first relates to the statutory requirement which states that induction tutors should be adequately prepared and supported in the role so that they are fully aware of and can apply the Induction Standards to design support programmes and make assessment judgements (Table 5.4).

Box 5.5 Headteacher, special school

We had been advised that if we were to employ an NQT there could be problems in meeting statutory induction requirements and that there would be some additional requirements for the school to fulfil. We acknowledged that NQTs should be appointed to posts for which they have been specifically trained and, since there are no initial teacher training courses with a special education specialism, that our new teacher, James, would need extra support.

We were also advised that we would need to take particular steps to ensure that if he did not have sufficient opportunities to meet all the Induction Standards in our special school setting, we should arrange opportunities for him to do some of his teaching in a mainstream school.

In this sense the Induction Standards were extremely helpful. We could see where we needed to arrange for additional support – for example, so that James could teach higher-attaining pupils in the nearby primary school. The Standards also indicate the level of performance which should be achieved by an NQT at the end of the induction period, i.e. we should not expect him to be able to attain this standard at the outset. This made us realise that in our school, with so many specialist teaching assistants, James would need particular support early on in working with his classroom team. We were not expecting him to take full responsibility for deploying the team until later on in his induction period. Without the Induction Standards we might have had unrealistically high expectations from September and James could have felt as if he was failing, which he certainly was not.

Table 5.4 Preparing and supporting induction tutors

School level	Appropriate Body level	National level
Appropriate selection of induction tutors	Assuring itself that schools are able to meet their induction responsibilities	TTA pack – *Supporting Induction for Newly Qualified Teachers* (TTA 1999)
Access to preparation and training for induction tutors	Either offers directly or brokers appropriate development opportunities for induction tutors which focus on interpretation of Induction Standards	TTA document – *The Role of Induction Tutor, Principles and Guidance*, (TTA 2001) TTA video packs – *Supporting Assessment for QTS*
Management overview to ensure consistency for all NQTs at the school	Responding to schools' requests for support and guidance in interpretation of Induction Standards	TTA/DFES/GTCE seminars and conferences for LEA Induction Co-ordinators

The second example relates to the statutory requirement that there must be systems in place that assure fair treatment and enable NQTs to raise any concerns, including that NQTs must have fair opportunities to meet the Induction Standards (Table 5.5).

Table 5.5 Ensuring fair treatment for NQTs

School level	Appropriate Body level	National level
Overview of induction programme for each NQT at the school	Overview of where NQTs are employed. Aware of and take action in cases where NQTs could be disadvantaged	TTA document – *Into Induction* (TTA 2002), provided for every NQT before beginning induction
Moderation systems to ensure consistency of assessment decisions for each NQT within the school	Quality assurance procedures for making the decision on receipt of headteachers' recommendations at the end of induction	TTA forum for sharing effective practice – closed website for Induction Co-ordinators, conferences, seminars
Provides a way for NQTs to raise concerns	Designates a named person with whom NQTs may raise concerns, ensuring no conflict of interest	Appeal procedures to the GTCE

Using the Induction Standards to clarify issues and resolve problems

When one part of the system is found not to be meeting its responsibilities for induction, application of the Induction Standards to the issue can very often identify the means of resolving the problem. For example, if an NQT is insufficiently committed to his or her own induction, that NQT will benefit from close consideration of the Induction Standards to review the evidence of how far he or she is meeting each standard. The NQT will then need to take full advantage of further development opportunities linked to the standards to enable movement forwards towards satisfactory completion of induction.

Similarly, if an induction tutor is not considered to be making fair assessment judgements, the tutor will benefit from making detailed consideration of the Induction Standards, to discuss his or her interpretation with others and then to review the assessment judgements in the light of new insights. Headteachers and LEAs also need to pay close attention to the Induction Standards in determining the nature of the quality assurance arrangements they put in place, and continually to refer back to the requirements for satisfactory completion of induction and the circumstances which best permit NQTs to meet those requirements.

There are two further ways in which the Induction Standards have been used and applied: to contribute to the development and sharing of good practice in induction of new teachers, and as a way of celebrating achievement.

Using the Induction Standards to share good practice

Because the Induction Standards represented a new way of working, their introduction has provided a stimulus to teachers, LEAs and ITT providers to find new and improved ways of learning from each other. Collaboration and information sharing has taken place in various ways, including:

- between and across teachers in individual schools;
- between schools within consortia and other groupings;
- between schools and LEAs;
- between LEA induction co-ordinators;
- between LEAs and ITT providers;
- between all of the above and the TTA, DfES and GTCE.

The main focuses of information sharing and partnership working have been on how the Induction Standards are being used on a day-to-day basis with NQTs. Interest is also centred on the practical ways in which the Career Entry and Development Profile is used to bridge between initial training and induction, and how induction tutors are prepared and developed in the role. Induction tutors in particular have been interested in sharing ways in which NQT support programmes can best be developed to present the appropriate levels of support and challenge. Additionally, because the Induction Standards and QTS Standards are so interlinked, the introduction of the Induction Standards (together with the Career Entry and Development Profile), has generated greater understanding, within schools, of initial teacher training. This is particularly the case for those schools that are not currently involved in partnership schemes with ITT providers or in training teachers on employment-based routes.

One effective method of collaboration to develop and disseminate good practice in NQT induction has been the development of regional groupings of LEAs, ITT providers and schools. The TTA has supported and encouraged the development of these groupings, to facilitate the sharing of good practice in induction. Conferences for induction tutors and NQTs across regions have been organised by groups of LEAs, Training and Beacon schools, and ITT providers, and summaries of approaches to effective induction have been published.

The Induction Standards and celebrating achievement

By the end of their induction period, newly qualified teachers are expected to have demonstrated that they have met the Induction Standards. Supported by their induction tutors, NQTs will have gathered and collated evidence to demonstrate their achievement and will be recommended by their headteacher as having met the requirements for satisfactory completion of induction. Their LEA (or, for independent schools, the ISCTIP) considers all the evidence, and makes the decision based on headteachers' recommendations. This information is then submitted to the GTCE for registration purposes.

Success will be the case for the vast majority of NQTs, and represents a substantial achievement for these new teachers. They have met challenging demands with commitment and determination, and deserve praise for their achievements. There has been success, too, for their induction tutors and other colleagues in school who have worked intensively with them. At the same time, induction tutors will want to be very critical about their own contribution to the NQT's induction so as to ensure that the learning from one year contributes to school-wide improvements in induction systems in subsequent years.

The Induction Standards – looking to the future

The future for newly qualified teachers

Newly qualified teachers who have worked in a constructive, formative way with the QTS and Induction Standards will look ahead to the next stages of their career with commitment to their own continuing professional development and a positive approach to the National Standards. If they have been able to access one of the growing number of accreditation schemes as part of their NQT experience they will also have gained some credits towards higher qualifications, which can then be used within the next five years as part of a higher qualification through a university or higher education institution.

The individualised support and challenge that NQTs have benefited from during their induction period leads smoothly into the professional development opportunities available later on in their careers. NQTs finish induction with high expectations of their continuing professional development. At the same time, we know that too many teachers are leaving teaching after just a few years in the profession. There is therefore an urgent need to provide ongoing support and development opportunities for our keen and enthusiastic new teachers to build on their induction year, and to support them to continue to develop their confidence and competence as teachers and as subject leaders. The DfES is responding to these needs and is currently funding early professional development pilot schemes which build on this individualised style of professional development, planning to enable teachers in their second and third years of teaching carefully to select and follow the professional development paths which best meet their own identified needs. Evaluation of these pilot schemes is currently being undertaken to determine if, when and how the early professional development programme might be extended beyond the twelve pilot LEAs. Many other LEAs, ITT providers and other sources of continuing professional support for teachers are also offering support programmes for this crucial group of teachers – the future leading professionals in schools.

The future for the Induction Standards

Following the introduction of the new Qualifying to Teach Standards in 2002, the Minister for School Standards asked the Teacher Training Agency to undertake a complementary review of the Induction Standards. This review provided an opportunity to take account of developments since the current Induction Standards were framed – for example, the threshold standards and the DfES continuing professional development strategy, including the emphasis on early professional development for teachers in the first few years of their careers as discussed earlier.

The review was an opportunity for all stakeholders to reflect on some key questions about the Induction Standards. For example, how should they support NQTs to meet the challenges they are facing in schools in the early twenty-first century? Do the Induction Standards:

- help NQTs establish themselves as effective members of school teams, with support staff and other professionals?
- set out how NQTs should develop their own professional knowledge and skills, and the knowledge and skills of adults with whom they work?
- establish appropriate expectations for effective management of pupils' behaviour?

Proposals for a new set of Induction Standards were developed to mirror the structure and emphases of the new professional standards set out in *Qualifying to Teach* (DfES 2002). The TTA consulted widely on the revised standards, and the finalised version was published in Spring 2003 so that the new Standards could take effect from September 2003.

Wide consultation was important, since the new Induction Standards had to be appropriate expectations of newly qualified teachers, and enable them to make maximum impact in their first year with their first classes. Much had been achieved since 1999 by the introduction of the Induction Standards in terms of ensuring quality of entitlement and responsibility for induction. However, it was also important to take this opportunity to look at the Standards again and to check their content and scope against the demands of schools and teaching today, so that learning from the first year of teaching sets the strongest foundations for continuing and career-long professional learning patterns.

In conclusion, the Induction Standards can be viewed as a major contributor to good practice both within and beyond induction. Having a set of National Standards for the first year of teaching confirms within new teachers the practice of reflection, review and objective setting which is begun during initial training. Focused reflection, coupled with monitoring and assessment against clear criteria, sets the climate for career-long learning. It also places value on workplace learning, confirming that a whole range of learning opportunities, from observation of colleagues at work to focused reflection on one's own experiences, can and do lead to significant learning outcomes for teachers.

Most of all, newly qualified teachers who have had the benefit of a positive, successful induction will look back positively on their first year of teaching, and use their learning from it to move forward with confidence to the new roles and new challenges which lie ahead of them in their teaching careers.

References and further reading

Bubb, S. (2001) *A Newly Qualified Teacher's Manual: How To Meet The Induction Standards*, London: David Fulton.

Department for Education and Skills (2002) *Qualifying to Teach Professional Standards and Requirements for Initial Teacher Training*, London: DfES.

DfES (2001) *Guidance 582/2001: The Induction Period for Newly Qualified Teachers*. Available at: www.dfes.gov.uk/circulars/5_99/.

Essex LEA (2002) *Professional Development Portfolio for Newly Qualified Teachers*. Available at: www.pubs@essexcc.gov.uk.

Ofsted (2000) *The Induction of Newly Qualified Teachers*, London: Ofsted.

Simco, N. (2000) *Succeeding in the Induction Year*, Exeter: Learning Matters.

Teacher Training Agency (1999) *Supporting Induction for Newly Qualified Teachers*, London: TTA.

Teacher Training Agency (2001) *The Role of Induction Tutor, Principles and Guidance*, London: TTA.

Teacher Training Agency (2002) *Into Induction: an Introduction for Trainee Teachers to the Induction Period for Newly Qualified Teachers*, London: TTA. Available at: www.tta.gov.uk/induction.

Chapter 6

The threshold standards and their use in performance management

Trevor Yates

Background

The Green Paper, 'Teachers – meeting the challenges of change' (DfES 1998) set out the Government's proposal to improve the teaching profession. In the foreword, Tony Blair, Prime Minister, commented that:

> It addresses the critical issues of training, recruitment, leadership and support for teachers in the classroom and beyond. It also describes our proposals for pay and performance. We must reward good teaching better, recognising its vital role in raising standards.

The Green Paper proposed a much closer link between pay and appraisal than had previously been the case. A performance threshold to 'provide an opportunity for teachers to advance to a significantly higher professional level, with an immediate salary increase of up to 10 per cent and access to a higher pay range' was a key element of these proposals.

It recognised that the then statutory scheme of teacher appraisal had become largely discredited because, in most schools, it was seen as a pointless additional burden rather than an integral part of the school's performance management arrangements. Consequently, proposals were made to introduce a new, properly focused system of teacher appraisal which had clear objectives and outcomes. A thorough and annual assessment of the performance of every member of staff, which would result in setting targets for improvement and development over the next year, was seen as being at the heart of good performance management aligned to appraisal. In future this should:

- take place annually;
- involve classroom observation and other objective evidence of performance;
- take pupil progress into account; and
- result in the setting of individual targets for each teacher, at least one

of which should be directly linked to the school's pupil performance targets.

A pay range leading up to the performance threshold was envisaged. Teachers would normally expect increments in their early years of teaching, but their rate of progress would depend on their performance as monitored through induction and annual appraisal.

The performance threshold

The performance threshold was to be set at the then nine-point maximum available for experience and qualifications (DfES 2000a). This would lead to a significant rise in salary after some five to seven years for high-performing teachers, i.e. those with a track record of consistently strong performance meeting higher professional expectations. Once teachers reached the performance threshold, it was anticipated that the vast majority would exercise their right to apply for performance assessment.

In the first round of threshold assessment, 200 853 teachers actually applied – representing 80 per cent of the eligible cohort based on the DfES estimate of 250 000 eligible teachers.

Success at the performance threshold would depend on high quality and sustained levels of competence, achievement and commitment. Successful applicants would need to demonstrate that they had consistently achieved new national standards centred on classroom performance resulting in positive pupil outcomes.

Teachers' Standards Framework

The Green Paper initiated consultation on a new set of professional standards that would be required to meet the proposed performance threshold assessment. These new standards would provide the missing rung in the Teachers' Standards Framework which, it was envisaged, would form a coherent ladder of professional competencies to enable teachers to plan their professional development throughout their careers. The Framework (DfES 2002a) includes the following key milestones:

- the Standards required for successful completing of training (Qualified Teacher Status, QTS);
- the Standards required by newly qualified teachers after the first year in the profession (Induction);
- the new Standards for the proposed performance threshold assessment;
- the Standards for SENCOs, Subject Leaders and Fast Track teachers;
- the Standards for Advanced Skills Teachers; and
- the Standards of Headship.

Threshold assessment

The Green Paper was followed by a technical consultation document on pay and performance management (DfES 1999). This technical paper formed the basis of an extensive consultation exercise which ran until 31 March 1999.

The technical paper established a number of principles, most of which stood the test of consultation: teachers who are at the top of the main scale will be eligible to cross the performance threshold; achieving the threshold standards will be demanding and may take more than one attempt; threshold assessment will be made against National Standards characterising experienced and high-performing classroom teachers. In particular, a rigorous and clear assessment procedure at threshold including a combination of external and internal assessment was proposed, involving:

- demonstration by the teacher of proven and sustained high-quality teaching, resulting in positive outcomes for pupils' performance;
- clear evidence of a commitment to professional development and the impact this has had on classroom performance;
- a robust and careful assessment by the head of the quality of the teacher's performance against the National Standards, based on classroom observation and the reports of line managers; and
- a check on the head's judgement by an external assessor, who would review the evidence for every applicant (including appraisal judgements), discuss every applicant with the head, and observe a sample of candidates.

In addition to confirming or challenging decisions on the performance threshold, the external assessors would provide the necessary degree of national consistency and monitor the head's overall operation of the new pay system as a whole.

Threshold standards

Annex 1 of the technical paper contained the first draft standards for threshold assessment. These set out 'the high level of performance and expertise required of those teachers wishing to pass the **performance threshold**. They represent high expectations appropriate for a majority of teachers'.

Four threshold standards were proposed:

1   Pupil performance;
2   Use of subject/specialist knowledge;
3   Planning, teaching and assessment;
4   Professional effectiveness.

In proposing these standards, the paper took account of current research findings on teacher effectiveness (TTA 1998). Teachers meeting the threshold standards are 'highly effective practitioners in their classroom who command a wider authority with pupils across the school'. Such teachers will have:

> an established track record of good results and make a significant contribution, through their teaching, to the school's targets, policies, ethos and aims. They have kept up to date with developments in their subject(s)/specialism and how to teach it/them. They have a wide repertoire of teaching techniques and used relevant evidence and data to improve their teaching in order to raise standards of pupils' achievements. They demonstrate professional insights into the effects of their teaching and assessment approaches and are proactive in working with others inside and outside the school to secure their pupils' progress'.
>
> (DfES 1999)

Following consultation, the initial four standards were extended to create eight standards. These eight threshold standards for England are grouped into five areas which relate directly or indirectly to classroom teaching:

1   Knowledge and understanding
2   Teaching and assessment

   2.1 Teaching and assessment – planning lessons
   2.2 Teaching and assessment – classroom management
   2.3 Teaching and assessment – monitoring progress

3   Pupil progress
4   Wider Professional Effectiveness

   4.1 Wider Professional Effectiveness – personal development
   4.2 Wider Professional Effectiveness – school development

5   Professional characteristics.

The characteristics of effective teaching, and the professional characteristic standard in particular, were drawn from the research conducted by the Hay Group Management Consultants. This research, commissioned by the DfES was designed to provide a framework describing effective teaching (see Chapter 3). Its purpose was to help take forward the proposals in the Green Paper.

   The Hay Group set out to create a vivid description of teacher effectiveness, based on evidence of what effective teachers do in practice at different stages in the profession. The report of their findings (DfES 2000b) begins with the following quotation from a Year 8 pupil:

> A good teacher ...
> is kind
> is generous
> listens to you
> encourages you
> has faith in you
> keeps confidences
> likes teaching children
> likes teaching their subject
> takes time to explain things
> helps you when you're stuck
> tells you how you are doing
> allows you to have your say
> doesn't give up on you
> cares for your opinion
> makes you feel clever
> treats people equally
> stands up for you
> makes allowances
> tells the truth
> is forgiving.

The Hay Group found three main factors within teachers' control that significantly influence pupil progress:

- teaching skills;
- professional characteristics;
- classroom climate.

Each provides distinctive and complementary ways that teachers can understand the contribution they make. None can be relied on alone to deliver value added teaching.

They also found that sixteen characteristics contribute to effective teaching. These professional characteristics fall into five clusters.

1 Professionalism

- Respect for others
- Challenge and support
- Confidence
- Creating trust.

2   Thinking

- Analytical thinking
- Conceptual thinking.

3   Planning and setting expectations

- Drive for improvement
- Initiative
- Information seeking.

4   Leading

- Managing pupils
- Passion for learning
- Flexibility
- Holding people accountable.

5   Relating to others

- Understanding others
- Impact and influence
- Team working.

Hay established that this is not a static 'one-size-fits-all' picture. Effective teachers need to have some strengths in each of the five clusters, and they show distinctive combinations of characteristics that create success for their pupils.

Hay found that pupil progress is most significantly influenced by a teacher who displays both high levels of professional characteristics and good teaching skills that lead to the creation of a good classroom climate. Above all, the research re-emphasises how important and influential the teacher is in raising standards in schools, whatever the existing situation.

Meeting the Standards

To cross the Threshold, teachers in England must meet all eight of the national standards of effective teaching.

The Threshold Standards build on the standards expected of teachers at the end of their induction period and embody high expectations appropriate for the majority of experienced teachers. Any teacher, including part-time or peripatetic staff, should be able to show the required expertise.

Threshold assessment process

The introduction of Threshold and the new upper pay scales were two of the main changes included in the School Teachers' Review Body (STRB)

2000 (DfES 2000c) recommendations which, after due consultation, were embedded in the School Teachers' Pay and Conditions of Employment Document (STPCD) 2000. The key recommendation was that qualified teachers in England who applied for threshold assessment by 5 June 2000 (or 14 July where certain conditions applied) and were successful would be paid on the first point of the new upper pay scale as of 1 September 2000. Subsequent STRB and STPCD documents include annual amendments to the process.

However, the introduction of the threshold process did not run entirely smoothly. On 14 July 2000, a High Court judgement quashed the threshold assessment process. This led to the Secretary of State making an order bringing the School Teachers' Pay and Condition Document into effect from 1 September 2000 and removing from it all reference to threshold assessment.

The High Court ruling meant that the standards and procedures for threshold assessment must be the subject of examination and report by the School Teachers' Review Body, and must be given statutory force by a Pay and Conditions Order under the School Teachers' Pay and Conditions Act 1991. The Secretary of State subsequently made a further order which met these requirements. Teachers' pay and conditions were thus set out in full in the 2000 document, the School Teachers' Pay and Conditions Order No. 3 (DfES 2000d), which deleted reference to the threshold from the document, and the School Teachers' Pay and Conditions Order No. 4 (DfES 2000e), which restored the reference to the threshold and added the threshold assessment standards and procedures.

Implementation

With an estimated 250000 teachers eligible to apply during the first round, Cambridge Education Associates (CEA) was awarded the contract in January 2000 to implement the Government's performance threshold arrangements for teachers in England. The implementation of the first round of threshold assessment involved over 20000 schools and more than 200000 teachers, and required the deployment of just over 2000 threshold assessors.

Whilst CEA was responsible for the recruitment and deployment of the external threshold assessors, the initial training of external assessors and headteachers was subject to a separate contract which was awarded to the Confederation of British Teachers (CfBT).

The approach adopted by CEA was one of central operational management, supporting a closely linked network of regional and area co-ordinators. This allowed for the flexibility required to implement the arrangements and respond to situations locally, while at the same time retaining the essential national consistency required of a 'national framework of standards'. There were 24 regions, each with a named co-ordinator working in the field, and a designated regional deployment officer based centrally in the Cambridge office. Each region had approximately 1000 schools spread across three to twelve local authorities. Regions were grouped into five major geographical areas, with a named area co-ordinator working in the field and an area team leader based in the Cambridge office.

The key responsibility of regional co-ordinators was the quality assurance of the threshold process implemented by threshold assessors. Regional co-ordinators provided continuing support and guidance to threshold assessors and monitored the quality of their work. They also liaised with schools, professional associations, local authorities and other agencies in order to ensure the smooth implementation of threshold arrangements.

Threshold process guidance

Detailed guidance on the threshold process produced annually by DfES (DfES 2000f, 2001a, 2002d, 2003b) explains the performance threshold assessment process as set out in the relevant STPCD. It also explains other administrative and procedural rules determined by the Secretary of State.

Eligibility

Threshold assessment is open to all qualified teachers who meet specific criteria. The annual DfES guidance defines the specific eligibility criteria for each round of assessment. In round 1, for example, this included teachers who:

- were legally covered by the School Teachers' Pay and Conditions Document;
- were paid on the Qualified Teacher pay scale;
- on 1 September 1999 had nine years' teaching experience as defined by numbers of experience points, or were good honours graduates with seven years' teaching experience as defined by numbers of experience points.

Pay increases for all successful applicants in the first year were backdated to 1 September 2000. A key element of the success of the statutory threshold assessment process is the fact that there is no financial quota on successful assessments.

Application deadlines for teachers

The DfES guidance gives a deadline for applications to cross the threshold.

Threshold standards

To cross the threshold, teachers must meet all eight of the national standards of effective teaching. Effectiveness in each standard contributes significantly to teachers' overall effectiveness and the total picture may be summed up as follows:

> Effective teachers **know** their subjects and **understand** their pupils' needs. They **keep up to date** in their specialisms and in relation to national development. They apply their knowledge and understanding in **effective planning** of the curriculum and in their **teaching strategies,** based on a careful **assessment** of pupils' prior attainment, in order to ensure that pupils make **good progress.** Effective teachers understand this as central to their work. In order to achieve the best outcomes for pupils, effective teachers take appropriate responsibility for their **professional development** and **use the outcomes to further improve** their teaching, and to improve **pupils' progress.** They make an active **contribution to achieving the school's aims,** and **reflect the school's policies** in their teaching. The work of effective teachers is underpinned by a number of **professional characteristics,** those ongoing patterns of behaviour that underpin what they do. Effective teachers approach their work with **high aspirations** and **expectations** for their pupils; they **inspire trust and confidence** in pupils and colleagues; they work **collaboratively** for the good of pupils and the school, and are constantly **striving for improvement.**
>
> (DfES 2001f)

Assessment is against these national standards based on evidence of performance with a principal focus on teaching in the classroom.

Confidentiality

The contents of threshold applications and all other documents associated with an applicant's application are confidential. They should not be disclosed to anyone who is not involved in assessing or reviewing the application. The only people who may see all or parts of teachers' applications are:

- the head (and other members of the school leadership group);
- other teachers with management responsibility for the applicant;
- the external assessor;
- any other person with responsibility for quality assurance of assessments or monitoring of equal opportunities.

Equal opportunities

All individuals involved in the assessment process must act fairly and, in particular, must not discriminate unlawfully on the grounds of a person's sex, disability, part-time working, fixed-term contract or trade union activities.

Applying for threshold

A teacher wishing to apply for threshold assessment is responsible for making the application. This involves summarising evidence – in the form of concrete examples from the applicant's day-to-day work – to show that he or she has worked at the standards indicated over the last two to three years.

The DfES guidance includes action to be taken in specific circumstances, such as long-term sickness, in-service career breaks or maternity leave, where an individual teacher is unable to cite evidence covering the last two to three years.

Duty on managers

The Pay and Conditions Document places a duty on teachers who manage staff to assist the head or assessor to carry out threshold assessments of the teacher he or she manages.

Duty on headteachers

Heads have a duty to assess threshold applications in line with their professional responsibility for evaluating the standards of teaching and learning in the school. Heads also have a duty – which may not be delegated – to record in writing on the application forms whether each of the standards has been met.

Where there may be a real or perceived conflict of interest (e.g. the head is related to the applicant), the head is required to inform the assessor when forwarding the batch of applications so that the application can be included in the sample as a guarantee of impartiality.

Role of the assessor

The role of the external assessor is to verify, through sampling and discussion with the head, that the head has applied the performance threshold standard correctly, fairly and in line with national practice. Assessors undertake detailed scrutiny of the evidence provided, looking at different aspects of applications in the sample, and may conduct discussions with team leaders and other line managers in the school to come to a view about all the aspects of the process. In some cases this may involve a structured conversation with applicants in the sample and, in exceptional circumstances, a classroom observation.

The assessor may decide:

- to approve the assessment process and endorse all the head's assessments; or
- to take further action before approving the assessment process – this may include discussing assessments with heads and/or asking heads to change their assessment of some or all applications and/or substituting their assessments of some individual applications for those of the head; or
- not to approve the assessment process.

If not satisfied that the threshold assessment process has been followed properly, the assessor informs the head of the grounds for the concern and may request that the head re-assesses some or all of the applications. The assessor also agrees a date with the head for a return visit to the school.

Feedback to teachers

Heads should promptly notify teachers of the outcome of their application once the assessor has approved the assessment process. All teachers must have their assessed original application forms returned to them. All teachers are entitled to oral feedback from their heads on the reasons for the outcome of their application, standard by standard, and advice on aspects of performance that would benefit from further development. Where the assessor has substituted his or her judgement for the head's, the teacher will be given a copy of the assessor's reasons together with any comments the head wishes to add.

Although DfES provides detailed guidance on the nature of feedback, this is an area which has given rise to significant concern – especially in the case of unsuccessful applicants.

Individual teachers' right to review

One of the outcomes of the 2000 judicial review was the introduction of a right to review. Teachers who, after feedback from the head, believe that they have been wrongly assessed as not yet meeting the threshold standards have the right to apply to have the decision reviewed.

Teachers need to establish legitimate grounds for review. The grounds for review are that the teacher would have passed the threshold if the head or assessor who made the assessment:

- had taken proper account of the evidence presented; or
- had not taken account of irrelevant or inaccurate evidence; or
- had not been biased or had not discriminated against the classroom teacher in question.

Critically, this is a right to review by a review assessor (who will be an assessor who was not involved with the original decision) and not an appeal. The teacher does not have the right of representation.

Complaints about the external assessment process

There is provision for heads to complain about professional misconduct or gross incompetence on the part of the original assessor. If a complaint is upheld, the original assessment might be considered null and void and a new assessor assigned to repeat the process.

There is also provision for complaint against discrimination by the review assessor. If the review application confirms the original assessment and the teacher feels that he or she has suffered unlawful discrimination, that teacher may complain to his or her employer (the Local Education Authority or, at voluntary aided and foundation schools, the governing body) about the handling of the review by the review assessor. If a complaint is upheld, the employer refers the case, giving their conclusions and the reasons for their decision, to the review co-ordinator at CEA, who refers it to a replacement review assessor.

Teachers in different circumstances

Guidance is also provided by the DfES for teachers in different circumstances, including unattached teachers, outsourced teachers and teachers with more than one workplace.

Outcomes of performance threshold assessment

The statistics of the work undertaken by CEA (CEA 2001, 2002, 2003) in connection with the performance threshold assessment show a positive response to the implementation of the process despite challenges along the way (see Table 6.1).

In addition to 'met' and 'not yet met', there are two other possible outcomes of assessment:

- withdrawn – this decision can be taken by the applicant at any stage;
- ineligible – the head must ensure that all applications meet the eligibility criteria.

Table 6.1 CEA statistics for performance threshold assessment

	Round 1	Round 2	Round 3
Applications			
Schools with applicants	21 674	12 397	13 399
LEAs with centrally-employed applicants	148	84	96
Total number of applicants	200 849	31 221	37 956
Percentage of teachers applying by phase			
Nursery	0.25	0.38	0.21
Primary	37.3	46.8	44.38
Secondary	52.4	43.25	49.64
Special	4.4	4.14	3.01
Local Authority Secure Units		0.38	0.06
NSS (LEA units)	5.5	5.03	2.67
DA/DV (direct assessment/verification)	0.24	0.03	0.04
Met applicants			
Total number of successful applicants	194 216	28 726	36 382
Percentage of applicants deemed met	96.7	95.11	97.02
Percentage of not yet met applicants			
Percentage of applicants deemed not yet met	2.88	4.89	2.93
Percentage NYM by phase			
Nursery	3.49	3.36	1.28
Primary	2.5	3.16	2.13
Secondary	2.8	5.11	3.38
Special	2.97	4.31	3.94
Local Authority Secure Unit		1.67	14.29
NSS (LEA centrally employed)	5.38	8.93	5.22
DA/DV (direct assessment/verification)	22.39	42.86	21.43

Table 6.2 Equal opportunities statistics

	Round 2		Round 3	
	No. of teachers	No. met	No. of teachers	No. met
Gender				
Not given (%)	4.9	5.1	0.9	0.8
Male (%)	24.9	23.6	26.0	25.4
Female (%)	70.2	71.3	73.1	73.8
Full/part-time				
Not given (%)	12.5	11.9	2.6	2.4
Full-time (%)	66.2	66.2	81.6	81.8
Part-time (%)	21.3	21.9	14.2	14.3
Supply (%)	Not available	Not available	1.6	1.5

These categories accounted for 0.42 per cent of applications in round 1, 3.14 per cent in round 2 and 0.97 and 0.62 per cent of applications in round 3.

From the outset, a number of issues were raised in relation to perceived differences in pass rates between male and female teachers and full-time versus part-time staff. Whilst detailed records are not readily available for round 1, an analysis of round 2 and round 3 statistics show that, in fact, there is little or no difference in the percentage of teachers 'met' for each of these categories.

Standards not yet met

Analysis (CEA 2001, unpublished *Threshold Assessment Overview of Cycle One – Summary for STRB*) of those applications that were judged as 'not yet met' in round 1 shows that the standards most often judged to be 'not yet met' were standards 2.1, 2.2, 2.3 and 3. These standards may be described as those most closely related to teachers' classroom practice and outcomes for the pupils. It should be noted that many applicants judged as not yet meeting the performance threshold standards failed to meet several standards. The percentages given Table 6.3 refer to the analysis of each individual standard, and not of each application overall.

Applications for review

The total number of applications for review in round 1 was 2001. This represents 34.7 per cent of the 5 790 applicants deemed not yet met.

Outcomes of reviews

The review process outcomes for round 1 are shown in Table 6.4.

Table 6.3 Percentage of applicants judged as not yet meeting threshold standards

Standard	Percentage not yet meeting standard
1 Knowledge and understanding	18
2.1 Teaching and assessment – planning lessons	45
2.2 Teaching and assessment – classroom management	50
2.3 Teaching and assessment – monitoring progress	46
3 Pupil progress	49
4.1 Wider professional effectiveness – personal development	27
4.2 Wider professional effectiveness – school development	29
5 Professional characteristics	33

Table 6.4 Outcomes of reviews, round 1

Setting	Reviews	Met	Not yet met	Not yet resolved
Schools	1718	559 (32.5%)	1157 (67.3%)	2 (0.1%)
NSS (LEA units)	238	71 (29.8%)	167 (70.2%)	0 (0%)
DA/DV	45	7 (15.6%)	38 (84.4%)	0 (0%)

Table 6.5 Outcomes of reviews, round 2

Setting	Reviews	Met	Not yet met	Not yet resolved
Schools	262	59 (22.5%)	197 (75.2%)	6 (2.3%)
NSS (LEA units)	36	11 (30.6%)	24 (66.7%)	1 (2.8%)
DA/DV	1	0 (0%)	1 (100%)	0 (0%)

Table 6.6 Grounds cited for review

Ground	Applicants citing (%)
Ground 1 (taken proper account of the relevant evidence)	96.7
Ground 2 (not taken account of irrelevant or inaccurate evidence)	58.4
Ground 3 (not been biased or had not discriminated against me)	30.7

The decline in the number of review applications has been repeated in round 3.

It should be noted that many applicants applying for review cited more than one ground. The percentages in Table 6.6 refer to the overall percentage of cases in which the ground was cited in round 1 and round 2.

Post-visit questionnaires

Headteachers were asked to analyse nine aspects of the assessor's work on a post-visit questionnaire, ranking each aspect on a five-point scale. The nine aspects were: pre-visit arrangements; sample construction; awareness of school context; quality of preparation; evidence scrutiny; effectiveness of communication; professional conduct; clarity of judgement; and consistency of judgement. CEA received responses from approximately 50 per cent of schools visited.

The summary analysis across all nine aspects indicates a very high level of satisfaction by headteachers. There were no major differences in heads' responses to each aspect. All summary comments for each aspect were in the good/excellent category. The breakdown of overall responses for round 1 is shown in Table 6.7.

Table 6.7 Post-visit questionnaire: analysis of assessors' work

Category	Percentage of responses
Excellent	63.8
Good	31.0
Satisfactory	4.7
Weak	0.4
Unsatisfactory	0.1

Table 6.8 Formal complaints received regarding threshold assessors

Complaints	No. of complaints
Complaints on administrative procedures	30
Complaints on threshold professional process	28
Complaints on content of Final Report	15

A similar pattern emerged in round 2 and round 3 with the number of unsatisfactory responses falling to 0.04% and 0.05% respectively.

Complaints received

From 21 674 school visits by threshold assessors in round 1, formal complaints received were as shown in Table 6.8.

In total, 73 formal complaints represented 0.3% of threshold visits to schools in round 1.

In rounds 2 and 3 the number of complaints received declined even further:

- Round 2 – 7 complaints from 12 789 visits – 0.05 per cent
- Round 3 – 8 complaints from 13 939 visits – 0.06 per cent

Developments

STRB recommendations

The STRB 2002 report (DfES 2002a) made a number of recommendations which were adopted for round 3 and beyond. The most significant of which was the introduction of a selective visit regime.

Selective visit regime

While external assessors will scrutinise all applications, visits are now confined to schools/services and units in which:

- the headteachers had no previous experience of threshold assessment; or
- external assessors had significant reservations about a headteacher's approach to assessment; or
- the school/unit was part of a representative sample to be assessed in depth.

The introduction of a sampling regime resulted in 20 per cent–25 per cent of schools in round 3 receiving a visit; in future rounds this is expected to level out at 10 per cent–15 per cent.

In round 3, discretionary visits were made to 9.18 per cent of schools. This compares to the need for mandatory visits where the headteacher had not previously been responsible for threshold assessment in 12.17 per cent of the total number of schools. Discretionary visits are only made for sound professional reasons. An analysis of the reasons for round 3 discretionary visits to schools drawn from 100 batch sheets indicated the following most common reasons:

- 46 per cent – weak applications citing little evidence.
- 28 per cent – applicant/s in current post less than two years and headteacher use of prior evidence unclear.
- 27 per cent – applicants deemed NYM by the headteacher present in the pack.
- 24 per cent – few or no headteacher assessment comments.
- 20 per cent – administrative errors or omissions on the application form/s.
- 17 per cent – no contextual data supplied.
- 16 per cent – few or no headteacher developmental comments.
- 11 per cent – variance between threshold assessor initial judgements and headteacher assessments.
- 10 per cent – headteacher assessment and/or developmental comments were general and not specific.

An analysis of round 3 headteacher post-visit questionnaires indicates that the introduction of distance verification had little impact on the perceived

Table 6.9 Round 3 visits by external assessor

Phase	Number of packs	Visit (%)	Distance (%)
Primary	9387	21.23	78.76
Secondary	3317	21.61	78.38
Special	626	25.07	74.92
Nursery	69	43.47	56.52
LEA sevices	506	39.92	60.07

Table 6.10 Outcomes of Round 3 review cases

Direct assessment (1)	1 met	100%
Visit cases (57)	1 ineligible	
	1 withdrawn	
	15 met	26.3%
	40 not yet met	70.2%
Distance cases (52)	1 ineligible	
	1 withdrawn	
	9 met	17.3%
	41 not yet met	78.8%

quality of the process. 96.9 per cent of respondents said they were satisfied or very satisfied with the process compared with previous rounds. 97.8 per cent of respondents indicated that they were satisfied or very satisfied with the round 3 process.

Similarly the introduction of distance verification did not result in an increase in the number of review cases. In fact, the decline in cases which emerged in round 2 has continued in round 3.

A total of 110 cases have been completed so far, of which:

- 1 case was a direct assessment;
- 57 were visit-based verifications; and
- 52 were distance verifications.

There are currently a further 73 cases under completion.

The outcomes of the review process for round 3 so far are shown in Table 6.10.

The other 2002 STRB recommendations required the department to hold consultations on:

- guidance and wording of the standards;
- recognising the professional standards in sixth form colleges as being equivalent to the threshold;
- ensuring effective feedback arrangements are implemented;
- continuing to improve and simplify the application process;
- ensuring that the review process operates more quickly in future.

Performance management

One feature of the external threshold assessors' role in round 1 was to comment on the performance management systems in the school. In round 2, this became a requirement to comment on how the head had managed threshold assessment within the school's performance management arrangements. From round 3 onwards, with the advent of sampling, it was agreed that this reporting requirement will no longer form part of the external assessors' role. Instead, information will be obtained through Ofsted Section 10 inspections. However, the principle of light touch external verification of performance management in a school is under review as part of the January 2004 pay recommendations.

Upper pay spine

Progression on the upper pay spine has produced a degree of confusion within the teaching profession. The original legislative requirements for progression were that:

- there has been a review of performance of the post-threshold teacher; and
- the achievements of the post-threshold teacher and his or her contribution to schools has been substantial and sustained.

However, despite the department making it clear that there will be no external assessment on a par to the performance threshold, a number of teachers have continued to submit 'threshold application forms' to seek further progression on the upper pay spine. There have also been consistent calls from heads and governors for clearer guidance on criteria for upper pay and leadership group progression, and in particular the need for a reliable system which defines what is meant by *sustained* and *substantial* in relation to the school.

In response to these calls, and concerns from the government regarding the percentage of teachers progressing to UPS 2 and beyond, the 2003 STRB made the following recommendation:

> We recommend that consultations take place urgently on a new framework for progression to U3 in both England and Wales, including:
>
> - rigorous criteria which enable schools to identify those teachers who are performing at the highest level;
> - a grading system which enables schools to rank the performance of teachers in their school in relation to those criteria; and
> - a system of external assessment, using the threshold model.

The STRB prefaced these recommendations by setting out a compelling vision for schools, in which:

> - governors, heads and teachers are comfortable with the concept of rewards related to performance;

- schools are able to make decisions without detailed rules and guidance;
- high-quality performance management and professional development are available to all teachers to help them improve standards;
- schools have the confidence and capability to assess performance and reward staff; and
- performance and reward systems are managed effectively, transparently and fairly.

In a Parliamentary Statement on the proposed changes to schoolteachers' pay for 2004 to 2006 the Secretary of State welcomed this statement and the detailed commentary provided in the STRB report on where we are with the upper pay scale. He also welcomed the STRB statement that:

> We wish to ensure that further progression up the scale is clearly based on merit. We believe this should result in a tapering pattern of progression in which teachers will have the opportunity, on performance grounds, to move up the scale but progressively fewer of them will do so. We see a more substantive role for continuing professional development in this model.

The Secretary of State added that:

> In all walks of life people may perform competently, or highly effectively, or outstandingly well. We have the best ever generation of teachers. But to be clear that some are positively outstanding is no insult whatever to their able colleagues. The notion that every teacher is performing identically well fails to pay proper tribute to our very best teachers and defies common sense. I am grateful to those schools which have recognised this and showed the courage to administer UPS2 with appropriate rigour. The fact that some awarded points to only a minority of teachers disproves the argument made by others that this was impossible.
>
> I now look to the pay partners to rally behind the STRB's proposals for where we should go now on UPS3.

The response to this invitation was extremely swift and highly positive and led to the publication on 9 January 2004 of joint pay proposals by the Government, employers and unions. The parties to this agreement supported

> both the STRB's long-term vision and the importance of securing workable transitional arrangements. We believe that it is essential for schools to have a clear framework for rewarding our ablest and most

experienced teachers and this agreement seeks to provide it. It will enhance harmony in schools and provides a constructive solution to a long standing issue.

Rewarding our good and excellent teachers

A key concern for this agreement has been the need to agree a realistic affordability framework for rewards related to performance. We have agreed an outcome which spans not only UPS3 but also other payments to our best classroom teachers; and also pay rewards related to performance for members of the school leadership group.

The agreement affirms two important principles:

- the first is that good classroom teachers should be able to aspire to a salary which reflects their important achievements in raising standards. Consequently, we see UPS3 as the salary to which all good classroom teachers can aspire;
- the second is that the highest rewards for classroom teachers should be awarded for excellence. Consequently, we propose that a new scheme for excellent teachers should be introduced. On the basis of existing assumptions this will take effect from September 2006.

As a consequence of these two decisions, we agree that UPS4 and UPS5 should be deleted from the upper pay scale and that excellent classroom teachers who have achieved UPS3 can have access to a new excellent teachers scheme.

The excellent teachers scheme would be likely to benefit some 20 per cent of those reaching UPS3. We agree that it will require high standards to be set, drawing on the Advanced Skills Teacher Standards where appropriate. The details of this scheme have yet to be finalised but we see it being about rewarding excellent teachers for their work in the classroom and supporting colleagues within the same school.

The application of criteria

We recognise that schools and teachers are currently working under a set of published UPS criteria, that these should not be changed for UPS3 progression and that UPS3 should not be subject to a quota.

We acknowledge that the STRB has said:

> that we expect teachers to progress at different speeds on the upper pay scale and that their progression should be linked to performance. It is clear from the experience of U2 that our expectations of the system are not being met, partly because of widespread unease about

linking pay and performance management and partly because many schools have found it difficult to make rigorous judgements about their teachers' readiness to progress.

We acknowledge that UPS progression was never envisaged as automatic.

Validation of performance management systems

We are agreed that there is a need to ensure consistency of performance management systems and to ensure that they are fully embedded in all schools. To secure these objectives we think that, for as long as is necessary to deliver the vision in the STRB's report, there should be a light touch external validation system to endorse the operation of a school's overall performance management system, including how pay decisions are linked to performance.

External assessment for excellent teacher scheme

Additionally, in relation to the excellent teachers scheme, we think independently appointed external assessors should sit with those making decisions about who will benefit from the scheme. This takes account of the STRB view that heads, governing bodies and teachers would find reassurance for a transitional period in the appropriate operation of these external assessment arrangements.

Progression on UPS should be based on two successful consecutive performance management reviews, other than under the exceptional circumstances as set out in STPCD.

A successful performance review as prescribed by the appraisal regulations involves a performance management process of:

- performance objectives;
- classroom observation;
- other evidence.

To ensure that the achievements and contribution have been substantial and sustained, that performance review will need to assess that the teacher has:

- continued to meet threshold standards; and
- grown professionally by developing their teaching expertise post-threshold.

In light of the experience and expertise which has been gained from performance threshold assessment, CEA have worked in partnership with a number of schools and LEAs to produce the 'Rewarding Teacher Performance (RTP)' publication which sets out a performance management framework for threshold assessment and post-threshold progression. The CEA framework builds on the requirement for reviewing the overall performance of a teacher and provides a set of descriptors to support each threshold standard, which reflect the full range of teachers' strengths and expertise, and acknowledges the professional development that teachers have achieved in their work since threshold.

The framework does not require an application by a teacher. It can be used as a management tool – by the headteacher to exemplify 'sustained and substantial' performance – and can be fully integrated with Performance Management. Using the descriptors, teachers can undertake self-evaluation and team leaders can evaluate the teacher by comparing outcomes with evidence gained through the school's performance management systems. The headteacher can use the outcomes to support judgements made.

Conclusions

The introduction of performance threshold assessment was a massive undertaking which has proved to be very successful. To date, over 250 000 teachers have successfully applied to pass through the threshold.

Threshold has gained increasing status. An ever-growing number of employers from outside the maintained sector are now enabling teachers, who are not statutorily covered by the School Teachers' Pay and Conditions Document, to apply for threshold. This is despite the fact that funding increased pay awards for such teachers rests solely with the individual employer.

With the development of coherent systems of performance management, there are ever-increasing links between the threshold standards and wider aspects of school self-evaluation. Performance management and the threshold standards are increasingly at the heart of school improvement and the promotion of more effective teaching and learning.

References and further reading

CEA (2002) *Rewarding Teacher Performance*, Cambridge: CEA.
DfES (1998) Green Paper: 'Teachers – meeting the challenge of change', London: HMSO.
DfES (1999) 'Teachers – meeting the challenge of change, technical consultation document on pay and performance management', London: HMSO.
DfES (2000a) *The School Teachers' Pay and Conditions Document,* London: HMSO.
DfES (2000b) Research into Teacher Effectiveness *A Model of Teacher Effectiveness Report by Hay McBer to the DfES*, London: HMSO.

DfES (2000c) *The Ninth School Teachers' Review Body*, London: HMSO.

DfES (2000d) *School Teachers' Pay and Conditions Statutory Order No. 3*, London: HMSO.

DfES (2000e) *School Teachers' Pay and Conditions Statutory Order No. 4*, London: HMSO.

DfES (2000f) *Guidance on Threshold Process in 2000 (round 1) England*, London: HMSO.

DfES (2000g) *Threshold Assessment in 2000 (round 1) in England, complaints against discrimination by Review Assessor*, Available at: www.dfes.gov.uk/teachingreforms/rewards.

DfES (2001a) *Guidance on Threshold Process in 2000 (round 1) England*, London: HMSO.

DfES (2001b) *The Tenth School Teachers' Review Body*, London: HMSO.

DfES (2001c) *The School Teachers' Pay and Conditions Document 2001*, London: HMSO.

DfES (2002a) *The Eleventh School Teachers' Review Body*, London: HMSO.

DfES (2002b) *The Framework of National Standards for Teachers*, London: HMSO.

DfES (2002c) *The School Teachers' Pay and Conditions Document 2002*, London: HMSO.

DfES (2002d) *Guidance on Threshold Process in 2001 (round 2) England*, London: HMSO.

DfES (2003a) *The School Teachers' Pay and Conditions Document 2003*, London: HMSO.

DfES (2003b) *Guidance on Threshold Process in 2002 (round 3) England*, London: HMSO.

DfES (2003c) www.teachernet.gov.uk/Management/pay and performance.

TTA (1998) *Teacher Effectiveness by Professor David Reynolds TTA Corporate Plan Launch 1998-2001*, London: TTA.

Unpublished

CEA (2001) *Threshold Assessment Overview of Cycle One – Summary for STRB*.

CEA (2002) *Project Report to DfES*.

CEA (2003) *Project Report to DfES*.

Chapter 7

Advanced Skills Teacher

Maureen Lee

Introduction

Historically, career progression in schools in England had begun with classroom teaching and then proceeded through middle management to school leadership posts. Successful, ambitious teachers with enthusiasm and commitment to classroom teaching found that if they wanted to continue to work in schools but also take on roles with more responsibility and better pay, they would need to become heads of faculty or department, senior teachers or deputy headteachers. LEA advisory teacher roles were another route, but fewer of these posts became available during the 1990s as LEAs restructured and reorganised their advisory and inspection services. It was often said that the net result of organisational structures in schools was that too many good teachers were being promoted out of the classroom.

This is not to suggest that promotion to senior management positions moves teachers completely away from classrooms. In primary schools most deputy headteachers and headteachers, including in particular those who are headteachers of small schools, retain a very substantial class teaching commitment. However, it is certainly the case that for primary headteachers and deputy headteachers the non-teaching time they do have is usually committed to management and organisational responsibilities. Similarly, for teachers in secondary and middle schools, promotion through the management structure is usually accompanied by significant increases in non-contact time. Of course, time spent on school leadership and management impacts strongly on pupils' progress and standards, but it could certainly be argued that the effect of school career structures was that many of the best teachers were having the least direct impact on the quality of pupils' learning experiences.

At the same time, at national level, the raising standards agenda became increasingly high profile – with imperatives to improve pupil attainment levels across the whole school system, in both primary and secondary phases. In addition, for some schools, and particularly in some parts of the country, recruitment and retention of teachers was becoming increasingly problematic – not only were the best teachers being promoted to managerial roles, but too many teachers were leaving the profession or moving schools too frequently to make a lasting impact on raising achievement. Temporary staff were increasingly filling staffing gaps until suitable permanent appointments could be made.

It was against this backcloth that in 1998 a new career pathway for excellent teachers was introduced. The new professional grade of Advanced Skills Teacher (AST) was created so that the best teachers could concentrate on using and sharing their skills in classroom teaching, and at the same time have access to higher salary levels:

> The Advanced Skills Teacher (AST) pathway offers teachers who want to stay in the classroom a new career route. AST posts concentrate on good teaching and benefit the profession by helping to raise standards more widely, both within and beyond the teacher's school. Colleagues will have an opportunity to learn from best practices, build on strengths and look at areas for development.
>
> (DfES, AST Guidance 2001)

What characterises Advanced Skills Teachers – how are they different from other good teachers?

The main focus and responsibility of Advanced Skills Teachers is to maintain and promote excellence in their own teaching and in the way they support and challenge the colleagues with whom they work, both in their own and in other schools. ASTs spend 80 per cent of their time teaching their usual classes in their own schools and up to 20 per cent working in what is known as an 'outreach role'. This means that for the equivalent of one day a week, ASTs are engaged in activities which focus on the training and development of other teachers. All Advanced Skills Teachers are expected to be able to advise and guide others on effective approaches to teaching and learning, as well as having their own individual specialism – for example, in a subject or subjects, a particular phase of education (such as early years), or an aspect of education (such as personal and social education).

Examples of successful AST outreach activities over the past five years have encompassed an impressive range of activities, including:

- advising other teachers in classroom organisation and teaching methods;
- providing demonstration lessons;
- leading learning networks and working groups;
- planning and leading in-service development programmes – in schools, for LEAs and ITT providers;

- spreading good practice and disseminating research findings;
- producing high-quality teaching materials, often using ICT;
- supporting teachers who are experiencing difficulties, often through observation of their teaching, and providing constructive, developmental feedback;
- contributing to the induction and mentoring of newly qualified teachers;
- working as a school-based tutor in initial teacher training.

What are the AST Standards?

A set of specific professional standards for Advanced Skills Teachers has been introduced by the DfES to underpin the selection process for the new AST career pathway. Only those teachers who can demonstrate that they fully meet the challenging expectations of the role can go forward to become ASTs. This chapter sets out to explore the detail of the DfES Advanced Skills Teacher Standards. It will attempt to make connections between the AST Standards and the other professional standards for teachers, and will look at how the Standards have been used and applied in schools and LEAs over the past five years.

Key features of the Advanced Skills Teacher Standards

There are six professional standards which aspiring Advanced Skills Teachers must demonstrate that they meet before gaining accreditation for the role. Table 7.1 sets out the specific areas of professional practice outlined by the standards.

In summary, it is clear that these standards describe excellence in levels of professional expertise and performance. They set out the highest possible standards of knowledge and understanding about teaching, together with an expectation of extremely high levels of professionalism and interpersonal effectiveness. The expectations of the last standard are particularly important, since the nature of outreach support work in other schools, often with teachers who are not day-to-day colleagues, means that ASTs must have extremely good communication and influencing skills. They need to be able to establish effective and productive working relationships within short periods of time – it is vital that resentment or hostility are not inadvertently created.

How are Advanced Skills Teachers viewed?

The introduction of an AST professional grade was not initially greeted with unanimous positive acclaim by the teaching profession. Some teachers

Table 7.1 Standards and expectations of Advanced Skills Teachers

AST standard	Expectations
Excellent pupil results and outcomes	• Consistent improvement on pupils' prior attainment; • motivated and enthusiastic pupils; • consistently high standards of behaviour; • consistent records of parental satisfaction and involvement in their children's learning
Excellent subject or specialist knowledge	• Up to date in subject/specialism; • full understanding of progression in the subject; • quick understanding of pupils' misconceptions; • effective use of ICT within the subject(s) taught
Excellent ability to plan	• Lessons prepared with clear objectives; • ensure successful learning by all pupils; • set consistently high expectations for homework; • ensure teaching builds on the current and previous achievement of pupils
Excellent ability to teach and manage pupils and maintain discipline	• Understand and use the most effective teaching methods; • display flair and creativity in engaging, enthusing and challenging groups of pupils; • use skilful questioning and explanation to secure maximum progress; • develop pupils' literacy, numeracy and ICT skills; • provide positive and targeted support for pupils, including those who lack confidence, have behavioural difficulties or are disaffected; • maintain respect and discipline, consistently and fairly
Excellent ability to assess and evaluate	• Use assessment effectively to diagnose pupils' needs; • set realistic and challenging targets for improvement; • plan future teaching and improve teaching through evaluating own practice in relation to pupils' progress, school targets and inspection evidence
Excellent ability to advise and support other teachers	• Provide clear feedback, good support and sound advice; • provide examples, coaching and training to help others become more effective in their teaching; • help others to evaluate the impact of their teaching on raising pupils' achievements; • analyse teaching and understand how improvements can be made; • highly developed inter-personal skills; • role model for pupils and other staff through their personal and professional conduct; • plan and prioritise own time and activity effectively; • highly respected and able to motivate others.

expressed caution, others outright scepticism. Why was an elite league of 'super teachers' being created, and why should they be paid at a higher level than other excellent teachers? Was this yet another criticism of teachers, another indication that teachers generally were not perceived as doing a good job? Why was it necessary to differentiate so unhelpfully between Advanced Skills Teachers and the teaching force in general?

Against this background, the importance of an AST's approach to the colleagues with whom he or she works was going to be crucial. However excellent an Advanced Skills Teacher's ability to plan, teach and assess, and however well such teachers relate to pupils in their own classes, if they cannot also work constructively with adults, their support and advice will not have maximum impact. Teachers who observe an expert at work or who receive advice about their classroom management and teaching must view the expertise and support positively. Each individual AST's credibility and reputation is crucial to the collective credibility and reputation of the whole AST programme.

Ofsted looked at this issue in summer 2000, as part of its evaluation of the employment and deployment of ASTs in the first two years of the scheme. In relation to their work in their base school, Ofsted reported that:

> the attitudes towards ASTs of other teachers, of headteachers and of members of the leadership team of schools, are largely good or very good. Positive attitudes usually derive from the AST's existing strong reputation in the school.

On the other hand, in relation to ASTs' work with colleagues in other schools, the survey found that in the first two years of the programme responses had been more mixed. Some teachers expressed suspicion that the introduction of ASTs was another form of inspection. Others were cautious about displaying any enthusiasm for what might be just a short-lived initiative, with no lasting impact. The Ofsted report highlighted the need for greater transparency and explanation of the role, concluding that: 'Whilst most reactions have been positive, a minority of teachers has been hostile or sceptical until the role of the AST has been fully explained'.

Important issues had been identified and a challenge set to LEAs and schools to ensure better deployment of ASTs and better explanation of the ways in which they can support teachers and improve schools.

How do the AST Standards relate to the other professional standards for teachers?

The AST Standards are similar to the national professional Standards for Headteachers, in that they apply directly to only those teachers who decide that they wish to move into a particular role in schools.

This means that the AST Standards are used in different ways from most of the other standards. For example, the QTS Standards (Chapter 4) and Induction Standards (Chapter 5) apply to all teachers, in initial training and in the first year of their career. All beginning teachers must by the end of their induction year meet both sets of standards in order to be eligible to continue to teach. The Standards are an entry requirement to the profession. The Subject Leader Standards (Chapter 10) have general application, too, in that they set out expectations which are relevant to most (if not all) teachers. The Standards help teachers prepare for and evaluate their subject leadership and co-ordination work in schools, although there is no formal or statutory assessment process involved in becoming a subject leader. The Threshold Standards, which do involve an assessment process (Chapter 6), also set out expectations which are relevant to large numbers of teachers – in this case, those with five to seven years' experience in the profession.

In terms of content and progression, the AST Standards lead on directly from the Threshold Standards. In particular, as discussed earlier in this chapter, because of the nature of the work Advanced Skills Teachers will be undertaking, the AST Standards set out very high expectations in terms of the ability to work effectively with other colleagues. ASTs must have excellent interpersonal skills and very high levels of expertise in coaching, mentoring and guiding other teachers.

The following sections of this chapter set out the ways in which the AST Standards have been used and applied since their introduction five years ago.

The AST Standards and the assessment of aspiring ASTs

The main way in which the AST Standards are used is to structure the assessment process for entry to AST status. As demonstrated earlier in this chapter, the AST Standards are deliberately challenging and set out expectations of excellence. An aspiring AST must first be assessed as meeting the AST Standards before being appointed to an AST post. Prospective candidates are subject to rigorous assessment procedures in order to establish and maintain the credibility of both individual ASTs and the AST teaching force more generally.

The assessment process

The assessment process is demanding, and requires critical reflection and analysis of an aspiring AST's work before successful accreditation for the role is awarded. All six standards must be fully met before AST status is awarded, and assessment is triangulated through:

- self-assessment by the aspiring AST and compilation of supporting evidence, usually in portfolio form;
- recommendation by the candidate's headteacher;
- on-site assessment by an external assessor.

The on-site assessment takes place over one day at the candidate's school and is conducted by an externally appointed assessor, arranged through the DfES-appointed agency which organises and quality assures the assessment process. Selection and training of appropriately qualified assessors is rigorous and detailed – many of the assessors are Ofsted registered inspectors or serving headteachers. All assessors are specifically trained for the role of AST assessor, and use purpose-designed assessment and reporting procedures.

Assessment against the AST Standards draws on different forms of evidence and involves a significant number of people. The on-site assessment day will include the following:

1 Analysis of the application form
2 Classroom observation
3 At least one interview with the aspiring AST
4 A review of documentary evidence, including a completed portfolio of evidence
5 Discussions with:

- the headteacher;
- other staff familiar with the candidate's work;
- an LEA adviser or colleague from another school where the candidate has provided support;
- a group of between four and eight pupils who know the candidate well;
- a small group of parents/carers whose children have been taught by the candidate.

In preparation for making an application to become an AST, candidates are advised to review and collate substantial and wide-ranging evidence that they have consistently met the high expectations of the Standards. This is because not only are the AST Standards unequivocal in their expectations of exceptionally high levels of performance, but they also require that a range of evidence must be made available to demonstrate a candidate's claim that he or she is consistently operating at this high level of performance. For example, parental satisfaction must be proven for more than one class and over a period of more than one year.

Similarly, to be assessed as having met these challenging standards, teachers must provide evidence that they are working effectively with the full range of pupils, including higher achievers, those who are difficult to engage with learning, and pupils with special educational needs. This will involve presenting evidence across more than one class and from current and previous years. Evidence must also demonstrate that pupils have made good progress, as demonstrated through analysis of performance data. In order to gain accreditation, aspiring ASTs must demonstrate that they are highly effective teachers who are also effective in disseminating their expertise to other colleagues.

For the assessor, it will be crucial that this information is comprehensive and wide-ranging. From a one-day assessment, a skilled assessor will be able to make judgements about an aspiring AST's level of performance against the six standards, but in terms of the consistency of an AST's competence, the AST's self-assessment and the headteacher recommendation will also be essential evidence bases.

Aspiring ASTs are informed at the end of the on-site assessment day whether or not they have fully met all the standards. If they have been successful, candidates are recommended for AST status and can then be appointed to an AST post. If there is insufficient evidence that each standard is fully met, AST status will not be awarded. It is possible for candidates to re-apply at a later date, once they have provided positive evidence of achievement of all the standards. Unsuccessful applicants will receive a report which gives them a clear indication of the areas where evidence was judged to be insufficient, to help them towards subsequent collation of evidence for assessment should they decide to re-apply.

Portfolios of evidence of AST competence

Professional portfolios have provided both aspiring and accredited ASTs with a way of reviewing and reflecting on their career development and selecting the best examples of evidence across the breadth of their professional practice. A rigorous and reflective portfolio is formative for the AST, as well as providing summative evidence of his or her qualification for the role.

Over the past five years, many interesting approaches to developing an AST portfolio have emerged. Once successfully assessed and operating in the AST role, ASTs have continued their portfolios, seeing them as a useful bank of evidence demonstrating their impact in the outreach role. Most ASTs have chosen to arrange their portfolio in sections, one for each standard, selecting and reflecting on the evidence which best demonstrates their experience and expertise to support their achievement and progression in that standard. Both paper-based ring binder and electronic portfolios have been developed, with many ASTs using a combination of the two formats.

Table 7.2 is a summary of the range of evidence that ASTs have included in their portfolios.

Table 7.2 A structure for an AST portfolio

AST standard	Evidence of achievement
Excellent pupil results and outcomes	• Pupil progress data, including external assessment results with value added analysis • Individual, departmental and whole-school analysis, graphs, trends • Reports to the department, headteacher or governors about standards and progress as a result of own teaching
Excellent subject or specialist knowledge	• Logs of professional qualifications and professional development activities undertaken, with attendance certificates from courses • Evidence of membership of working groups at local, regional and national levels • Evaluations and letters testifying to the quality of support a candidate has provided for other colleagues within specialism
Excellent ability to plan	• Samples of schemes of work and lesson plans • LEA review reports • Reports from school or departmental self-evaluation and monitoring
Excellent ability to teach and manage pupils and maintain discipline	• Ofsted teaching profiles • Reports from school or departmental self-evaluation and monitoring • Evidence from Ofsted, LEA reviews and school self-evaluation reports • Behaviour management evidence – school or class 'incident' records, records of positive reinforcement and rewards given, systems and approaches developed
Excellent ability to assess and evaluate	• Examples of assessed pupils' work, demonstrating accuracy of assessment and quality of constructive feedback • Samples of assessment criteria for school modules or courses • Self-evaluation and reflection, showing insights gained from evaluation have been used to improve own teaching • Indication of how a range of sources of evidence is used – action research, Ofsted reports, published research
Excellent ability to advise and support other teachers	• Details of support provided for other teachers – e.g. INSET plans, demonstration lessons, minutes of meetings • Evaluations and comments from teachers and others with whom the candidate has worked in a developmental capacity • Analysis of training course evaluations • Headteacher testimonies

How are AST posts established?

Any school may create one or more AST posts, and will usually advertise externally for suitable candidates. LEAs are asked by the DfES to designate an AST Co-ordinator, and will supply details of funding arrangements and application forms. Aspiring ASTs can only be assessed in relation to a designated AST post but, logistically, interviews may have to be held prior to assessment taking place. Headteachers will make the decision on appointment to the advertised post in their usual way, and based on the evidence presented, to indicate the best candidate for the post. This means that some ASTs may gain accreditation as an AST but not secure an AST post immediately and, conversely, that some appointments may be made prior to AST status being awarded.

There are two separate pay scales for ASTs. The national AST pay scale runs from £29 757 to £47 469 (from April 2003), and the Inner London pay scale runs from £35 700 to £53 412. ASTs move to this pay spine from the classroom assistants' spine. Management allowances are not payable to ASTs; nor are allowances for recruitment and retention and special needs.

Once assessed and appointed, ASTs go on to the AST pay spine, with the level of pay determined by the Governing Body in accordance with the School Teachers' Pay and Conditions Document and the advice provided in the DfES AST Guidance Pack. The Governing Body should select a 5-point pay range within the 27-point AST pay spine to allow for appropriate pay increases in line with the school's overall pay policy. This means that the AST pay range is financially attractive to teachers who might otherwise be considering applying for posts on the leadership group pay spine. The top of the AST scale equates to point 18 on the spine for the leadership group.

Full details can be found in the School Teachers' Pay and Conditions Document 2003, at www.teachernet.gov.uk/pay. Full details of current arrangements for the creation and funding of an AST post can be obtained from www.dfes.gov.uk/ast

Funding for AST posts is available to all maintained schools through the Standards Fund, and is currently allocated to LEAs for each financial year. Schools are able to claim the additional costs of placing an AST at an appropriate point on the AST pay spine, and £1900 per term towards the costs of outreach work. The DfES will either contribute half of these additional costs while LEAs provide matched funding or, for some posts 100 per cent DfES funding may be available within a limited time scale, often twelve months.

A school may also fund AST posts using its own budget, provided all ASTs have been successfully assessed by the national assessment agency. In such cases outreach work is still a requirement.

Employment and deployment of ASTs

Once successfully assessed and having secured an AST post, ASTs will embark on their new career path of classroom teaching for 80 per cent of their time and outreach support and development work for the remaining

20 per cent. Part of the AST outreach time can be used for preparation and reporting purposes in relation to the activities undertaken.

The DfES recommends that ASTs do not also hold management responsibilities, so that they can concentrate fully on their new role. However, since the AST role has a clear remit for curriculum and pedagogic leadership, it is also recommended that, wherever possible, ASTs should be leaders and be part of (or have access to) the senior management team. In practice, involvement (or not) in the leadership team and attendance at management meetings varies enormously from school to school. Some ASTs feel that they became ASTs because of their commitment to the classroom rather than any interest in involvement in school management. Others make a considerable input to their senior management team and take a strong leadership role in the school, for example through:

- full membership of the school leadership team;
- regular reports to senior management on the strategies ASTs are developing for improving teaching and learning;
- being invited to senior management meetings as appropriate to the topics for discussion and decision;
- leading teaching and learning teams drawn from across departments, faculties and key stages.

Some headteachers have used the creation of an AST post in their school to take a new look at their school's approach to leadership, and to review and restructure how the leadership team is formed and operates. There is growing in commitment to dispersed or distributed leadership, where leadership and management responsibility is spread across the school in a flexible way according to the needs and focus of the school's improvement plan. ASTs can play an important part in the development and success of this approach, through both their own leadership and their coaching and mentoring of middle managers to take a wider leadership role.

Management of AST outreach across an LEA is usually through an appointed AST Co-ordinator, who liaises with those schools who wish to appoint ASTs. Co-ordinators are also instrumental in the induction of ASTs and their deployment in their outreach role, for example, negotiating their work in schools facing challenging circumstances or, with newly qualified and other teachers, leading INSET, conducting demonstration lessons and providing feedback on teaching.

In schools judged to require special measures by Ofsted, it is possible for an Advanced Skills Teacher to be appointed to work primarily within that school – i.e. the outreach work is focused on the 'inreach' needs of the employing school. However, DfES advice in these circumstances is that ASTs should do some outreach work to develop their ability to share their expertise, as part of their own continuing professional development planning.

ASTs also use their specialisms across other activities – for example, planning and leading training courses for newly qualified and other teachers, or working alongside them. Some are engaged specifically in promoting partnerships for initial teaching training on a regional basis. Others may lead an aspect of the curriculum across an LEA or a region, for example, promoting good practice in the teaching of citizenship or personal, social and health education, drawing together working groups of expert teachers, producing guidelines and teaching materials, and liaising with LEA advisers and consultants. LEAs, ITT providers, Beacon and Training schools often arrange for ASTs to drive forward their key priorities through their inreach and outreach work, for example support for teaching assistants, including candidates for Higher Level Teaching Assistant Status.

What has been the impact of the AST role?

How has this new career path benefited the teaching profession? Have the scheme's objectives been met – are the best teachers being retained in the profession, are standards rising as a result?

In summer 2000, Ofsted undertook an evaluation survey of the employment and deployment of Advanced Skills Teachers. They found the early signs to be largely positive. The ASTs in the survey's sample of schools were found to be 'experienced, skilled and conscientious teachers who are able to provide effective support for other teachers without overwhelming them with their expertise'. Some difficulties had been experienced in the logistics of organising the outreach role, but in spite of this:

> the impact of the outreach work of two-thirds of the ASTs was judged at least good and for two-fifths it was very good or excellent. Where the impact was judged to be less than satisfactory, this was principally because of the limited amount of work which had taken place.

The report goes on to look at the motivational effects of their new role on the ASTs themselves. Some said it was 'a dream job', others that it had considerable advantages over being an LEA adviser. Ofsted concluded that '... the variety of work, coupled with the additional financial reward for most, has been effective in giving the ASTs' careers a new impetus'.

The following comments from different parts of the country are not taken from the Ofsted evaluation survey, but are similar in tone and show how being an 'advanced skills' teacher has positively impacted on individual ASTs, their own schools, the 'outreach' schools in which they have worked, and the wider community of the LEA and schools.

> I was in my fifth year of teaching and in my second school when I became an AST. After three years in the role, I am now moving on to

deputy headship and will greatly miss the opportunities being an AST has given me. I have had to respond to so many professional challenges, working in situations and with colleagues where all my skills were taxed to the full. At the same time, I have had the enormous benefit of working with so many schools and their various approaches to common issues. In particular, my AST experience has helped me to develop my analytical and problem-solving skills. I now feel much more confident to see my way through difficult issues.

(AST, Middle school)

I have taught in a small rural primary school for six years. There are tremendous advantages to our type of school – being part of a close community, the teamwork and knowing all the pupils and their families so well. On the other hand, there are definite disadvantages, mainly the demands of providing subject leadership across the whole curriculum (when there are only four teachers) together with our geographic isolation from other schools. My becoming an AST has really helped our whole cluster of small schools – I now have time to work with the other schools and to build working links. I organise joint professional development events, and advise subject leaders across all the schools on ways of leading the improvement of teaching and learning.

(AST, Primary phase)

I became an AST in the first year of the scheme. I had been second in department for several years, but had never wanted to take on a lead departmental role. Since becoming an AST I have felt that my teaching career has been completely re-energised by bringing me new and very welcome challenges. I work as an AST in my outreach role for two afternoons a week – mainly with newly qualified teachers across the LEA, modelling lessons, observing NQTs teaching and providing feedback. I also organise and lead a subject network group for teachers in the first three years of teaching, and have tutored trainee teachers in my own school and elsewhere across the training partnership schools. An LEA Senior Adviser co-ordinates AST outreach work, and is currently meeting all the LEA's ASTs to evaluate our impact. We will then negotiate our outreach commitments for next year.

(AST, Secondary school)

Our school was found to have serious weaknesses by Ofsted and, as a result, maintaining staff morale throughout the implementation of our action plan has been a significant challenge for our leadership team. However, for a day a week we have been fortunate to have the time of an AST from a neighbouring school – her influence on the staff has been tremendous. She has given our teachers clear and very helpful feedback on their planning and teaching and has sensitively, but very constructively, pointed out where our expectations of the children could and should be higher. The school has made very good progress over the past six months, and I attribute much of that to the AST's skilful and committed input.

(Headteacher, Primary school)

The Strategic Partnership has moved forward considerably from the LEA's previous performance. As part of that drive for improvement, we have set out to increase our numbers of ASTs. The effects of having teachers who are officially recognised as 'excellent' have been far reaching, raising the morale of the individual teachers and the schools where they work, and of the area as a whole. My role involves the effective induction of the ASTs, and also ensuring that their head-teachers are fully aware of the potential and possibilities of establishing an AST post in their school.

Headteachers and teachers in other schools are proud that we have recognised and retained teachers of this calibre who can demonstrate cutting edge thinking about effective teaching and learning. We take confidence in the fact that we have a quality assured pool of specialists who can operate successfully in challenging situations.

We are now planning to operate more broadly across the region and expand the AST roles to address aspects of the different authorities' Education Development Plans.

(AST Manager, Strategic Partnership)

It would seem reasonable to conclude that there is growing evidence that the establishment of a force of Advanced Skills Teachers across England is beginning to make a significant impact on the very issues the initiative was intended to address. For individual ASTs the benefits are also considerable, and include:

- an enhanced profile across a number of schools;
- opportunities for further career enhancement and financial reward;
- renewed personal motivation;
- unique professional development opportunities gained by working alongside other teachers, school leaders and colleague ASTs.

For schools, the appointment of one or more ASTs can play a vital role in school improvement, enhancing the profile and prestige of the school and broadening the available skills base to support teaching, learning and professional development. Through enthusiastic and skilful teaching, an AST can have a substantial motivational effect on colleagues, injecting new ideas and approaches and driving forward a collaborative learning culture.

Through outreach work, ASTs also foster close working relationships with other schools and through this collaboration can take forward initiatives which schools on their own often find difficult to sustain. ASTs are in a position to be key players in the establishment of professional learning communities, where teachers can come together within and across schools to share what works and to consider and refine the most effective approaches to raising achievement levels.

A greater range of career options within teaching

There is now a range of career options within teaching, not all of which will necessarily lead to headship. For new entrants to the profession this is often a significant additional recruitment factor – new teachers often say that they come into teaching to be teachers, to teach in classrooms. Some say that they do not want to take a management role, and so they welcome the opportunity for the different kind of career progression which the AST route offers. Similarly, Fast Track teachers are also encouraged by the DfES guidance to see becoming an AST as one of their later career options – an alternative or perhaps a precursor to deputy headship and headship. To have a range of options is healthy for the teaching profession; it signals that teaching is a dynamic profession which responds to new demands with creativity and drive.

Encouragement and rewards for excellence

Teaching is now increasingly viewed as a profession which welcomes and rewards excellence. This is in part due to official recognition that there are 'advanced skills' professionals who can command pay scales which are at least comparable with the higher pay levels of other public (and some private) sector professions. This recognition of excellence should help the profession to retain its excellent teachers – they may be less likely to seek professional challenges outside teaching if they can see that their efforts will be rewarded from within.

The application of the AST Standards to teachers who are not ASTs

The AST Standards set out measures of excellence, and as such have been used by teachers, their team leaders and line managers to set challenging objectives within the performance management system. The AST standards can be used individually or collectively for this purpose for teachers who are not at that point seeking AST accreditation. However, if a teacher has identified the AST route as a career option within the next two or three years, using the AST standards to frame that teacher's performance management objectives can enable him or her to prepare gradually and progressively for assessment at some later stage.

The AST Standards: issues for the future

As with many other initiatives in education, the positive effects of change must become evident before anything approaching enthusiasm for the initiative is even tentatively mooted. It is true that initially there was suspicion of this new band of 'super teachers'. However, now that ASTs have been working in schools and LEAs for five years, their worth is becoming more widely acknowledged. The ASTs themselves have consistently demonstrated their enthusiasm and expertise, as well as their commitment to supporting colleagues.

As of November 2002, 2760 ASTs had been successfully assessed, although not all of that number are currently in AST posts. The Government is committed to creating more AST posts, so that over a period of time their numbers rise to 3–5 per cent of the teaching force. In addition to posts attached to specific schools, there are also opportunities for ASTs to focus on a range of issues – for example, initial teacher training, music and modern foreign languages in primary schools, and, for ASTs whose work is focused on the Key Stage 3 strategy, citizenship within secondary schools. As new initiatives and developments are introduced in schools, excellent teachers, including ASTs, will be increasingly needed to take these drives forward.

Newly qualified teachers enter the profession having already considered progressing their career in this way. There are now many leading mathematics and literacy teachers, experts in teaching the Numeracy and Literacy Strategies, who have been gaining experience in working with other teachers to demonstrate and discuss good practice in their teaching. Becoming an AST would be a direct career progression for these teachers. Similarly, experts in the Key Stage 3 strategy are realising their wider potential for influencing whole-school improvement through expert teaching and expert subject leadership. Inceasingly more headteachers are creating AST posts, and more teachers are considering taking the AST career route. The DfES is currently supporting an expansion in numbers of ASTs. LEAs have designated an AST Co-ordinator to formulate and implement an AST strategy to co-ordinate and target AST outreach activity on the schools with greatest need. LEA AST Co-ordinators also work with headteachers and ASTs to evaluate and further develop the quality of the ASTs' work.

The challenge for the future will be to ensure that ASTs receive the professional support they themselves need to continue to develop effectively in the role. In some areas there are very few ASTs, and so face-to-face networking is difficult. Regional and virtual networks which cut across LEA boundaries are a way forward for sharing practice, problems and issues. Access to high-quality professional development programmes for ASTs is also a priority – starting with induction to the role, and continuing with challenging, developmental feedback, and participative and interactive development programmes. The DfES Continuing Professional Development Strategy, the changing role of the LEA, public–private partnerships and the growth of private sector education consultancies have all impacted on the resource available to schools for teacher development and in-service training. Advanced Skills Teachers are a rich resource on which schools can draw in order to meet their teachers' specific development needs – they provide a resource bank of professional expertise, which is quality assured against rigorous professional standards.

The Advanced Skills Teacher Standards are clear and describe a broad spectrum of teacher excellence, but may need further refinement and review within the next two or three years, particularly in the light of the review of the entry standards to teaching. For example, they will need to take account of the way learning is likely to be organised for pupils in the future, and so there will probably be a need to place much more emphasis on ICT – for example, on an AST's confidence and expertise in using virtual learning environments to support and guide pupils' learning.

What is not likely to change is the value teachers place on advice from real experts, from other teachers who are engaged in teaching on a day-to-day basis. The Advanced Skills Teacher Standards have injected greater credibility and rigour into the professional learning process for teachers – the challenge will be to expand the numbers of ASTs as well as opportunities for their own continuing professional development. In this way, more of the teaching profession will be able to benefit from working alongside Advanced Skills professionals to take forward the next stages of curriculum development and school improvement.

References and further reading

DfES (2002a) *Advanced Skills Teachers: Induction Handbook*, London: HMSO.
DfES (2002b) *Advanced Skills Teachers: Building on your Strengths*, London: HMSO.
Ofsted (2000) *The Appointment and Deployment of Advanced Skills Teachers – A Survey by HMI*, London: Teacher Education and Training Division, Ofsted. www.hlta.gov.uk.

Chapter 8

Fast Track

David Brunton

Introduction

This chapter is concerned with a particular set of National Standards that are not yet well known in the teaching profession. These are the Fast Track competencies and values, a key part of the Fast Track teaching programme that was launched in 2000:

> The aim of the programme is to attract new entrants (recent graduates and career changers) and serving teachers with excellent leadership potential and provide a structure to assist them in reaching leadership positions – from within the classroom as Advanced Skills Teachers, as members of the Leadership group, or in the wider world of education – as quickly as possible.
> (www.teachernet.gov.uk/Professional_Development/fasttrackteaching/)

The first part of the chapter sets out the policy context of the Fast Track teaching programme and describes the selection and recruitment strategy of the initiative. The focus then moves onto the Fast Track standards themselves; the competencies and values that underpin the programme. There is an analysis of these standards and a comparison with other models and approaches to be found in educational settings. The Fast Track competencies and values are seen to conform most closely to the 'personal characteristics' model of defining occupational standards.

The Fast Track Standards are in many respects quite different from the other National Standards, and do not even specify competencies that are focused directly upon school leadership or teaching practice. The key question explored in this chapter is: what is the significance and further potential of this distinctive set of generic standards in the context of leadership development and school improvement?

Finally, the chapter evaluates the possibilities for the further development and application of the 'characteristics' approach to defining professional expertise in setting national standards and shaping leadership practices in schools.

Context: the inception and implementation of the Fast Track teaching programme

The proposal to develop a Fast Track initiative for the teaching profession was first mooted by the Department for Education and Employment in the 1998 Green Paper 'Teachers: meeting the challenge of change'. This document proposed a series of changes to the teaching profession that were deemed necessary to produce a 'world-class education service that achieves consistently high standards'. It set out 'a new vision of the teaching profession – with good leadership, incentives for excellence, a strong culture of professional development, and better support for teachers to focus on teaching – to improve the image and status of the profession' (DfEE 1998: 6).

The Green Paper described what it saw as the 'imperative of modernisation' to tackle poor school leadership, address recruitment problems, improve retention rates, create new incentives for excellence, and provide new structures for career and professional development. The document described more than 40 proposed reforms for a 'modernised teaching profession', including several designed to tackle recruitment problems and introduce more rigour and flexibility into initial teacher training. It stated, however:

> But we are under no illusions about the scale of the longer-term challenge. Stated simply, the present reality of teaching too often compares unfavourably with the growing range of alternative careers for successful graduates.
>
> (DfEE, 1998: 14)

One of the key proposals to tackle these concerns about quality and quantity in teacher recruitment was the establishment of a Fast Track initiative to attract able graduates into the profession and provide opportunities for enhanced professional development and career progression.

In the following year, the DfES published *A Fast Track for Teachers* (DfES 1999), setting out its proposals for the initiative in more detail, stating:

> We will launch a national training programme to recruit, stimulate and support highly-talented trainee and serving teachers and offer them clear, rapid career progression ... We will target, attract and select the best. They will be committed to teaching, academically strong, talented communicators and ambitious to make an impact.
>
> (DfES 1999: 1)

The Fast Track programme would offer successful candidates an arranged series of teaching posts, offering intensive experience and challenging objectives, matched by additional development and support. It was also recommended that teachers who gain from the Fast Track package should have the limitations on their working hours relaxed, 'so that they can commit themselves to the intense professional development that the fast track offers' (DfES 1999: 2).

Policy objectives of the Fast Track initiative

The Fast Track initiative was designed to attract able candidates into the profession by offering them enhanced opportunities for professional growth, career development and pay progression. In particular, the initiative is intended to be attractive to those who might not otherwise be prepared to consider a career in teaching. This policy objective should be set within the context in which it is still the case that 'the more prestigious your university, the less likely you are to become a teacher' (*Guardian* 19 January 2002). The Institute for Public Policy Research recently completed a statistical analysis of the percentage of undergraduates from UK universities progressing to teacher training, and discovered that the percentage from elite universities fell far short of the national average. The report concluded:

> In order to reach the government's aim of quantity and quality, these universities should be leading the recruitment drive into the teaching profession, rather than lagging behind.
>
> (IPPR 2002, cited in the *Guardian* 19 January 2002)

The initiative has benefited from a high level of influential political support. One of the key architects of the initiative was Andrew Adonis, policy adviser to the Cabinet Office, who had observed the effectiveness of other programmes in other public sectors, including the 'Faststream' initiative in the Civil Service.

The Fast Track teaching programme claims to be 'the first accelerated development programme for teachers anywhere in the world' (DfES 2001). It aims to attract more high-calibre graduates into teaching, and also to identify talented existing teachers for participation in the programme. Therefore, within the Fast Track, both serving teachers and those new to the profession are able to apply, and the latter stages of the selection process are common for both categories.

It is, however, the decision to seek to identify the leadership potential of candidates without any teaching experience that has proved contentious for some within the profession. This reflects a view that the personal credibility and professional effectiveness of teachers and managers in schools rests fundamentally upon their teaching skills, curriculum knowledge and classroom management.

This is less of an issue for candidates who are serving teachers, in that they are required through the application process to provide 'evidence of ... high level skills as a classroom practitioner' (Fast Track teaching application form: What You Need to Know, DfES 2002). This evidence is also verified through the reference process, which requires the first referee to be someone such as a headteacher or performance management team leader (who can objectively assess the evidence and has access to information about the candidate's performance).

However, as shall be seen below, the key challenge for the team designing the selection process and criteria for participation in the Fast Track teaching programme was how to assess candidates' potential for school leadership when they frequently had little or no experience of classroom practice.

The launch of the Fast Track initiative

Following a tendering process, a DfES contract was issued in February 2000 for the development and management of the Fast Track recruitment and selection programme. This contract was secured by a partnership between two organisations, Interactive Skills Ltd, a company employing occupational psychologists and human resource specialists, and QAA, a company providing training, inspection and consultancy services in education. QAA is now part of Serco Learning.

The initiative was launched in October 2000 to recruit applicants who were new to the profession and did not yet have Qualified Teacher Status. A first cohort of undergraduates and career-changers started their initial teacher training in September 2001. This first group of Fast Track teachers subsequently completed their PGCE programmes at nine selected providers of Initial Teacher Training, and became Newly Qualified Teachers in September 2002.

From November 2001, applications were invited from serving teachers, and successful candidates joined the programme in September 2002. Meanwhile, a further cohort of aspiring teachers was recruited during 2002 and began their Initial Teacher Training in September 2002. Further cohorts of both aspiring and serving teachers will continue to be recruited. When the programme was launched, it was envisaged that up to 5 per cent of the teaching force might become Fast Track Teachers.

Responses to the Fast Track initiative

The number of Fast Track Teachers is still comparatively low; the two cohorts of 2002, taken together, numbered less than 300, although the number of enquiries from aspiring teachers has been considerable. It may be useful to consider briefly how the perceptions and responses of aspiring teachers and serving teachers towards the programme have been influenced by external factors.

There are two distinct categories of aspiring teachers and career-changers towards which the FT is oriented: those who have already considered teaching as a career option and will evaluate FT as a potential route into the profession, and those who have not previously considered it for financial or other reasons.

Undergraduates and career changers will investigate the personal and practical costs and benefits of the Fast Track programme in comparison with other entry routes into teaching. This investigation may lead some to enter the teaching profession, but by other routes. Since the inception of the Fast Track, there have been a number of parallel policy initiatives to create more diverse routes into the teaching profession. At the heart of these initiatives is a shift away from the traditional one-year full-time PGCE programme and towards employment-based and/or flexible approaches. The Graduate Teachers Programme has been expanded over the past two years. This means trainees can be paid a salary to train in a school and then apply to FT later if they wish. From a financial point of view this is an attractive option to a career-changer, who also might not want to 'go back to university', preferring the more individualised school-based training of the GTP.

The Teacher Training Agency has also increased the number of places across the country on Flexible Modular PGCE programmes. These programmes are based upon an initial individualised analysis of the development needs of each student, and can in some cases be completed within one term. The revised QTS Standards and requirements for providers also state that all programmes will now be required to be responsive to the needs of individual students. A new TTA initiative also provides students with the opportunity to gain credits towards QTS whilst they are still undergraduates. The increased flexibility of these routes may lead some potential FT applicants to consider that, whilst the initiative may ultimately lead towards rapid pay progression, there are more rewarding or convenient routes into teaching initially.

The responses of those within the teaching profession

The response to the Fast Track initiative will also be shaped by the profession's perceptions of the social values and policy intentions that underpin the initiative. These perceptions in turn will be mediated by the public responses of the professional associations and educational publications.

There may be some scepticism within the teaching profession towards the values that underpin the Fast Track initiative. These values give primacy to individual ability and enterprise, and reinforce the view that exceptional individuals should progress rapidly towards management posts in schools. In previous decades, most commentators have suggested that the teaching profession has been dominated by communitarian and egalitarian social ideologies that are inimical to individualist and competitive approaches. There may also be scepticism within the profession about the validity of the Fast Track selection processes. This scepticism is based upon a pragmatic world-view that assesses the competence of serving teachers by virtue of their experience and stamina, and rejects the view that successful teachers may be identified by their intellectual potential or simulated social skills.

The Professional Associations have expressed antipathy towards some of the reforms in the 1998 Green Paper 'Modernising the teaching profession', and a number of articles have been published in the educational press which are hostile to the core principles of Fast Track. Some coverage in the *Times Educational Supplement* has focused directly upon the use of psychometrics within the Fast Track selection and recruitment strategy.

Finally, it is important to recognise the cautious outlook of many teachers; they may view new initiatives with scepticism and make a pragmatic decision to postpone involvement until such time as the initiative has been 'successfully implemented'. However, the reaction to Fast Track should also be viewed as one aspect of the profession's emergent response to the re-structuring of the career progression of teachers and the introduction of performance review systems. In the absence of systematic data concerning this changing response, it may be suggested that attitudes towards threshold assessment and performance-related pay are softening as these initiatives are mediated in practice.

Teachers will also consider pragmatic issues in any decision to apply for the Fast Track initiative. Their decision will rest upon a calculation of the perceived costs and benefits of an application for the initiative. The perceived costs and benefits are related to pay differentials, contractual requirements, career progression, training opportunities, professional status and personal risk. Equally, headteachers will make a similar calculation of the costs and benefits, opportunities and constraints in their decision to apply for a Fast Track appointment in their school.

Serving teachers will be aware of current concerns about the workload of staff. The DfES Teacher Workload survey has enhanced this awareness of comparative workloads, and is likely to make teachers reluctant to enter a contract which exceeds normal working hours. Serving teachers will also weigh the costs/benefits of Fast Track against other opportunities for early promotion and financial gain. In those parts of the country where the recruitment and retention of promoted posts is poor, headteachers are willing to offer management points to good teachers early in their careers (i.e. the first three years). Alternatively, they may deploy recruitment incentives to attract and retain staff. Headteachers may find this preferable to creating a FT post with the potential loss of an effective member of staff after two years. New teachers who receive positive feedback on their performance may calculate that they are likely to be promoted to head of department or assistant/deputy head in a primary school within four or five years without recourse to the Fast Track initiative.

Serving teachers who have completed their induction year successfully may make a cautious appraisal of their ability to perform consistently at a level which warrants two points on the pay scale per annum. They may also have a sanguine view of the responses of other teachers towards such rapid pay progression. However, under the revised model of performance management and pay progression in schools, teachers may be awarded additional points for excellence, whether or not they are on the Fast Track.

The mechanisms for the creation of Fast Track teaching posts, and the centralised administration of the programme, may also reduce the attractiveness of the initiative to teachers, especially the requirement that they move posts every two years. There may be some anxiety about the uncertainty and inconvenience that this could cause, especially for teachers with familial responsibilities. Finally, new initiatives to provide teachers with ICT equipment and CPD opportunities in their early years of teaching may also reduce the distinctiveness of those aspects of the Fast Track teaching programme.

It is important, however, to recognise that the Fast Track teaching programme is likely to develop and be refined over time, as it adapts to new policy contexts and change strategies. This chapter seeks to illuminate what has been achieved thus far, particularly in terms of the strategies for selection and recruitment, and to analyse the significance of the Fast Track competencies and values.

Overview of the Fast Track selection process

> Getting on to Fast Track won't be easy. We're looking for the very best people who can achieve the high standards we've set, and who want to raise those standards even higher. You'll have the intellect, commitment and passion to inspire others, and the resilience to respond to all the challenges teaching offers.
>
> (Fast Track Application Pack 2001: 2)

A key task in the implementation of the Fast Track initiative was to develop and trial a selection recruitment process that would identify appropriate candidates for participation in the programme. This section of the chapter summarises the processes through which candidates are selected. The selection process is made up of a number of stages, as shown in Figure 8.1.

This process combines what may be called an 'educational sift' with a

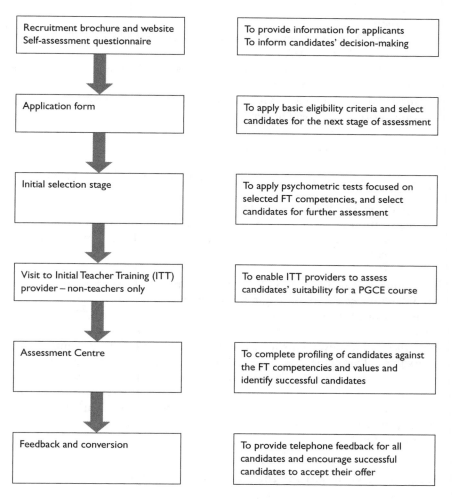

Figure 8.1 Overview of the stages in the Fast Track selection process.

'competency sift'. Through the educational sift, applicants' academic qualifications and basic eligibility are assessed. It is based upon two sets of 'educational criteria', depending on whether the applicant is currently qualified as a teacher.

Eligibility for the Fast Track initiative

In 2001, the eligibility criteria for those who had yet to train as a teacher (i.e. undergraduates and career-changers) were:

- a 2:1 degree or a 2:2 with a relevant higher degree (e.g. Master's degree);
- at least 22 UCAS points (a summative score of the overall performance of students at A/AS level);
- grade C or above at GCSE in English and Maths (General Certificate of Secondary Education);
- for primary teaching, a GCSE Science Grade C or above (for applicants born after 1 September 1979).

The eligibility criteria for serving teachers were:

- a 2:1 degree or a 2:2 with a relevant higher degree (e.g. Master's degree);
- Qualified Teacher Status (QTS);
- registration with the General Teaching Council for England (GTCE);
- current remuneration at no more than point 8 on the main teachers' pay scale.

This 'educational sift' is completed at the application stage, to ensure that candidates meet the basic eligibility criteria. The competency sift is conducted through a number of stages in the selection process. Through the application form, candidates are also asked to provide evidence of their expertise and achievements in relation to selected Fast Track competencies and values. This evidence is assessed to determine whether applicants self-report that they possess the right skills and attributes, and whether they are suitably motivated. This stage of the process is different for candidates who already have qualified teacher status, in that it based upon evidence verified by a referee, rather than upon self-report alone. This is discussed in more detail below.

Stages of assessment for the Fast Track initiative

Successful candidates then progress to the initial stage of assessment. This is administered through regional centres, takes half a day, and comprises three tests. These psychometric tests profile candidates' abilities against selected FT competencies, and are administered at an assessment venue via networked PCs. Candidates complete a Personal Styles Questionnaire (PSQ), which explores the personal motivations, interests and values that are identified as important to success as a Fast Track Teacher. They also complete a Reasoning and Problem-solving Test (RPT), that tests verbal and numerical problem-solving skills based on a series of educational scenarios that candidates might face in school settings. Finally, candidates complete a Critical Evaluation Test (CET), designed to assess their ability critically to evaluate information about a number of educational scenarios.

Candidates who are successful at this initial stage of assessment then progress to a Fast Track Assessment Centre. This is described in the application pack for candidates:

> ... you'll be invited to a two-day residential assessment centre, where your potential to succeed on Fast Track will be measured. It'll be challenging and demanding, and the feedback – whatever the result – will give you unprecedented detail on your performance and information about your developmental needs.
>
> (Fast Track Application Pack 2001: 10)

During the Assessment Centre, candidates are involved in a series of different exercises designed to assess their performance against the Fast Track competencies and values.

Use of assessment centres in the selection processes

Assessment centres are increasingly used within both private and public sectors, mainly within large organisations (Woodruffe 2000: 10). The key principle underpinning assessment centres is that the most effective way of predicting performance in a professional role is through the observation of candidates in activities which simulate that role. The assessment is conducted in a highly controlled setting through which candidates can be observed and evaluated. The activities are also replicable, thereby adding to the reliability of the assessment. Assessment centres are regarded as one of the most reliable methods of selection, so long as the design of the Centre conforms with certain characteristics (see Woodruffe 2000 for a discussion of the 'seductiveness of assessment centres' and competing claims for their validity and reliability).

Characteristics of Assessment Centres

The design of the Fast Track Assessment Centre complies with what are regarded by occupational psychologists as the key characteristics of an effective centre. Each of these characteristics (Roberts 1997; Woodruffe 2000) is discussed below, with examples of the design of the Fast Track model.

The first of these characteristics is that the assessment is based upon the direct observation of behaviours demonstrated by candidates. In a Fast Track Assessment Centre, assessors observe and record the behaviour of candidates in each of the exercises. They seek to capture as much evidence as possible, including direct quotations of what the candidate said and descriptions of non-verbal behaviour. After each exercise, the assessor classifies this behaviour in relation to each competency and value, and then evaluates it using a rating scale. The evidence and judgement are captured in a written report form.

Secondly, a number of trained assessors are used to assess each candidate participating in the Assessment Centre. This is to ensure that bias is minimised and that judgements are based upon objective evidence. In the Fast Track Assessment Centres, six assessors are involved normally in the assessment of a group of twelve candidates. All assessors are required to complete an initial seven-day training and accreditation programme, and then undergo periodic refresher training and quality assurance.

The exercises in the assessment are designed to replicate the scope and nature of the professional role the candidate will fulfil (Roberts 1997: 200). The validity of the judgements formed about the performance of candidates at an assessment is dependent upon the degree to which the exercises are based upon an evaluation of role requirements. In the Fast Track Assessment Centre, the exercises are based in a fictitious case-study school, and create the kind of challenges and situations a Fast Track Teacher is likely to encounter in school settings. This has two additional benefits: it increases the 'face validity' of the assessment and the perception of candidates that they have been engaged in a pertinent assessment process, and it also provides candidates with a deeper insight into what is involved in being a Fast Track Teacher.

The assessment of candidates draws upon a number of different techniques (Roberts, 1997: 197). A range of different types of exercise is used to generate evidence, and each competency is assessed through two or more exercises. In the Fast Track Assessment Centre, the exercises include a written decision-making exercise, a group exercise, a structured interview, and two role-plays.

Several candidates participate in the Centre at the same time (Woodruffe 2000: 10). This provides an opportunity to observe candidates working together in groups, and is more cost-effective than the assessment of candidates on an individual basis. It should be stressed that the assessment is criterion-based rather than normative, in that the performance of candidates is assessed against the competencies and values, and is not based upon comparison with others. There is no set quota for the number of successful candidates at each Centre; success of each individual in gaining a place on the Fast Track programme is dependent upon their performance at the Centre.

The evidence collected through the exercises is synthesised to produce a comprehensive assessment of the candidates' performance (Woodruffe 2000: 186). In the Fast Track Assessment Centre, selection decisions are based upon an integrated view of the performance of each candidate in relation to each competency and value. A full day is spent during which the assessors share the evidence they have recorded and arrive at judgements about the overall performance of each candidate.

Finally, candidates receive feedback on their performance at the centre (Woodruffe 2000: 207). This is generally regarded as good practice, whether the centre has been held primarily for selection or development purposes. Feedback may be given either orally or in writing, and should be designed to summarise key strengths and areas for development. In the Fast Track Assessment Centre, detailed feedback is given to all candidates orally through a telephone interview. The feedback is provided by one of the assessors who was present at the Centre.

Assessment centres in education

Assessment centres have not been used widely in the selection, recruitment and development of staff working in educational settings, partly because of the costs of setting up and managing centres. However, the National Educational Assessment Centre, established in 1990, provides development centres for headteachers and other senior and middle managers in schools (Hewitt 2000). Like the Fast Track Assessment Centres, these centres are competency-based and use a range of techniques to assess participants. However, they are 'development centres' rather than 'selection centres' in that their fundamental purpose is to generate evidence that is used to agree an action plan for the participants' professional development. Governing bodies have also increasingly drawn upon assessment centre techniques to inform the selection of headteachers and other senior staff in schools, often with the support and guidance of an external agency such as NEAC.

Apart from the Fast Track programme, the National Professional Qualification for Headship provides the only other example of extensive use of assessment centres in education. All candidates completing this programme provided by the National College for School Leadership undertake a series of school-based assessment, but also participate in a one-day final assessment. This takes the form of an assessment centre, and conforms closely to the general characteristics of such centres outlined above. It is a competency-based process, focused upon criteria derived from the National Standards for Headteachers.

The Fast Track competencies and values

As an individually tailored development programme, Fast Track's been designed specifically to inspire, attract, retain and reward the most dedicated, enthusiastic and able people. People who have the authority, energy and drive to fulfil their potential by setting high standards, motivating others and managing their own development. People who value high quality training and development and are willing to tackle the challenges that will give them the scope to advance their careers rapidly. Above all, people who are committed to working with and for children.

(Fast Track Application Pack 2001: 2)

Given the high expectations for participants on the Fast Track programme, how might their characteristics be defined? There is a close correlation between the assessment techniques that are used for selection processes and the criteria that are used to inform judgements about selection. Increasingly, the selection and recruitment of staff in both public and private sector organisations is based upon explicit criteria, stated as professional competencies. This reflects a growing recognition of the strategic significance of the selection and recruitment of staff, particularly leaders and managers. It is argued that the identification of key skills and attributes (and the selection, promotion and development of employees with these skills and attributes) is central to managerial efficiency, organisational effectiveness and cultural change (Iles and Salaman 1995).

When the DfEE indicated its intention to launch the Fast Track teaching programme, it stated that it would 'invest heavily in the selection process, to ensure that we are able to identify those with the highest potential'. It stated that selection for participation in the programme would be competency-based:

... selection will be based on the characteristics that we expect of fast track entrants ... and on the skills and competences of excellent teachers and heads.

(DfEE 1999: 7)

The selection of Fast Track Teachers is based upon a set of competencies and values that were developed for the initiative in 2000 and subsequently refined in 2001. The competencies fall into three clusters: thinking style, interpersonal style and personal style. Each of the competencies and values is supported by a set of more specific behavioural indicators, and these are used to inform judgements in the Fast Track selection process. The competencies and values are set out in Table 8.1.

There are certain observations that can be made immediately about these competencies and values:

- none of the competencies specifically cites school teaching or school leadership;
- all of the competencies could be demonstrated in occupational settings other than teaching;
- they are comparatively complex and describe what might be called 'higher order' characteristics and abilities;

Table 8.1 Fast Track competencies and values

Thinking style	
Analysis and problem solving	Identifies solutions to problems and takes responsibility for making decisions
Conceptual thinking	Thinks beyond the immediate situation and identifies new and improved ways of doing things
Ensuring the delivery of quality results	Sets high standards for themselves and others and ensures they are achieved
Interpersonal style	
Communicating effectively	Communicates effectively both orally and in writing, capturing the interest and enthusiasm of different audiences
Influencing others	Is able to persuade and influence other people
Developing and enabling others	Continually encourages others to perform to the best of their abilities and challenges under performance
Teamworking and building relationships	Builds and contributes to highly effective working relationships with individuals, within and across teams
Personal style	
Confidence and resilience	Demonstrates self-confidence in their ability to succeed, maintaining energy and enthusiasm in highly challenging situations
Commitment to self-development and learning	Shows a commitment to own learning and takes responsibility for their own professional development
Values	
Integrity and fairness	
Commitment to working with children	
Passion for learning and education	

- they imply a certain set of personal motives, convictions and commitments;
- they are oriented towards high levels of achievement, with an emphasis on challenge, success, performance and innovation;
- a discrete set of professional values is outlined, and values are also implicit in the definition of the competencies.

Design of the Fast Track Standards

It is worthwhile to discuss some of the factors impacting upon the design of the Fast Track competencies and values. The standards needed to be used as the basis for the assessment of candidates' potential for teaching and for educational leadership, and therefore needed to focus upon the characteristics required for successful classroom practice and also encompass those needed for leadership, capturing the common characteristics that underpin working successfully both with children and with other adults.

The team that drafted and refined the FT standards realised that they would need to be different from the other standards in the teaching profession. However, they also needed, at some level, to be complementary to them. Finally, the standards needed to be credible within the profession; they required 'face-validity' for serving teachers.

The key issue about the Fast Track selection process is that it was designed to measure potential for progression to leadership roles in education. This need to assess potential impacted directly upon the framing of the standards and the design of the selection process. It was seen as vital that the standards should relate to skills and behaviours that a candidate could have developed in contexts other than teaching. The standards also needed to be drafted in such a way that the competencies could be observed at an appropriate level, for example, through an assessment centre.

For this reason, the assessment centre exercises are 'located' in a school setting, but are structured in a way to ensure that candidates without teaching experience are not disadvantaged. The assessment centre is intended to permit the detailed profiling of strengths, development needs and potential for leadership on the basis of evidence captured about the candidate's behaviours and perceptions.

The Fast Track competencies and values were developed with close reference to the other sets of National Standards, and the research by the Hay Group for the DfES on the characteristics of highly effective teachers and school leaders. They also drew upon typical criteria used in Fast Track graduate recruitment programmes in the private sector. Focus groups and structured interviews were also used to gauge the response of stakeholders to the validity of the draft standards. It was emphasised to stakeholder groups that these standards were focused upon the characteristics of Fast Track Teachers, capturing the additional qualities and skills needed to progress to leadership roles in education. The groups were also assured that all candidates on the Fast Track programme are expected to demonstrate high levels of performance in relation to other National Standards as they enter the profession and work towards threshold assessment. The focus groups and interviewees were therefore asked to comment on the utility of the standards in terms of predicting potential for leadership and their likely credibility for the teaching profession. Amendments were made in the light of feedback, although the overall structure and focus of the standards were not changed fundamentally.

The Fast Track competencies and values as National Standards: initial analysis

The Fast Track competencies and values are not well known across the profession, but are displayed on the Fast Track website. They are also included in the guidance pack for applicants (*Develop the potential*), and the notes for headteachers who may consider creating a Fast Track post in their school. They do not, however, appear in the Teachers Standards Framework, which maps the national standards for teaching, 'setting out the expectations for effective performance in different roles within a school'.

These National Standards are designed to inform decisions about career progression, performance management and professional development. Some have a statutory basis and underpin formal procedures for pay progression; others have an advisory status and are primarily designed to inform decisions about professional development. Taken together, they define the structure of the profession and impact directly upon the majority of teachers and leaders in the state sector. To a lesser or greater extent, they have come to shape accepted definitions of roles in teaching and been absorbed into the consciousness of those working in the teaching profession. From this perspective, the Fast Track standards are national standards in that they underpin the selection, recruitment and progression of all Fast Track Teachers in England. They are not, however, 'National Standards' in the sense defined above. They apply only to a very small group of teachers.

The Fast Track standards were primarily designed to inform the selection process but are also used to monitor and support the work of FT Teachers as they progress through the programme. Through a DfES contract, a Central Support Team manages the FT Teachers, provides core development opportunities and operates a job brokerage scheme.

> ... Fast Track teachers will be expected to perform to a high standard at all times .... If a teacher does not perform to the standard expected, the headteacher should notify the central support team, who would liaise with the school and the teacher. If the teacher continues to fail to meet the standards, the central support team will issue a formal warning that the individual might be removed from the programme if there is no improvement in performance. Any decision on whether to remove a teacher from the programme would be made by the central support team.
>
> (DfES 2001)

Fast Track Teachers, however, are also subject to other standards, each of which may impact far more directly upon them at specific stages in their career. If they enter the programme as undergraduates or career-changers, they are required to complete a PGCE programme (provided by an approved set of providers) and meet the Standards required to achieve Qualified Teacher Status (and subsequently the Induction Standards as newly qualified teachers). If they enter the programme as qualified teachers, they will be required to prepare to meet the Threshold Standards within three years. Fast Track Teachers are also included in the school's normal performance management procedures, and are expected to achieve annual objectives and perform at a level that warrants double increments. This means that whilst the FT competencies and values shape the selection and progression of candidates on the programme, other sets of standards may be of greater significance in shaping the professional practice and assessing the competency of FT teachers, particularly in the early stages of their careers.

The Fast Track standards and the Teachers' Standards Framework

It is salutary to map the FT standards against the generic headings provided in the Teachers' Standards Framework. This was developed to provide a coherent overview of the National Standards and define 'the expectations for effective performance in different roles in a school' (Teachers' Standards Framework Issue 1, DfES 2001). They show progression in relation to ten different dimensions of teaching and leadership.

In Table 8.2, the ten dimensions are listed in the first column. A summary of the degree of fit between the ten dimensions and the Fast Track standards is provided in the second column. Columns three and four identify pertinent FT standards, and give examples of FT behavioural indicators.

Table 8.2 demonstrates that a high degree of inference is often required to make the link between the FT standards and the ten dimensions of the National Standards. This is primarily because the ten dimensions are 'school-specific', and very much focused on the daily work of the school, whilst the FT standards are generic, and could be exercised in a number of organisational settings. It is also interesting to note that whilst the Fast Track initiative is designed to secure the rapid promotion of participants to leadership roles in schools, there is no explicit reference to strategic leadership and resource management in the Fast Track competencies and values, although a relationship can be inferred.

The FT standards are different from most of the other National Standards in that the latter were not developed to predict potential, but to measure competence and inform development. This is particularly the case with those Standards that have a statutory basis, and are subject to formal assessment, verification and certification. The comparison with the other National Standards also reveals just how distinctive the Fast Track competencies and values are, primarily because they operate at a comparatively

Table 8.2 Mapping the Fast Track competencies and values against the main elements of the National Standards

Main elements of National Standards	Degree of fit of FT competencies and values with National Standards	Related FT competencies and values	Examples of FT indicators
Knowledge and understanding	None; no specific areas of knowledge and understanding specified		
Planning and setting expectations	Inferred fit; generic analytical and planning skills	Analysis and problem-solving Ensuring delivery of quality results	Sets stretching and achievable tasks for themselves and others Continually monitors and evaluates progress, taking action to revise priorities, overcome obstacles and problems
Teaching and managing pupil learning	High degree of fit; emphasis upon personal qualities and convictions	Communicating effectively Commitment to working with children Integrity and fairness	Adapts style and content of communication to appeal to the listener or reader Able to build rapport with many different groups of children
Assessment and evaluation	Inferred fit; specifies generic skills, not explicitly related to educational context	Analysis and problem-solving Ensures delivery of quality results	Systematically gathers up-to-date information from a wide range of relevant sources and perspectives Continually monitors and evaluates progress, taking action to revise priorities, overcomes obstacles and problems
Pupil achievement	High degree of fit; focus upon underlying convictions and attributes	Passion for learning and the development of others	Believes in the ability of everyone to fulfil their potential Has high expectations of self, pupils and others in relation to achieve potential
Relations with parents and wider community	Inferred fit; specifies interpersonal skills relevant to a range of settings	Influencing others Confidence and resilience	Effectively negotiates with others to find a way forward Appears confident and self-assured in a wide range of social and professional situations

continued

Table 8.2 Continued

Main elements of National Standards	Degree of fit of FT competencies and values with National Standards	Related FT competencies and values	Examples of FT indicators
Managing own performance and development	High degree of fit; Pertinent skills and attributes identified	Commitment to self-development and learning; Integrity and fairness	Admits mistakes when he/she got it wrong
Managing and developing staff and other adults	High degree of fit; pertinent skills and attributes identified	Teamworking and building relationships; Developing and enabling others	Brings problems that hamper teamworking into the open and works with others to resolve them; Continually challenges and encourages others to perform to the best of their abilities
Managing resources	Inferred fit; no explicit reference to different aspects of resource management	Ensuring the delivery of quality results	Identifies what needs to be achieved, by when, by whom and in what order. Continually focuses energy and effort on achieving the best possible results with the time and resources available
Strategic leadership	Inferred fit; no explicit reference to leadership	Innovative thinking; Ensuring the delivery of quality results	Is able to take an overview of situations, standing back from detail; Is able to anticipate future possibilities

high level of generality and do not encompass specific sets of professional knowledge, technical skills or classroom practice.

The distinctive nature of the FT standards is a reflection of the very particular purposes for which they were designed. However, it is useful to reflect upon whether they have pertinence beyond the specific requirements of the Fast Track teaching programme, particularly as they appear to be so distinctive. Before this question can be addressed, Fast Track competencies will be located more precisely within the spectrum of different approaches to the definition and application of competencies currently to be found in education and training.

The Fast Track competencies and values: the assessment of professional performance and potential

This section of the chapter looks at how the Fast Track competencies and values fit in with broader perspectives on the assessment and development of professional achievement and expertise. It seeks to locate the competencies and values in relation to a number of different approaches to defining competency. There are a number of key questions that may be asked to define more closely the nature and purpose of competency frameworks in occupational settings:

- Are they concerned with threshold or superior performance?
- What consideration do they give to cognitive processes, analysis and understanding?
- What consideration do they give to moral dimensions and value issues?
- Do they focus on specific occupational skills or generic professional characteristics?
- Are the frameworks used primarily for the purposes of selection, promotion or professional development? (Bennett 1997; Roberts 1997; Brundrett 2000)

Within education, it is possible to identify three broad approaches to defining professional expertise and achievement (see Figure 8.2). These three approaches have, either singly or together over the last two decades, tended to displace a previous approach that was based primarily upon the academic assessment of theoretical and propositional knowledge, both within initial teacher education and in continuing professional development.

These three approaches may be briefly characterised as follows:

1   The definition of the *occupational competencies* needed to achieve at an appropriate standard in a specific role and setting

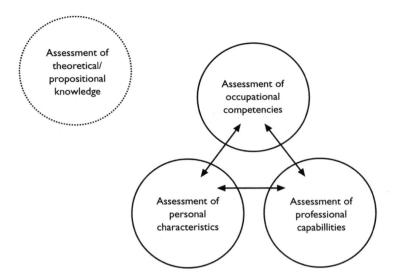

Figure 8.2 Competing approaches to the assessment of professional achievement and expertise in UK education settings.

2   The identification of the underlying *personal characteristics* needed for high levels of professional effectiveness in a range of related roles and settings

3   The search for the *professional capabilities* and conceptual skills needed to manage ambiguity, exercise good judgement and demonstrate capacity for further development.

Each of these approaches will be considered in turn. This analysis will seek to clarify the different ways in which they define competency, and to locate the Fast Track competencies and values in relation to this spectrum of approaches. The key differences in the definition of competency are summarised in Table 8.3.

Occupational competencies

This approach to the definition of occupational competence underpins the National Vocational Qualifications in the UK and the Management Charter Initiative, which has defined national standards of managerial competence (Brundrett 2000) for use within both private and public sector organisations. From this perspective, competence represents a threshold level of performance required to fulfil a role satisfactorily. Each key role comprises a set of competencies in which a given set of observable skills and behaviours are needed to complete that unit of competence to a

Table 8.3 Comparison of different models of competency and capability in educational settings

Occupational competencies	Personal characteristics	Professional capability
Competence defined as basis of satisfactory performance	Competency defined as basis of superior performance	Capability defined as basis of professional expertise and capacity for personal learning
Competencies are possessed or they are not possessed	Competencies possessed consciously or unconsciously	Capability based upon person's propositional knowledge and personal knowledge (in part tacit)
All competencies at a given level have to be demonstrated for satisfactory performance to be achieved	Certain competencies are necessary as 'threshold' competencies to permit further development of superior performance	No concise definition of what would constitute a satisfactory level of performance – focus on improvement and development
Competences related to the requirements of a specific job	Competencies related to the characteristics of persons who are highly effective in a job	Capability related to different kinds of knowledge and expertise that are embedded in a professional role
Competencies defined by specific roles and tasks that make a job	Competencies are made up of clusters of skills and attributes needed to fulfil different aspects of a job	Capability defined in terms of different types of professional knowledge and expertise needed to fulfil a role
Each set of competencies incorporates and extends those at lower level of seniority	Competencies required for senior managers are different from those needed by those at different levels in the organisation	All forms of profession capability are underpinned by specific types of knowledge and higher levels of thinking
Assessment designed to ensure that a threshold level of competence has been achieved	Assessment designed to identify strengths and areas for development	Assessment designed to assess capability for further professional learning and career progression

Note
Adapted from Bennett 1997

satisfactory standard. A complex framework defines units and elements of competence, performance criteria, range statements and required evidence.

Competencies are identified through a functional job analysis that is designed to analyse the core components of a specific role This means competencies are job-specific rather than person-specific, in that the focus of analysis is upon the tasks and functions required to perform a role, rather than upon the characteristics of individuals fulfilling that role (Iles and Salaman 1995: 216).

The Fast Track competencies do not conform to this model, in that they are concerned to define high levels of effectiveness, rather than satisfactory performance. They are not job-specific, and could be pertinent in a range of occupational settings. They were not defined through a functional analysis of different tasks that teachers perform. They are supported by a set of behavioural indicators, but these reflect the characteristics of persons rather than requirements of a role.

Personal characteristics

The second approach is based upon the identification of the personal characteristics of high-performing professionals. This 'person-oriented' approach to job analysis was pioneered by Boyatzis, a consultant working with Hay McBer, whose research into managerial competence has proved enduringly influential, particularly in the USA. He defined competency as 'an underlying characteristic of a person which results in effective and/or superior performance in a job' (Boyatzis 1982: 21).

The aim of this approach has been to identify the personal characteristics of managers that lead to excellence: what Boyatzis called 'superior managerial performance'. From this perspective, the key task in defining standards is to differentiate between adequate levels of performance and those that characterise excellence. Such standards are more likely to be used in an aspirational or developmental way within an organisation or profession rather than to assess individuals against a threshold of acceptable performance.

This approach involves defining standards that are related to the characteristics of the person in a specific role rather than the role itself, and 'are generic to a quality of performance at a given level of seniority' (Bennett 1997: 71). The personal characteristics that a leader demonstrates may operate at a number of different levels within the leader's psyche. They may inform the behaviour of the leader unconsciously as underlying personality traits or motives; they may be consciously owned as a self-image or espoused values; or they may be demonstrated as specific behaviours or skills (Bennett 1997: 71; Torrington and Hall 1998).

It is this approach to defining professional competency that is most closely related to the Fast Track competencies and values. As seen above, the Fast Track framework describes the personal characteristics of individuals with the potential to become highly effective teachers and school leaders. The Fast Track competencies focus directly upon habitual behaviours, knowledge of self, and embedded forms of conduct. The Fast Track values reflect a set of personal motives and professional convictions concerned with high levels of commitment and achievement.

The FT standards also have some similarity with the generic model of management competency identified by Boyatzis (1982) through research conducted over some years into over 40 management roles and 12 organisations. The model was based on five clusters of competency that include: goal and action management, leadership, human resource management, focus on other, and directing subordinates. They operate at a very high level of generality, and are applicable to a broad range of professional roles and organisational settings. The question of the apparent generality of the FT standards is discussed further below.

The models of effective teaching and excellence for school leaders developed more recently by the Hay Group under contract to the DfEE (now the DfES) were also developed using the approaches pioneered by Boyatzis and McLelland (Chapter 3). The research conducted by the Hay Group to produce the 'Models of Excellence for School Leaders' is described as follows:

> The characteristics are drawn from research about what high-performing individuals in different settings actually do in their schools and in their communities. In-depth interviews, panel discussions and questionnaires were used with a representative sample of school leaders from each phase and type of school in England, together with individual interviews with representatives of education bodies and other stakeholders, to identify the characteristics that drive performance.
> (www.ncslonline.gov.uk/programmes/haymodels)

The models produced by the Hay Group are sophisticated in that they include the juxtaposition of the different personal characteristics of effective school leaders and relate these to the specific challenges posed by a variety of settings and sizes of school. There are similarities between the Fast Track standards and those defined by Hay; these are mapped out in Table 8.4.

Professional capability

The Fast Track competencies and values also bear a passing resemblance to the 'professional capability' model. This approach is informed by philosophical perspectives, and is concerned with a search for a new epistemology that defines professional knowledge and expertise (Eraut 1993: 62). It draws heavily upon Schon's model of the reflective practitioner and the desire to understand the tacit, personal and intuitive forms of knowledge that effective professionals draw upon. It is based upon the

Table 8.4 Similarities between Fast Track standards and those defined by Hay

Fast Track competencies and values / Hay characteristics of effective school leaders	Thinking style		Interpersonal style					Personal style			Values	
	Analysis and problem-solving	Conceptual thinking	Ensuring the delivery of quality results	Communicating effectively	Influencing others	Developing and enabling others	Teamworking and building relationships	Confidence and resilience	Commitment to self-development and learning	Integrity and fairness	Commitment to working with children	Passion for learning and development of others
Personal values and passionate conviction												
Respect for others		✓		✓			✓			✓✓	✓	✓✓
Challenge and support			✓✓	✓	✓	✓					✓	✓✓
Personal conviction		✓								✓✓	✓✓	✓
Creating the vision												
Strategic thinking	✓✓	✓										
Drive for improvement	✓	✓	✓✓	✓		✓						
Initiative	✓							✓✓	✓			✓
Planning for delivery and monitoring												
Analytical thinking	✓✓	✓										
Transformational leadership						✓✓	✓					✓✓
Teamworking						✓✓	✓✓					
Building commitment and support												
Impact and influence			✓✓	✓	✓✓	✓						
Holding people accountable			✓✓	✓								
Gathering information and gaining understanding												
Social awareness		✓								✓		
Scanning the environment	✓✓											

conviction that the complex and ambiguous challenges of professional practice cannot be reduced to specific competencies and procedural recipes, but instead demand recourse to a set of cognitive skills, deliberative processes and reflective behaviours. These include the ability to:

- articulate, apply and question conceptual frameworks;
- analyse complex dilemmas/exercise good professional judgement;
- engage in appropriate professional discourse in an objective and impartial manner;
- reflect on one's personal behaviour and professional performance;
- apply professional learning to new problems and settings.

It is argued that these skills and behaviours are also controlled by meta-processes concerning self-knowledge and self-management. These meta-processes also shape the 'professional capability' of an individual: his or her ability to transfer learning to new situations and demonstrate the potential for further professional growth and career development (Eraut 1999). This approach, particularly through its links with Argyris and Schon's work on reflective practice, theory-in-use and double-loop learning (Argyris and Schon 1978; Schon 1983), can still be discerned in many initial teacher education and continuing professional development programmes offered by higher education institutions in the UK.

This approach to defining capability and potential does resonate with some aspects of the Fast Track competencies and values. The eligibility criteria for Fast Track places a high importance on the cognitive skills of candidates, as reflected in its academic requirements. There is also within the Fast Track standards an emphasis on thinking style: analytical and problem-solving skills, creative thinking, and ensuring the delivery of quality results. Thus candidates, in terms of analysis and problem-solving, are assessed on their ability to gather data systematically, assimilate different types of information, identify key issues, use sound judgement and make timely decisions. In terms of conceptual thinking, candidates are expected, for example, to integrate ideas into meaningful concepts and models, look at situations from different perspectives, anticipate future possibilities, and continually look for new and improved ways of doing things. In terms of ensuing quality, candidates are expected, for example, consistently to focus their energy and effort on achieving the best possible results, to set stretching and achievable objectives, anticipate obstacles, develop contingency plans, and so on. The Fast Track competencies emphasise cognition, deliberation and analysis in much the same way as the capability approach.

There is also an emphasis in the Fast Track competencies upon personal responsibility, professional learning and self-knowledge. These resonate with the meta-processes of self-knowledge and self-management. There is a clear focus upon continued professional growth and a search to fulfil potential through a commitment to learning. Finally, the Fast Track values also resonate with the professional values that implicitly underpin the capability model; integrity and fairness, commitment to working with children, and a passion for learning and education. Each of these celebrates values that accord with a particular philosophy of teacher professionalism that involves earned autonomy, a commitment to public service, objectivity and judgement, and a duty to exercise self-regulation.

However, it could be argued from the perspective of 'professional capability' that within the Fast Track competencies and values, there is also a celebration of what has been called 'managerialism'. This is characterised by a generic set of management prescriptions that its proponents would apply in any organisational setting, whether private, public or voluntary. It is possible to conclude that the Fast Track standards are based upon a generic model of leadership and management that does not take into account apparent differences in the public and private sectors, and seeks to replace traditional forms of teacher professionalism with one based upon centralised control and market forces (Grace 1995; Kydd 1997). This is in stark contrast to the implicit orientation of 'professional capability' towards protecting and defining the specialist knowledge, expertise and values that are enshrined within professional communities dedicated to public service.

Conclusion: defining the personal characteristics of superior performance

What then are the possibilities for the further development and application of the 'characteristics' approach to defining professional expertise in setting national standards and shaping leadership practices in schools?

The Fast Track competencies and values are, by definition, concerned with superior levels of professional performance. The 'personal characteristics' approach to defining competency is oriented towards high levels of performance and therefore readily aligned with the standards agenda in education and initiatives designed to raise levels of pupil attainment, challenge under-performance and transform the school workforce. The role of such competencies within education policy can also be seen as aspirational in that they may be used to crystallise approved sets of values and shape the perceptions of teachers and managers working in the sector.

Competency, innovation and excellence

A criticism of many models of competency is that they are focused on the present requirements of organisations or the elements of past success, rather than defining what is likely to be successful in relation to changing context and future needs (Iles and Salaman 1995: 217). The search for excellence orients researchers towards examples of outstanding professional performance that reflect innovatory practice and successful outcomes. Such examples may also be identified because they resonate with government policy objectives and relevant research findings.

If it is accepted that the main thrust of current educational policy is now fundamentally forward-looking, (as reflected, for example, in the new organisational forms, professional structures, and leadership paradigms sponsored by the DfES Workforce Unit and the National College for School Leadership), it is necessary to adopt techniques which permit what has been called 'forward-looking strategic job analysis' to identify best practice, future trends and professional requirements (Iles and Salaman 1995: 215). Such techniques are predominantly qualitative, and may include behavioural event interviews, critical incidents, repertory grid analysis and participant observation to collect evidence about a small sample of high-performing individuals. Focus groups and structured interviews are also used to capture the perceptions of key groups of stakeholders, in order to evaluate the validity of draft standards and shape their further definition. These techniques reflect the methods used to define both the Fast Track competencies and values and the Hay Model of Excellence for School Leaders.

However, brief scrutiny of the current sets of standards and procedures for professional assessment and performance management in education reveals that they do not all reflect this futures-oriented commitment to superior performance and educational excellence. Instead, it reveals:

- the juxtaposition of objectives-based and standards-based models of performance assessment;
- a proliferation of different types of professional standards and competencies;
- a mixture of standards concerned with both threshold and superior levels of performance; and
- the application of a range of techniques for the collection of evidence and the formation of judgements about professional competence.

This complexity is in part the product of incremental systems development led by a number of departments, agencies and organisations over several years. It also reflects the contrasting functions that the various elements of the system of standards and procedures have been designed to perform, primarily in relation to professional accountability, progression and development. However, this summary also suggests the need for a review of the principles, coherence and co-ordination of the current system.

Towards a social process model of assessment

One source of inspiration for such a review of current standards and procedures could be what has been called the 'emerging social process model' for the assessment of professional competency. This draws upon research in social psychology to consider more closely the impact of selection techniques, professional assessment and performance management upon individuals and organisations (Iles and Salaman 1995: 222). These impacts relate to organisational health, professional effectiveness, personal motivation, career progression and self-esteem. Such an approach is based on a number of assumptions in its consideration of professional standards and assessment procedures – that:

- people change constantly in the course of their career and progress through a number of transitions;
- subjective self-perceptions are critical to people's work motivation and performance;
- assessment procedures impact directly either positively or negatively upon candidates' professional commitment and self-esteem;
- people increasingly work in multi-skilled, flexible, self-directed teams.

Within this kind of approach to assessment, the definition of standards as statements of aspirational performance and behaviour is best expressed through the 'personal characteristic' model outlined above. There is clearly scope for a review of current systems for the selection, recruitment, development and progression of school leaders based upon a coherent and integrated view of professional learning and accountability. From this perspective, the key significance of the Fast Track standards is their potential contribution to a new approach to defining the key competencies of school teachers and school leaders. Further research is needed, drawing upon that already conducted by the Hay Group, to capture the key personal characteristics required of teachers and leaders fulfilling different roles in schools, and to identify the underlying qualities, skills and values that are needed at all levels. The key contribution of the Fast Track standards is that they do capture what is needed to secure excellence across the school sector, and that they express this in a simple and direct manner. Such an approach could potentially engage those working in schools far more powerfully than the current range of complex, unwieldy and incoherent standards.

References and further reading

Argyris, C. and Schon, D. (1978) *Organizational Learning: A Theory of Action Perspective*, Boston MA: Addison-Wesley.
Bennett, N. (1997) 'Analysing management for personal development: theory and

practice,' in Kydd, L., Crawford, M. and Riches, C. (eds) *Professional Development for Educational Management*, Buckingham: Open University Press.

Boyatzis, R.E. (1982) *The Competent Manager: A Model For Effective Performance*, New York: John Wiley.

Brundrett, M. (2000) 'The question of competence: the origins, strengths and inadequacies of a leadership training paradigm,' *School Leadership and Management* 20: 3.

Department for Education and Employment (1998) Green Paper, 'Teachers: meeting the challenge of change' (Cm 4164), London: DfEE.

Department for Education and Employment (1999) *A Fast Track for Teachers*, London: DfEE.

Department for Education and Skills (2001) *The Fast Track Teaching Programme: Guidance for Headteachers*, London: DfES.

Eraut, M. (1993) 'Developing expertise in school management and teaching,' in Strain, M., Dennison, B., Ouston, J. and Hall, V. (eds) (1998) *Policy, Leadership and Professional Knowledge in Education*, London: Paul Chapman Publishing.

Eraut, M. (1999) 'Headteachers' knowledge, practice and mode of cognition,' in Bush, T., Bell, L., Bolam, R., Glatter, R. and Ribbins, P. (eds) *Educational Management: Redefining Theory, Policy and Practice*, London: Paul Chapman Publishing.

Goleman, D. (1998) *Working with Emotional Intelligence*, London: Bloomsbury.

Grace, G. (1995) *School Leadership: Beyond School Management. An Essay in Policy Scholarship*, London: the Falmer Press.

Hewitt, M. (2000) 'The work of the National Educational Assessment Centre,' *Professional Development Today*, Autumn.

Holmes, G. and Tomlinson, H. (2000) 'Fast track to school leadership,' *Professional Development Today*, Autumn.

Iles, P. and Salaman, G. (1995) 'Recruitment, selection and assessment,' in Storey, J. (ed.) *Human Resource Management: A Critical Text*, London: International Thompson Business Press.

Kydd, L. (1997) 'Teacher professionalism and managerialism,' in Kydd, L., Crawford, M. and Riches, C. (eds) *Professional Development for Educational Management*, Buckingham: Open University Press.

Roberts, G. (1997) *Recruitment and Selection: A Competency Approach*, London: Chartered Institute of Personnel and Development.

Schon, D. (1983) *The Reflective Practitioner*, New York: Basic Books.

Torrington, D. and Hall, L. (1998) *Human Resource Management*, 4th edn, London: Prentice Hall.

Woodruffe, C. (2000) *Development and Assessment Centres: Identifying and Assessing Competence*, 3rd edn, London: Institute of Personnel and Development.

Part 3

National Standards for school leaders

Chapter 9

Special Educational Needs Co-ordinator (SENCO)

Janet Tod

Context and content of the Special Educational Needs (SEN) Standards

Context of SEN Standards

> SENCOs play a pivotal role, coordinating provision across schools and linking class and subject teachers with SEN specialists to improve the quality of teaching and learning. We want schools to see the SENCO as a key member of the senior leadership team, able to influence the development of politics for whole school improvement.
>
> (DfES, 2004)

The Government's Programme of Action, *Meeting Special Educational Needs* (DfEE 1998a), set out a broad agenda to 'ensure that the needs of all pupils with SEN were met through greater access to the curriculum and specific training for teachers'. The Programme aimed to achieve successful inclusion of pupils with SEN by securing better training for teachers working with such pupils. Two key documents, National Standards for Special Educational Needs Co-ordinators (TTA 1998) and National SEN Specialist Standards (TTA 1999a), were published with the aim of improving the status and training of teachers of pupils with SEN and, consequently, improving the quality of education of pupils with SEN.

An important point to note concerning the two sets of SEN National Standards is that they were written during a time of rapid change in relation to provision and practice for pupils with SEN. The SENCO Standards were developed within a 'standards raising' context and housed within associated national priorities, particularly in support of the Government's key educational targets in relation to literacy, numeracy and ICT. The SEN Specialist Standards, arriving a year later in 1999, reflected that 'inclusion', with an anticipated increase of pupils with severe and/or complex learning needs in mainstream settings, was joining 'standards raising' as a national priority area for education. Interestingly the new Professional Standards for QTS (TTA 2001) have emphasised one particular aspect of inclusion rather than overtly continuing with the process of preparing teachers to meet the challenge of including more pupils with significant learning difficulties within mainstream settings:

> they will also ensure that training tackles issues such as behaviour management and social inclusion well.
>
> (Morris and Tabberer 2001)

This emerging emphasis, within the context of inclusion, on behavioural difficulties and disaffection may be redressed by the introduction of the Special Educational Needs and Disability Act (Disability Rights Commission 2002) that was implemented in different parts of the United Kingdom in September 2002. This act prescribes two main duties:

1   Not to treat disabled pupils less favourably and
2   To make reasonable adjustments in order to ensure that disabled students are not placed at substantial disadvantage.

These duties are intended to cover every aspect of the life of the school and ensure that disabled students should have the same opportunities as non-disabled students in their access to education.

The SENCO National Standards and the SEN Specialist Standards are both closely linked with the *SEN Code of Practice* (DfEE 1994; DfES 2001a). The *SEN Code of Practice* provides practical advice to Local Education Authorities, maintained schools, early education settings and others on carrying out their statutory duties to identify, assess and make provision for children's special educational needs. When effecting their roles, schools, LEAs, and SENCOs are also required to take on board the three key principles of inclusion (see Figure 9.1) described within the new National Curriculum (DfEE/QCA 1999).

Content and format of SEN Standards

The National Standards for Special Educational Needs Co-ordinators (SENCO Standards) were issued in 1998 after a period of consultation and revision:

> in the light of research by the DfEE (The SENCO Guide 1997) and a second survey of the implementation of the SEN Code of Practice carried out by HMI during 1996 and 1997.

The SENCO Standards are in the format of a fourteen-page document under the headings described in Table 9.1.

The SENCO Standards were accompanied by a booklet entitled *Using the National Standards for Special Educational Needs Co-ordinators*

Table 9.1 Areas of SENCO Standards (TTA 1998)

Areas of SENCO Standards	Flavour of the detail of areas of SENCO Standards (author selection from TTA SENCO standards document)
Core purpose of the SENCO.	'The SENCO takes responsibility for the day-to-day operation of provision made by the school for pupils with SEN and provides professional guidance in the area of SEN in order to secure high quality teaching and effective use of resources to bring about improved standards of achievement for all pupils.'
Key outcomes of SEN co-ordination.	Described under: a) pupils on the register, who make progress; b) teachers, who have high expectations, set realistic targets, monitor, review and provide appropriate support for pupils with SEN; c) learning support assistants (LSAs), who work collaboratively to support pupils such that achievement and independence are maximised; d) parents, who feel involved as partners in the education process; e) headteachers and senior managers, who take SEN into account when formulating policies; f) governors, who understand and effect their role in relation to SEN pupils; g) LEAs and other bodies, which receive information about progress made by SEN pupils including efficacy of externally provided support
Professional knowledge and understanding.	Effective teaching for both academic and social/moral development; systems for monitoring and evaluation; efficient and effective use of resources; enabling ICT for SEN pupils; interpretation and implementation of legislation for SEN; familiarity and use of national and local inspection evidence; effective communication internally and externally; professional development of staffing in relation to SEN
Skills and attributes.	Leadership and professional competence; decision-making and problem-solving; communication skills; self-management; personal attributes (impact, presence, adaptability, energy, vigour and perseverance, self-confidence; enthusiasm; intellectual ability, reliability and integrity, commitment)
Key areas of SEN co-ordination.	a) strategic direction and development of SEN provision in the school; b) teaching and learning; c) leading and managing staff; d) efficient and effective deployment of staff and resources

(SENCOs) (TTA 1999b), which is offered as guidance that is 'neither exhaustive nor prescriptive'.

The *National Special Educational Needs Specialist Standards* 'comprise an audit tool' issued in a 53-page booklet (TTA 1999a) and more recently in a CD-ROM (TTA 2002). They consist of:

- core standards, designed for all teachers and managers who work with pupils with severe and/or complex SEN;

- extension standards, for teachers who require specialist expertise to meet the needs of pupils with particular SEN;
- standards in relation to key SEN Specialist roles and responsibilities (elements of the Specialist Standards), for those who have roles and responsibilities for SEN linked to advisory, curricular or managerial positions;
- skills and attributes required by teachers working with pupils with severe and or complex SEN.

Figure 9.1 seeks to provide a diagrammatic explanation of how the specialist standards are organised.

The core standards are housed within key 'generic' areas, e.g. identification, assessment and planning, development of communication, literacy, numeracy skills and ICT capabilities, as seen on the left-hand side of the grid. The extension standards reflect the SEN Code of Practice categories, i.e. communication and interaction, cognition and learning etc., as described at the top of the grid. Components of the Specialist Standards for managerial, curricular and advisory roles are selected as appropriate as shown by the arrows on the right of the grid. Skills and attributes are relevant to all teachers involved in meeting the needs of pupils with severe or complex SEN as shown by the arrows at the bottom of the grid.

While the organisation and content of both sets of SEN Standards can be seen to be relevant, two emergent problems remain:

1   If the key purpose of the SENCO role is via management to ensure desired outcomes, what happens if the SENCO does not have any management status? (In many primary schools the SENCO role is part-time for an existing class teacher, and in some cases is an NQT).
2   Given that the SEN Standards are 'advisory', does this assure national parity of provision for SEN pupils and a national standard of professional competence?

Given that CPD providers and schools have to work within the constraints of any identified problems with the SEN Standards, the next section illustrates how the SEN Standards may be used in a practical way with teachers and schools.

Using the Standards – national and local perspectives

Government perspectives

In addition to publishing the Standards, the TTA set out some of the ways in which the National SENCO Standards might be used flexibly by

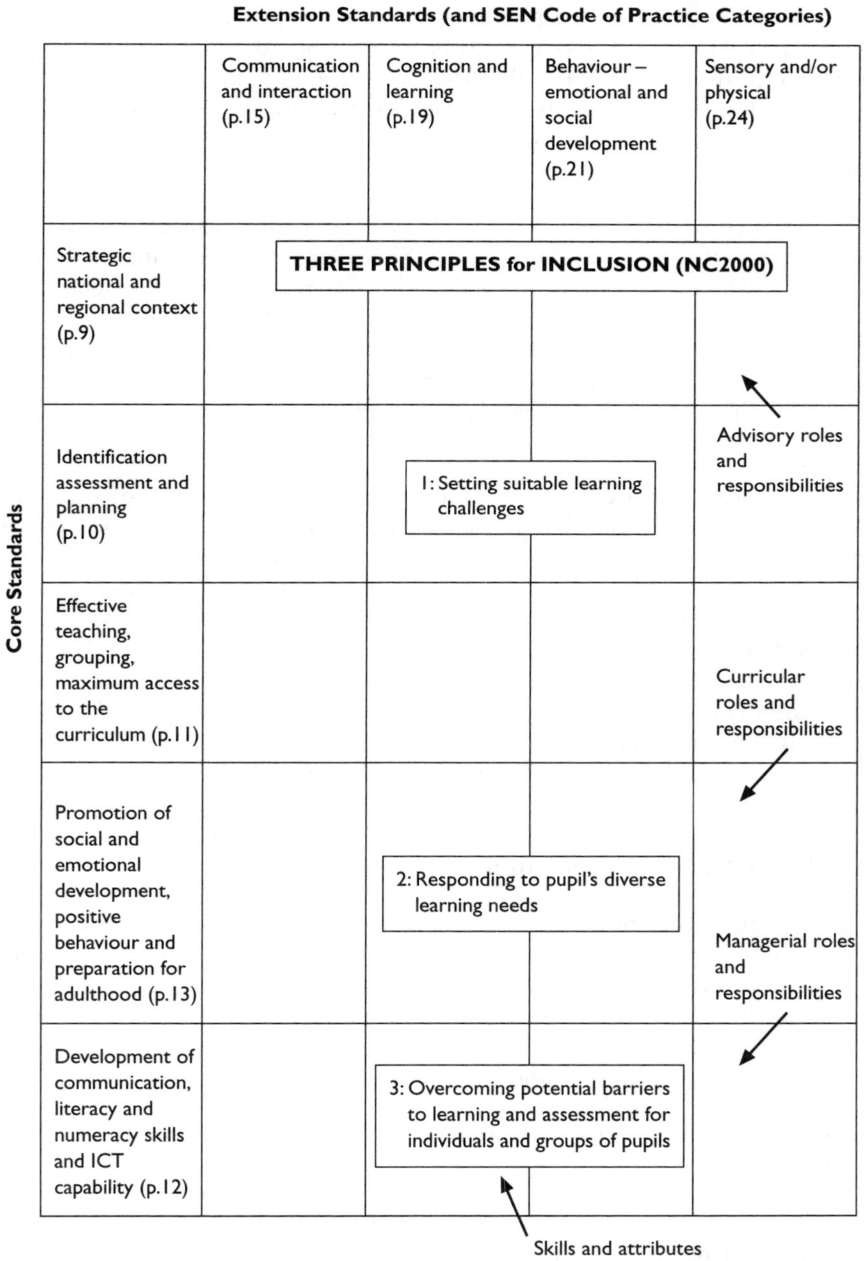
Extension Standards (and SEN Code of Practice Categories)
Communication and interaction (p.15)
Cognition and learning (p.19)
Behaviour – emotional and social development (p.21)
Sensory and/or physical (p.24)
Core Standards
Strategic national and regional context (p.9)
Identification assessment and planning (p.10)
Effective teaching, grouping, maximum access to the curriculum (p.11)
Promotion of social and emotional development, positive behaviour and preparation for adulthood (p.13)
Development of communication, literacy and numeracy skills and ICT capability (p.12)
THREE PRINCIPLES for INCLUSION (NC2000)
1: Setting suitable learning challenges
2: Responding to pupil's diverse learning needs
3: Overcoming potential barriers to learning and assessment for individuals and groups of pupils
Advisory roles and responsibilities
Curricular roles and responsibilities
Managerial roles and responsibilities
Skills and attributes

Figure 9.1 SEN specialist standards within the context of the Code of Practice and the National Curriculum statement on Inclusion (page numbers refer to the Specialist ISO Standards booklet, TTA 1999a).

schools, LEAs and training providers to secure improvement in the educational provision for pupils with SEN in line with the Government's Programme of Action (TTA 1999b). More recently, possibly in response to an agenda of increasing inclusion, the TTA has produced a CD-ROM to support schools in the use of the National SEN Specialist Standards. The material on the CD-ROM is:

> designed to help teachers and managers to identify aspects of teaching pupils with severe and/or complex SEN that inform training or further professional development needs. The CD-ROM contains video case studies in which teachers discuss the implications of that area for teaching pupils with particular needs in a particular setting. An associated commentary then explores the relevance of each area of the SEN specialist standards to teachers of pupils with different needs and in different settings.

This is a useful and creative addition to the booklet format of the SEN Specialist Standards in that it focuses on pupil needs to inform school development and training, and could be used by small groups of staff sharing a computer such that debate and discussion were generated.

Table 9.2 compares how the two sets of Standards may be used via reference to the guidance given by the TTA.

The Government, via the DfES (www.teachernet.gov.uk/Professional_Development), has provided guidance on Continued Professional Development (CPD) and, via the TTA (1999a, 1999b, 2002), on the use of SEN Standards. It makes sense for schools to combine these two sets of guidance when planning a coherent response to national requirements in relation to both CPD and the SEN Standards.

The CPD 'aim' of Standards is to:

> help providers of professional development to plan and provide high quality, relevant training which meets the needs of individual teachers and headteachers, makes good use of their time and has the maximum benefit for pupils. By 'professional development' we mean any activity that increases the skills, knowledge or understanding of teachers, and their effectiveness in schools.

The national ideals for CPD can support teachers and schools in relation to SEN by:

- *helping teachers to manage change.* In the case of SEN there is the need for teachers to manage change in relation to the increasing drive for inclusion set within the context of an ongoing standards-raising agenda for pupils at all levels (DfEE/QCA 1999; DfES 2001a, 2001b; Disability Rights Commission (2002).

Table 9.2 Suggested ways of using the SENCO and SEN Specialist Standards (TTA 1999a, 1999b)

	SENCO Standards	SEN Specialist Standards
Suggestions for use in TTA guidance documents	• support performance review; • deploy staff effectively; • inform job description/ recruitment; • inform policy and practice at school level and evaluate its effectiveness; • inform training; • inform strategic planning at regional level.	Audit in relation to core and extension standards such that development priorities for individual teachers and school /unit/service can be identified and met via 'objective, action, success criteria review' (p. 37) a) teacher working as junior member of team in a mainstream primary school wishing to specialise further in SEN; b) teacher in charge of special unit for pupils with a range of SEN including severe learning difficulties; c) senior teacher in a Pupil Referral Unit (PRU); d) area team leader within LEA SEN support service; e) a middle manager in a day special school

• *improving the performance of individuals and institutions as a whole.* This is now an important area for SEN in that schools and LEAs are required to provide data on the progress made by SEN pupils. Given the requirements for inclusion, SEN pupils will now be included in planning for whole-school effectiveness. The emerging emphasis that previously was on identification and assessment for SEN pupils is now on monitoring the outcomes of 'additional and/or extra provision' on the progress of SEN pupils, (DfES 2001).

• *increasing staff morale and sense of purpose.* In the SEN context, this can be achieved via effective CPD and recognition of additional responsibilities and 'specialist' training. Additionally, an emphasis on inclusion and collaborative working arrangements both within and between schools, particularly between special schools and mainstream settings (DfEE 1998a), may reduce processes and perceptions of the 'de-skilling' of teachers via pupils being removed from the school or classroom for 'specialist help' – particularly in literacy. Agreed aims, collaborative working arrangements and the monitoring of outcomes for SEN pupils should help to foster 'sense of purpose'.

- *lead to the personal as well as the professional development of teachers.* This is absolutely crucial in the SEN field, where teachers have not been involved in national planning for inclusion and indeed do not feel in a state of preparedness (Croll and Moses 2000, Garner 2001). Many teachers feel that they have not been trained to cope with the inclusion of all pupils, particularly those with severe emotional and behavioural difficulties or social communication difficulties – e.g. pupils on the autistic continuum. During a period of time when external monitoring and imposition of policy by the Government remains evident, there is a need to enable and empower teachers via CPD if teaching is to survive as a 'profession'. An emergent emphasis on 'evidence-based practice' and opportunities for teachers to engage in research that impacts upon their practice should serve to link personal and professional development.
- *promoting a sense of job satisfaction.* Many teachers simply want to 'make a difference'. Emphasis within legislation on 'monitoring outcomes' and 'reducing disaffection and exclusion' via effective CPD should help to address this important issue at a time when teacher retention (including that of SENCOs) is a necessary item on schools' agenda.
- *pulling together the school's vision for itself.* In relation to SEN and via initiatives to support inclusion (e.g. the *Index of Inclusion*, CSIE 2000), schools can use the impetus of external reform to improve or develop themselves (Hopkins *et al.* 1997) by working on common identified themes and principles.

Considering the ways in which CPD can help teachers and schools, Table 9.3 describes how this might be planned via reference to the SENCO National Standards. It can be seen from this that the SENCO Standards can be used to identify and inform individual CPD for existing or prospective SENCOs, but can also be used to identify areas for school and staff development in relation to SEN and inclusion.

Practical examples of how the SEN Standards have been used with teachers and schools

SENCO Standards

In this example, the SENCO Standards were used in an exercise to inform training for NQTs who have expressed a preference to work as SENCOs.

The main aim behind the task was to ensure that the students concerned actually read the Standards and examined their use in influencing the development and implementation of the role of the SENCO in a mainstream setting.

Table 9.3 Linking government aims for Continued Professional Development (CPD) with the aims for the National Standards via reference to the SENCO Standards

	Help teachers to manage change	Improve the performance of individuals and institutions as a whole	Increase staff morale and sense of purpose	Lead to the personal as well as the professional development of teachers	Promote a sense of job satisfaction	Pull together the school's vision for itself
Set out clear expectations for teachers at key points in the profession	The SENCO plays a key role in supporting, guiding and motivating colleagues	Have knowledge and understanding of research and national inspection evidence and implications for SEN	Create and foster commitment and confidence among staff to meeting the needs of pupils with SEN	Take responsibility for their own professional development and should draw upon attributes – self-confidence, energy, vigour and perseverance, etc	Contribute effectively to the development of a positive ethos in which all pupils have access to a broad, balanced and relevant curriculum	'SENCOs fundamental task is to support the HT in ensuring all staff give learning for all pupils equal priority'
Help teachers at different points in the profession to plan and monitor their development, training and performance effectively, and to set clear, relevant objectives for improving their effectiveness	Supports staff and encourages all staff to recognise and fulfil their statutory responsibilities to pupils with SEN ...	Work with pupils, subject leaders and class teachers with tutorial/pastoral responsibilities to ensure that realistic expectations of behaviour and achievements are set for pupils with SEN	Co-ordinate the professional development of staff to increase their effectiveness in responding to pupils with SEN	Help staff to achieve constructive working relationships with pupils with SEN	Develop systems for monitoring and recording progress made by pupils with SEN towards the achievement of the targets set	Provide regular information to the headteacher and governing body on the evaluation of the effectiveness of provision for pupils with SEN, to inform decision-making and policy review

continued

Table 9.3 Continued

	Help teachers to manage change	*Improve the performance of individuals and institutions as a whole*	*Increase staff morale and sense of purpose*	*Lead to the personal as well as the professional development of teachers*	*Promote a sense of job satisfaction*	*Pull together the school's vision for itself*
Ensure that the focus at every point is on improving the achievement of all pupils and the quality of their education	Collect and interpret specialist assessment data gathered on pupils and use it to inform practice	Support the identification of, and disseminate the most effective teaching approaches for, pupils with SEN	Develop systems for monitoring and recording progress made by pupils with SEN towards the achievement of targets set	Provide professional direction to the work of others	Support the development of improvements in literacy, numeracy and ICT ...	Ensure that the objectives of the SEN policy are reflected in the school development plan ...
Provide a basis for the professional recognition of teachers' expertise	Advise, support and contribute to QTS, Career entry profiles, and standards for induction	SENCO National Standards can be used to audit knowledge, understanding and skills, thus targeting areas for development/training and an evidence base for recognition of expertise either for accreditation or performance review	National Standards can be used to audit school policy and practices in relation to SEN, providing agreed targets, roles and responsibilities for whole-school development and a basis for objective evaluation of outcomes	SENCO Standards can be used to identify and audit personal attributes, e.g. self-confidence, enthusiasm, integrity, adaptability to change, etc., and these areas can be targeted for development	Standards can provide an impetus for the identification of individual or school-based research projects which can be externally funded (e.g. BPRS*) and/or used for accreditation of performance review	'contributes to a positive ethos in which all pupils have access to a broad, balanced and relevant curriculum' ... and in which teachers seek continually to enhance their own personal and professional development

Note
*DfEE Best Practice Research Scholarships

Students were set the task of carrying out a small-scale evidence-based enquiry to address the statement:

> The role of the SENCO is determined more by the immediate school context than by the perception of the individual SENCO and the requirements of the TTA National SENCO standards.

This was perceived to be an important area for professional development for NQTs, and was supported by the quotation by one student 'the co-ordination of SEN provision was an area that went largely untouched during my three-year teacher training'.

In order to address the question set, the group ($n = 15$) agreed the data collection strategy illustrated in Table 9.4.

Figure 9.2 illustrates one aspect of the data collected, i.e. 'how does the SENCO actually spend her time?'. The SENCO concerned was shadowed for one week in school, and her actions categorised and recorded.

While it is accepted that there were variations between individual case studies due to contextual and methodological factors, there was

Table 9.4 Example of use of SEN Standards: data collection strategy

	Question posed	Data collected
Documentary	What are the national and local *expectations* of the SENCO's role and responsibilities?	Review: TTA National Standards; SEN Code of Practice; the School's SEN policy
Interview	What are the *perceptions* of the SENCO's role in the school setting?	Interview with a) SENCO, b) class teachers, c) parent(s)
Observation	What is the *reality* of the SENCO's role in practice?	Shadowing the SENCO throughout a week using ten-minute charting of focus of activity-based DfEE categories (DfEE 1994): • liaising with and advising teachers; • co-ordinating provision for SEN pupils; • maintaining the school's SEN register and overseeing records of all pupils with SEN; • liaising with parents of children with SEN; • contributing to the in-service training of staff; • liaising with external agencies; • day-to-day operation of the school's SEN policy.

Categories	Hours in total	Percentage
Day-to-day operation of SEN policy	12	16.65
Liaison with and advising fellow teachers	14.75	20.46
Co-ordinating provision for children with SEN	9	12.48
Maintaining the school's SEN register/records	15.5	21.5
Liaison with parents of children with SEN	7.5	10.41
Contributing to the in-service training of staff	1.33	1.85
Liaison with external agencies	12	16.65
Total	72.08	100

Time management of SENCO

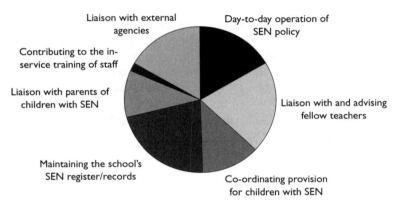

Figure 9.2 Time management of a SENCO, based on one week's observations (data taken from project work submitted by Hannah Ross, 2001).

consensus amongst the findings that have implications for the use of SENCO Standards in meeting the key aims that are taken from page 1 of the SENCO National Standards and set out in the left-hand column of Table 9.5.

From this small case study it seems reasonable to conclude that the SENCO Standards are being used to meet some of their intended aims via their use as a mechanism by which CPD providers identify and address professional development needs in order to meet LEA purchaser requirements. However, the use of SENCO Standards by schools to improve provision and practice for SEN pupils appears to be limited. The findings from this study suggest that Ofsted and LEA requirements and the immediate needs of the school are the prime influences on co-ordination and provision for SEN pupils. Priority is being given to the implementation of external directives rather than the evaluation of the impact of those directives. In an era of rapid change in relation to SEN provision, schools have been forced to

Table 9.5 Findings from CPD case studies, and their implications

Stated aims of Standards	Consensus of findings from CPD case studies (primary phase) described in text	Possible implications
Set out clear expectations for teachers at key points in the profession.	In the school setting the SENCO Standards had *not* been read by any of the practising SENCOs, or indeed heard of by most. SENCOs had instead referred to the Code of Practice (1994) and LEA advice in deciding on the school's SEN policy and their role within that policy	From this small-scale study it would seem that SENCOs and/or schools are not in fact reading or using the SENCO Standards. This may be due to the fact that 'external' monitoring (i.e. for schools Ofsted) refers to the SEN Code of Practice to which schools must 'have regard' when inspecting SEN practice and provision. Given that the SENCO Standards are 'advisory' for schools, it appears that this may have reduced their impact in a world where 'external monitoring' of Government policy takes precedence over initiatives that are 'advisory', however desirable such initiatives may be
Help teachers at different points in the profession to plan and monitor their development, training and performance effectively, and to set clear, relevant objectives for improving their effectiveness	This exercise allowed the students the time and opportunity to read the SENCO Standards. From this they were able identify that although many of the Standards were being met in school settings, the 'weighting' of aspects of the Standards varied. Of interest (see pie chart data in Figure 9.2) the SENCO role in contributing to the training of mainstream staff was allocated less time than some of the administrative aspects of the role (e.g. maintaining the schools SEN register) Similarly, liaising with parents was allocated less time than liaising with external agencies	Data from the small-scale investigative study suggests that although the four key aspects of SEN co-ordination are described in the SENCO Standards (p. 11), the outcome of such activity is not being systematically evaluated via reference to 'Key Outcomes of SEN coordination' (pp. 6–7). Examination of SENCOs' diaries plus observation suggested that SENCOs are too busy to systematically evaluate the *impact* of their role. This is done via the monitoring of Individual Education Plans (IEPs), and avoiding crises. Interview responses from teachers were unanimous in valuing the SENCOs
Ensure that the focus at every point is on improving the achievement of pupils and the quality of their education	As can be seen from the data, the SENCO spends the majority of her time in trying to *meet* the educational needs of SEN pupils (via advising teachers and liaising with external agencies) and *record* the response to any additional and/or extra provision (maintaining school's SEN register/records). Given the time allowed for the SENCO role and the demands for written evidence needed to secure any	It appears that, although the SENCO is fully aware (from interview data) that the key outcome of SEN co-ordination should be improved achievement and enhanced quality of education for SEN pupils, as with many government initiatives the focus for external evaluation and internal appraisal becomes focused towards the execution of the

continued

Table 9.5 Continued

Stated aims of Standards	Consensus of findings from CPD case studies (primary phase) described in text	Possible implications
	additional resources/funding/action, limited time could be given to systematic monitoring and evaluation of provision for individual pupils (i.e. written IEPs were in place but it was not known whether these were actually being implemented)	'mechanisms' rather than evaluation of effectiveness of those mechanisms. The recording and 'evidencing' of action taken to meet SEN is considerable for SENCOs particularly given IEPs (Ofsted 1997). IEPs were intended to be the mechanism via which 'improved achievement' could be evidenced, but they only record the meeting of targets set – not the appropriateness of the target-setting in improving the quality of education and the level of attainment for individual SEN pupils. Progress for individuals is not monitored by reference to age-related, Key Stage normative 'Standards'. This is being addressed by the revised Code, but remains contentious
Provide a basis for the professional recognition of teachers' expertise	SENCOs in the study reported attending a variety of INSET, mainly in relation to statutory requirements (Revised SEN Code of Practice 2001) and specific areas of SEN (e.g. autism). The majority of courses were less than one day, and did not carry accreditation	Although the SENCO Standards provide a mechanism for giving SENCOs an opportunity to have their professional expertise recognised, there was no evidence from this study that LEAs and schools are using the Standards in a systematic way to achieve this aim. (A national study examining the take-up and impact of SENCO training in relation to the Standards would be welcome.)
Help providers of professional development to plan high-quality relevant training which meets the needs of individual teachers and headteachers, making good use of their time and giving maximum benefit for pupils	Used as CPD resource within HE to inform training, the exercise ensured that NQT students read the Standards and examined their impact in practice. They were also able to audit their CPD needs in relation to SENCO training	Standards are used mainly by CPD providers and training agencies (LEA, Higher Education (HE) etc). These providers, in particular HE, are subject to external monitoring by funding agencies and QAA and Ofsted, who refer to the Standards when assuring quality and relevance. School-based training, if not accredited, may seek to address 'school' rather than 'government' agendas for SEN training, and thus schools do not feel the need to use advisory Standards to inform their staff and school development

be selective in their responses. It seems that the 'advisory' nature of SENCO Standards has limited their effectiveness in relation to school development.

National SEN Specialist Standards

In the following exercise, the SEN Specialist Standards were used as an audit tool to support the development of effective inclusive practices for pupils who experienced speech, language and social communicating difficulties. Students attending a Post-Graduate Diploma course for Speech, Language and Communication Difficulties following the publication of the SEN Specialist Standards (DfEE 1999a) and in the wake of Government initiatives for inclusion (DfEE 1998a, DfEE/QCA 1999) were required to address the following questions (i.e. improve professional knowledge within the context of LEA policy on inclusion):

1 How much do I know about teaching pupils with speech, language and communication difficulties, and what are my current CPD needs in relation to pupils with speech, language and social communication difficulties?
2 How well does the local 'special' school/unit/service match up to the SEN Specialist Standards in relation to speech, language and social communication (i.e. what is 'special' about special provision)?
3 How can mainstream provision be developed so that it can increasingly support the inclusion of pupils with speech, language and communication difficulties?

These are crucial questions which apply to teachers who seek to improve their ability to meet the learning needs of pupils who experience SEN within the context of policies which seek to reduce the numbers of pupils in special school /unit placements by encouraging mainstream schools to develop strategies and systems that are planned to meet a range of diverse learning needs.

The setting used was a Language Unit for seventeen pupils, all with Statements of SEN, located on the site of a 400-pupil primary school. Pupils are integrated for playtimes and swimming. On transfer to secondary school, most pupils go to a Specialist Language Unit.

SEN SPECIALIST STANDARDS AUDIT FINDINGS

Method: Observation using a 'grid' to reflect the information in the SEN Specialist Standards (see Appendix 1 to this chapter). Using the grid, an audit was undertaken of mainstream provision, the students' own professional development needs, and the Specialist Language Unit.

These three audits were then considered in order to identify areas for professional development. Table 9.6 provides an illustrative example of a small selection from the total audits.

In looking at Table 9.6, the task has allowed the teacher concerned to identify professional development needs for herself, her mainstream colleagues and staff from the Specialist Language Unit.

These include exploring:

- ways of reducing barriers to learning which arise from the pupil's language impairment, the curriculum and the social context of the classroom;
- ways of encouraging independent learning while still giving additional support;
- strategies to enhance and promote non-verbal communication;
- visual and auditory teaching approaches that can enhance social/communicative interactions;
- ways of minimising long-standing communicative difficulties on pupil's cognitive, emotional and social development.

Outcomes of audit

The school (mainstream) needs to focus training on supporting the particular needs of children within the school at the same time as embracing government initiatives on inclusion and the professional development needs of individual members of staff. The school needs to arrange training for all staff on cued articulation and Makaton with a view to cued articulation being adopted throughout the school as an inclusive teaching strategy promoting independent learning and minimising long standing communication difficulties. In addition, training on social communication difficulties to minimise the social communication difficulties for pupils with Asperger's syndrome and semantic pragmatic disorders. An area for development would be a staff room display to be used to highlight the visual teaching approaches that can be used to facilitate learning and social interaction skills.

Summary

As can be seen from the two practice examples described in this section, the SEN Standards have provided a focus for relevant staff and school development. Both these examples have been linked to CPD delivered within a higher education context, and point to the need for the impact of such CPD to be systematically monitored and evaluated within the school setting. Viewed in this light, there is a risk that the SEN Standards are more likely to impact upon the professional development of individuals (i.e. to inform the training of SENCOs or 'specialist' teachers) than upon

Table 9.6 Selection of observations referenced against TTA National SEN Specialist Standards via page numbers

	Core standards	Extension standards	Standards in relation to key specialist roles and responsibilities	Skills and attributes
Observation made	*Strategic direction of SEN* Teachers were unaware of how organisations were changing within and across schools . . . to maximise appropriate inclusive opportunities (p. 9)	*Knowledge and understanding* 'ways to minimise long standing communication difficulties on pupil's cognitive, emotional and social development' (p. 15). One autistic infant pupil had her own book of her own actions photographed to reinforce the understanding of her daily activities and how to describe them	*Advisory roles and responsibilities* 'Advise on the effectiveness of, and where necessary justify the use of specialist techniques and materials' (p. 28) Staff in the unit used TEACCH[1] and Social Use of Language Programme (SULP)[2] on a regular basis	'Analyse and if necessary modify own language, communicative capability/behaviour to meet the needs of the pupil' (p. 17)
What are my training needs?	Covered on present course and via LEA training and policy documents	Am fully aware of the need to use visual strategies; however, need training linked to enabling technology for pupils with communication difficulties	I need to be informed of a range of specialist techniques currently being used and know about the underlying rationale and any evidence/research base to support their use. Need to know cost and practical issues, such as how much training do staff/parents need to use it etc.	Need more skill in how to assess pupils with language and communication difficulties so that I can use information from assessment to modify demands on the pupil. Then I need to have opportunity via joint teaching, video etc. to analyse, change and evaluate my own language behaviour
Does the Speech and Language Unit meet the SEN Specialist Standards?	No – rather insular. Staff need to understand how they could support mainstream schools via outreach and team teaching	Yes	Yes, but some staff were not sure why they were using 'specialist' techniques	Yes

continued

Table 9.6 Continued

	Core standards	Extension standards	Standards in relation to key specialist roles and responsibilities	Skills and attributes
How can my own 'mainstream provision' be developed?	By staff from both mainstream and Specialist Unit working together on identified areas for increased inclusive practices	By exchanging ideas and joint INSET opportunities for staff from Unit and mainstream. Joint assessment and provision for IEPs	Need to work with Unit staff, pupils and their parents to see how 'different and/or extra' provision for individual pupils prescribed by the SEN Code of Practice could be met within mainstream context – possibly via joint training/development activities	By working with Learning Support Assistants (LSAs), pupils etc., by working collaboratively with LSAs etc. and by being rigorous in monitoring the impact on pupil progress and learning

Notes
Data from the work of Christ Church University College CPD student Bridget Watts (2000).
1 See Watson L.R. (1985) TEACCH = **T**reatment and **E**ducation of **A**utistic and related **C**ommunication handicapped **CH**ildren
2 See Rinaldi, W. (2001)

school development. The potential for impact is certainly within the content of the Standards documents. However, the take-up of the SEN Standards by schools as a mechanism to identify, plan, meet and evaluate the professional development of their staff suggests that the potential of the Standards for *'improving the achievement of (SEN) pupils and the quality of their education'* has yet to be fully realised.

Evaluation of the SEN National Standards:

It is clear that the Standards cannot be evaluated in isolation as a 'training tool' or 'staff development aid', but have to be contextualised in time and place. As such, there will be enduring issues concerning the nature and content of the SEN Standards and emergent issues reflecting the changing context in which they are housed.

From the evidence available from published research and the case studies described in this chapter, it is possible to identify issues concerning the nature and content of the SEN National Standards. These will be discussed under the following headings:

1 *Philosophy*: what are the philosophical/theoretical underpinnings (i.e. what is the thinking behind the SEN Standards)?
2 *Practice*: what is happening at the level of practice? Does the rhetoric match the reality?
3 *Power*: what is the impact – i.e. how effective are the Standards in meeting their aims?
4 *Potential*: how might we build upon the strengths identified from the brief history of the SEN National Standards and address identified weaknesses?

Philosophy

It is reasonable to assume that, like the other National Standards, the key thinking behind the SEN Standards was to bring about improved standards of achievement for all pupils, including those with SEN. This is an important aim following concerns about the education of pupils with SEN (Audit Commission and HMI 1992), which noted that: 'the delegation (of the SEN budget) should go hand in hand with accountability' (p. 57). The SENCO Standards (TTA 1998) seek to bring about improvements for SEN pupils by focusing on 'expertise in leadership and management' of SEN. The SEN Specialist Standards were designed to enable teachers and schools to 'identify training and development needs in relation to the effective teaching of pupils with severe and/or complex SEN' and to an extent build on the notion of Individual Education Plans (IEPs) which prescribe provision that is 'additional to or different from' for SEN pupils within the Framework of the SEN Code of Practice (DfEE 1994, DfEE 2001a).

Dominant ideologies for the organisation of special education are, historically, segregation, integration and inclusion. The SEN Standards, in a way, reflect aspects of all three ideologies. Notions of 'specialist provision' linked to labels or categories are evident within the SEN Specialist Standards, and reflect elements of the thinking behind policies for special schools. The SENCO Standards house the notion of a designated role (i.e. SENCO) for the co-ordination of provision for SEN pupils, including 'different and/or extra', and are thus consistent with an integrationist model. However, both sets of SEN Standards were launched at a time when inclusion was the emerging model of choice, and both consequently stress the importance of SEN provision being grounded within mainstream with consequent support for access and entitlement to the National Curriculum (DfEE/QCA 1999) and to National Strategies for raising achievement (e.g. DfEE 1998b, 1999a).

The SEN Standards thus seem to be ideologically linked to the viewpoint that some pupils do need 'specialist' provision that can be linked to broad categories of need (communication and interaction; cognition and learning; behavioural, emotional and social; and sensory and physical), and that this provision needs to be managed by a designated individual (i.e. the SENCO) such that an increasing number of SEN pupils, including those with severe and complex SEN, can be effectively 'included' in mainstream settings. But how sound is this ideology? ...

While there has been a consensus that initial teacher training (ITT) does not adequately prepare teachers to meet the challenges of increasing inclusion for pupils with SEN (Garner 2001) and therefore support for the SEN Standards to inform further SEN-related training, there is less agreement about the timing and content of such training. The new Qualifying to Teach Standards should help to prepare teachers more effectively for the challenges of special educational needs. The SEN Standards support an 'add on', compensatory model to training, which builds upon ITE either via a SENCO route or via the core and extension standards of SEN specialisms, while (somewhat paradoxically) supporting the rhetoric of inclusion. It could be argued that training teachers to deal more effectively with SEN pupils is a building block to breaking down barriers to inclusion. However, this viewpoint is not supported by findings from an extensive review of literature (Avramidis and Norwich 2002), which concludes that teachers' attitudes to inclusion were found to be more influenced by the nature and severity of the disabling condition presented to them (child-related variables) and the availability of physical and human support than by teacher-related variables.

There is also ongoing debate about notions concerning 'specialist' pedagogy (Norwich and Lewis 2001). Thomas and Loxley (2001) have questioned the validity of the theoretical underpinnings to special education. There is also considerable support for the view that specialist provision, specialist pedagogies, SENCOs (and associated SEN National Standards) act as a barrier to inclusion (Booth 1999), and, for some, a belief that 'most schools have the expertise needed to teach all pupils effectively' (e.g. Ainscow 2000). Central to the support for a 'SEN/specialist' pedagogy is the belief that it is possible to identify differences between learners by category or SEN group *and* link this identification with learner needs for differential teaching (Avramidis and Norwich 2002). The SEN Specialist Standards presume, for example, that it is possible to both identify and classify learners as having 'emotional and behavioural difficulties' (EBD) *and* then identify those 'intervention strategies appropriate for pupils with emotional and behavioural difficulties and their likely benefits to the pupil' (DfEE 1999: 21)

In seeking to address, via an extensive literature review, whether there is justification for a 'specialist' pedagogy for SEN, Norwich and Lewis (2001) conclude that there is lack of empirical evidence for distinctive SEN teaching strategies. However, there does seem to be empirical support for common pedagogic principles (see Wang 1990) that are relevant to the unique differences between all pupils, including those designated as SEN, although 'this position is ... qualified by some recognition of the need for more intense and focused teaching for those with SEN' – which leads Norwich and Lewis to conclude that a continuum of teaching approaches is useful with both 'normal' adaptations to class teaching and specialised adaptations called 'high-density' teaching.

Thus, in evaluating the 'philosophy' behind the SEN Standards it is true to say that they address a need (even if that need is perceived) for more SEN training for teachers during an era when schools are increasingly required take on the roles previously undertaken by 'special' schools/units. Although doubt is cast upon the utility and validity of categorising learners and linking these categories systematically to 'specialist' teaching, it is recognised that some learners need 'specialised adaptations'.

In conclusion, the SEN National Standards need not be incompatible with emergent research findings that question 'specialist' pedagogies and the function of the SENCO. Inclusion is a process, the policy for which has been prescribed to schools that are in various states of readiness. The SENCO role can be seen just as easily as a bridge rather than a barrier to that process, *provided* that school development is at the heart of that process and that staff are enabled and empowered to take on responsibility for all their learners, including those with SEN. Likewise, the SEN Specialist Standards, encompassing both core and extension standards, mirror the emergent notion for a continuum of teaching approaches using both generic and high-density elements. However, the division of the extension standards into categories (e.g. communication and interaction, cognition and learning etc.) remains a problematic area for the SEN Specialist Standards both by denying the complexity and overlap of SEN and by assuming that common categories share common learning needs. In practice, though, it might simply be too great a step for teachers to abandon categories and adopt instead 'a problem-solving culture including how to use one another's experience and resources in order to devise better ways of overcoming barriers to learning' (Ainscow 2000). Additionally, the emergent need for increased multi-agency planning and community-based practices requires some recognition that 'categories' of SEN are often linked to particular agencies – e.g. communication and interaction/autism to Health, EBD to Social Services, cognition and learning to Education etc. – and that some useful intervention strategies have often been developed using categorised samples (e.g. TEACCH for Autistic Children; see Watson 1985). In revising the National Standards, following consultation, the TTA merged some of the classic SEN groups into broader categories stressing commonalities between them (TTA 1998, 1999a). There is now the opportunity for teachers and schools critically to evaluate the conceptual framework underpinning commonality–differentiation of pedagogy (Norwich 1996), and to evaluate the use of the SEN Specialist Standards' broader categories in promoting the delivery and evaluation of effective teaching.

This leads on to considering the use of the SEN Standards in practice . . .

Practice

There is limited evidence available concerning the use of the SEN Standards in practice. Some identified areas of concern are not supported by a sound evidence base, and hopefully will be contested by some providers, schools and teachers.

These concerns include the following:

1   Given that one of the key aims for the SEN Standards was to 'bring about improved standards of teaching and learning for SEN pupils', it is of concern that their take-up by schools appears limited. Essentially, they are being used mainly by providers of CPD who have been funded through the *Standards Fund* (DfEE 1999b) and TTA INSET funding (TTA 1999c). There does not appear to be any evidence that they are being used within schools to support school and staff development. This limits the impact of the SEN National Standards and, coupled with the fact that they are 'advisory', suggests that evidence of their use is unlikely to be included in any school-based Ofsted evaluation. Given variations between LEAs in the organisation and provision of training (Moore 2000), it would seem that the SEN Specialist Standards have had little impact on reducing national inequalities

within teaching for SEN pupils – i.e. any individual SEN pupil is dependent upon the school in which he or she is placed, the existing expertise of the staff, and the availability of additional support.

2   The National Standards are unclear about 'how many standards will a 'specialist teacher' or SENCO be expected to have', and, given that the Standards are audited in context, 'will these Standards only be applicable to the current role or setting?' (Porter and Miller 2000). The illustrative case study provided by the TTA (1999a) of how the Specialist Standards might be used within the context of school or service development assumes that appraisers or line managers have a considerable familiarity with the Standards and can translate these into SMART (Specific, Measurable, Achievable, Relevant, Timely) objectives linked to school and personal development. There is as yet no evidence that schools have this assumed familiarity and understanding of the Standards, and therefore this limits the extent to which schools can help teachers to 'set clear relevant objectives for improving their effectiveness'. Indeed, some of the standards are particularly challenging and difficult to measure, e.g. 'teaching pupils to accept, initiate and maintain relationships with others, and how to communicate in social contexts' (Skills; Autistic spectrum disorder, p. 17, TTA SEN Specialist Standards, TTA 1999a).

3   The SENCO Standards are based on notions of 'effective co-ordination and management', although rather undermining phrasing is used: 'SEN co-ordination will provide a good grounding in many of the leadership and management roles necessary to take on broader and more senior leadership and management roles'. This suggests that the SENCO role is not as challenging or as important as other school management roles. The SENCO role, as prescribed by SENCO Standards and the SEN Code of Practice (DfEE 2001a), is not inconsiderable, and yet many SENCOs take on the role in a part-time capacity, with some being NQTs. As yet, there is no guidance for schools on time allocation or status that should be given to the SENCO role. Given the demands of the job and the lack of status (often needed to impact upon school development), it is not surprising that the drop-out rate for SENCOs is of concern (personal communication, J. Moore, Senior Advisor for Additional Educational Needs, Kent LEA, 2002).

4   The SEN Specialist Standards are designed to be an audit tool. However, practitioners who have tried to use them in this way have found its 53-page format somewhat unwieldy. Some have addressed this by designing a grid based on the Specialist Standards (see Appendix 1 to this chapter), or have used them to audit a particular area of concern for the school and inform training needs (see Appendix 2). The CD-ROM of the SEN Specialist Standards (TTA 2002) should prove to be more manageable as an audit tool within the school context.

5   Both sets of Standards cover a wide range of skills, knowledge and understanding, and presumably few teachers could meet 'all' the standards. However, within the Standards there is no idea of a distinction between the 'necessary' and the 'desirable', or indeed planning for progression – should it be assumed that 'extension standards' follow 'core standards' or vice versa, or should these elements be integrated? Presumably arriving at consensus as to what 'standards' are required to meet the learning needs of any particular category or grouping of SEN in any particular context would require negotiation between the provider, the funders, the teacher concerned, and the line manager/ headteacher.

Given these 'practical' concerns, it is perhaps surprising that the practical examples provided earlier in this chapter revealed benefits in the use of the SEN Standards for informing training and school development needs. It seems reasonable to conclude that concerns need to be identified and addressed if the aims of the SEN Standards are to be met more effectively and their potential for improving the quality and outcome of educational experiences for SEN pupils realised. In essence, the SEN Standards are a resource not a prescription, and schools need to use them with integrity and flexibility if the desired 'outcomes' are to be achieved.

The next section examines the power of the SEN Standards in achieving these outcomes.

Power

In essence, the SEN Standards are designed to impact on individual teachers, on school development in relation to SEN and, most importantly, on the recipients of this improved co-ordinated provision – namely the pupils who experience learning difficulty, difference and/or disability.

Individual teachers have been funded to undertake accredited CPD based on the SEN Standards. In addition, TTA-funded INSET is designed and inspected with reference to 'impact' on teaching and learning. However, due to the fact that the SEN Standards seem not to have been absorbed into school cultures for staff and school development, and given some ideological clashes between 'specialist SEN provision' and 'inclusion', there has to be concern about the efficacy of the SEN Standards in relation to their impact. One way of placing providers, funders, teachers and their schools on a shared agenda would be to concentrate on the element of the SEN Standards related to outcomes. In the case of the SENCO Standards these are noted on p. 6–7 (TTA 1998), and for the SEN Specialist Standards in Annex B pp. 52–53 (TTA 1999a). It would seem that by auditing the extent to which a school had achieved these outcomes, it would be possible to identify and target objectives for school development in relation to SEN/inclusion. The SEN Standards could then be used selectively in order to support the meeting of those objectives. For example, one of the outcomes for SENCO standards is 'parents who: ... understand the targets set for their children and their contribution to helping their children achieve them' (p. 6, section D, TTA 1998). This could provide a target for school development – say for pupils with EBD – and direct staff towards meeting the associated SEN specialist standards, thus contributing to school development designed to enhance existing school–parent partnerships.

Overall, there is, as with most educational initiatives, more emphasis on the meeting of standards than on the evaluation of their impact. Accreditation is linked more to evidence of 'can do' statements than relating these to evidence-based outcomes. It is this evaluative stance that will result in impact, and providers, schools and teachers must ensure that intrinsic to the meeting of SEN standards is an evaluation of their impact on pupil progress. Although providers can and do set coursework tasks that are linked to impact and school development, the timeframe of courses (e.g. termly, yearly etc.) often limits the extent to which impact can be evaluated. Teachers do need the involvement of their school and longer-term opportunities to evaluate the effect of any changes to their practice consequent on meeting the SEN Standards.

Potential

It is reasonable to say that the SEN Standards are now housed within a national educational context which is increasingly diverse, context-sensitive and process-driven (Stoker 2002). The SEN Standards need to reflect this changing context if they are to achieve their potential in enabling teachers to achieve recognition for increasing their own teaching repertoires and the learning repertoires of their pupils.

In reflecting upon the aims of the Standards, which are to:

- set out clear expectations for teachers at key points in the profession;
- help teachers at different points in the profession to plan and monitor their development, training and performance effectively, and to set clear, relevant objectives for improving their effectiveness;
- ensure that the focus at every point is on improving the achievement of pupils and the quality of their education;
- provide a basis for the professional recognition of teachers' expertise;
- help providers of professional development to plan and provide high-quality, relevant training, which meets the needs of individual teachers and headteachers, makes good use of their time and has the maximum benefit for pupils,

it can be seen that some of these aims have been met. The SEN Standards are being used by SEN training providers. This serves an important function in setting high expectations for SEN teaching and reducing inequalities in SEN provision. The funding of courses linked to the SEN Standards and associated inspection criteria prescribe that such courses should be designed to 'impact' upon pupil learning and progress. Thus, for those teachers who have attended courses linked to Standards Funding (DfEE 1999b) or TTA INSET funding (TTA 1999c), it is likely that their CPD will be planned and monitored and their coursework tasks linked to evidence-based outcomes for improved teaching and learning.

The biggest single problem for the SEN Standards is that they, like many other SEN initiatives, have not become absorbed into mainstream school cultures but appear to serve an 'add-on function'. It is of concern that, with the advent of policies for increased inclusion, the SEN Standards remain advisory and are not systematically linked to other National Standards – notably for QTS and Subject and Specialist Leaders. It follows that, as relatively few teachers opt to engage in SEN-specific training (and these are usually those who are already engaged in SEN practice), mainstream teachers and their schools are unlikely to develop sufficient expertise in teaching SEN pupils to assure that inclusion will lead to improved learning opportunities and outcomes for these pupils. In essence, the SEN Standards need to be further meshed with mainstream teacher training and concerned as much with the outcomes of Standards training as with the impact of that training on pupil progress and school development.

How might this be achieved? While not finding a simple solution, some achievable suggestions include the following:

1 Building from the positive experience of Higher Education Institutions (HEIs) and other providers in using the SEN Standards to inform and monitor CPD, it might be reasonable to consider delivering elements of this type of training to schools and/or clusters of schools with a view to accrediting school-based developments informed by the SEN Standards. This would be an innovative step from accrediting individual teacher's development, but would assure some embedding of the SEN Standards within school-based practice and evaluation.

2 The SENCO role should be seen as a management role with some explicit linking to other leadership and management roles. HEIs who deliver a range of National Standards-linked courses could consider shared issues and plan delivery accordingly. Within schools, the SENCO role should be allocated sufficient time and training, and SENCOs given the management status they deserve and need in order to effect their changing collaborative roles (Tod 2002) within the framework of the revised SEN Code of Practice (DfEE 2001a).

3 The thinking behind the SEN Specialist Standards, particularly in rela-

tion to 'specialist SEN pedagogy', should be kept under critical review by practitioners, researchers and policy-makers. Teacher research, via Best Practice Research Scholarships and MA/PhD study supported by HEIs, would provide a mechanism for this type of endeavour. Schools are required to monitor the progress of SEN pupils, and this could feasibly be linked to evaluating the impact of any changes in provision consequent upon SEN Standards-linked training.

4   If schools are to become more involved in the SEN Standards, then it might be worthwhile starting from the 'outcomes' sections of the Standards (pp. 6–7 of SENCO Standards (TTA 1998) and pp. 52–53 for the SEN Specialist Standards in Annex B (TTA 1999a)). Focusing on these 'outcome' measures, auditing the school in relation to how far these outcomes are being achieved, and then building a development plan based on this audit, would serve to harness whole-school interest and effort regarding SEN issues within the spirit of inclusion. Such activity could reduce the isolation of the SEN Standards and lead to more collaborative practices.

5   Core standards within the SEN Specialist Standards (pp. 8–13, TTA 1999a) should be taken into consideration when planning ITT experiences and training, with a view to them being met early on in a teacher's career. With increasing inclusion, all teachers will need to meet these generic specialist standards if they are to meet the challenges of increasing inclusion.

The SEN Standards brought a much needed 'national' dimension to SEN training, with optimism for consequent improvements in teacher expertise in the delivery and management of effective practice for SEN pupils. National Standards for SENCOs brought recognition of the importance of that role and some assurance that inequalities in provision for SEN pupils would be reduced. The SEN Specialist Standards gave credence to the belief that teachers would need more specialist SEN training if effective inclusion was to be secured for pupils with complex learning needs. The brief history of the SEN Standards suggests that some of their intended aims have been met. However, if the effort put into their development and dissemination is to reap just rewards for SEN pupils, their schools and teachers, then it must be recognised that they are an essential ingredient and not a recipe for success. The SEN Standards need to reflect the changing contexts in which they are housed, and be intrinsic to planning for inclusion and school development for all teachers and pupils. If the potential of the SEN Standards is to be more fully realised, then it would seem from this review that they would benefit from both a revision and a re-launch.

References and further reading

Ainscow, M. (2000) 'The next step for special education – supporting the development of inclusive practices,' *British Journal of Special Education* 27(2): 76–80.

Audit Commission and HMI (1992) *Getting in on the Act*, London: HMSO.

Avramidis, E. and Norwich, B. (2002) 'Teacher's attitudes towards integration /inclusion: a review of the literature,' *European Journal of Special Needs Education* 17(2): 129–147.

Booth, T. (1999) 'Inclusion and exclusion policy in England: who controls the agenda?' in Armstrong, D. *et al.* (eds) *Inclusive Education: Contexts and Comparative Perspectives*, London: David Fulton, pp. 95–99.

Croll, P. and Moses, D. (2000) 'Ideologies and utopias: educational professionals' view on inclusion,' *European Journal of Special Needs Education* 15(1): 1–12.

CSIE Centre for Studies in Inclusive Education (2000) *Index for Inclusion*, Bristol: CSIE.

Department for Education (1994) *Code of Practice on the Identification and Assessment of Special Educational Needs*, London: DfE.

DfEE (1998a) *Meeting Special Educational Needs: a Programme of Action*, London: DfEE.

Department for Education and Employment (1998b) *The National Literacy Strategy Framework for Teaching*, London: DfEE.

Department for Education and Employment (1999a) *The National Numeracy Strategy. Framework for Teaching Mathematics from Reception to Year 6*, London: DfEE.

Department for Education and Employment (1999b) *The Standards Fund: 2000–1* (Circular 16/99), London: DfEE.

Department for Education and Employment and Qualifications and Curriculum Authority (1999) *The National Curriculum: Handbook for Primary and Secondary Teachers*, London: DfEE.

Department for Education and Skills (2001a) *Special Educational Needs Code of Practice*, London: DfEE.

Department for Education and Skills (2001b) *Inclusive Schooling: Children with Special Educational Needs*, London: DfES.

Department for Education and Skills (2004) *Removing Barriers to Achievement – The Governments Strategy for SEN*, London: DfES.

Disability Rights Commission (2002) Code of Practice (Schools) www.drc-gb.org.

Garner, P. (2001) 'Goodbye Mr. Chips,' in O'Brien, T. (ed.) *Enabling Inclusion Blue Skies . . . Dark Clouds?* London: The Stationery Office, pp. 53–62.

Hopkins, D., Ainscow, M., West, M. and Beresford, J. (1997) *Creating the Conditions for Classroom Improvement*, London: David Fulton Publishers.

Moore, J. (2000) *Developments in Additional Resource Allocation to Promote Greater inclusion* (SEN) Policy Options Steering Group: Policy Option Paper 2 (Third Series) Tamworth: NASEN.

Morris, E. and Tabberer, R. (2001) Foreword to *Qualifying to Teach Professional Standards for Qualified Teacher Status and Requirements for Initial Teacher Training*, London: TTA.

Norwich, B. (1996) 'Special Needs Education or education for all: connective specialisation and educational impurity', *British Journal of Special Education* 23(3): 100–104.

Norwich, B. and Lewis, A. (2001) 'Mapping pedagogy for special educational needs,' *British Educational Research Journal* 27(3).

Porter, J. and Miller, C. (2000) 'Meeting the Standards?' *British Journal of Special Education* 27: 2.

Rinaldi, W. (2001) *Social Use of Language Programme*, NFER-Nelson.

Slee, R., Weiner, G. and Tomlinson, S. (eds) (1998) *School Effectiveness for Whom?* London: Falmer Press.

Stoker, R. (2002) *Educational Psychology: Diversity Led, Context Sensitive and Process Drive – a View of the Future.* DECP Debate Division of Educational and Child Psychology – The British Psychological Society No. 101, March 9–14.

Teacher Training Agency (1998) *National Standards for Special Educational Needs Co-ordinators*, London: TTA.

Teacher Training Agency (1999a) *National Special Educational Needs Specialist Standards*, London: TTA.

Teacher Training Agency (1999b) *Using the National Standards for Special Educational Needs Co-ordinators (SENCOs)*, London: TTA.

Teacher Training Agency (1999c) Criteria for second interim bidding round for TTA Inset Funding. http//www.teach-tta.gov/inset/criteria.htm.

Teacher Training Agency (2001) *Qualifying to Teach Professional Standards for Qualified Teacher Status and Requirements for Initial Teacher Training*, London: TTA.

Teacher Training Agency (2002) *National SEN Specialist: Standards Identifying Your Training Needs.* CD-ROM.

Thomas, G. and Loxley, A. (2001) *Deconstructing Special Education and Constructing Inclusion*, Open University Press.

Tod, J. (2002) *IEPs for Inclusive Educational Participation.* SENCO update March 2002 Issue 33, London: Optimus.

Wang, M.C. (1990) 'Learning characteristics of students with special needs and the provision of effective schooling,' in Wang, M.C., Reynolds, M.C., Walberg, H.J. (eds) *Special Education Research and Practice: synthesis of findings*, Oxford: Pergamon, pp. 1–34.

Watson, L.R. (1985) 'The TEACCH communication curriculum,' in Schopler, E. and Mesibov, G. (eds) *Communication Problems in Autism*, New York: Plenum Press.

Appendices

Appendix 1: Grid designed from SEN Specialist Standards

National SEN Specialist Standards	Extension Standards	Section A Autistic Spectrum	Communication and Interaction
Know/understand the characteristics of this disorder and their implications for communication and learning		Know/understand the range of individual differences within autistic spectrum	
The impact of co-occurrence of different types of difficulty e.g. dyspraxia and an autistic spectrum disorder		Have the ability to teach pupils to accept, initiate and maintain relationships with others and how to communicate in social contexts	
National SEN Specialist Standards	Extension Standards	Section B Knowledge and Understanding	Cognition and Learning
Know/understand the continuum/complexity of moderate, specific, severe and profound learning difficulties and how to provide curricular access through teaching that promotes active learning	Extend knowledge here	Know/understand difference between global learning difficulties and specific learning difficulties e.g. dyslexia, dyspraxia and specific language impairment	Revise
Know/understand the range of cognitive skills necessary for effective learning	Revise	Know/understand the effects of single/multi disabilities on functions such as perception, memory and information processing	Revise
Know/understand range of visual, motor and linguistic channels available to promote cognitive potential	Revise – extend knowledge here in light of SLSCD*	Know/understand the importance of assessing how pupils process auditory and visual information	Yes
Know/understand how cognitive difficulties impact on development of language and communication, and how this affects learning	More knowledge needed here with respect to SLSCD	Know/understand methods of ascertaining levels of cognition in pupils with severe and multiple difficulties	More knowledge and expertise needed here
Know/understand the impact of exceptionally high cognitive ability in conjunction with physical, communication, specific learning difficulties and/or autistic spectrum disorder	Yes	Know/understand the impact of different types of medication on cognitive and physical abilities, behavioural and emotional state	Yes

Notes
Based on the work of Mary Anthony, Canterbury Christ Church University College INSET student, 2001.
*SLSCD = speech, language and social communication difficulties.

Appendix 2: School-based monitoring sheet for 'Communication and Interaction', informed from the SEN National Standards (Communication and Interaction)

Taken from the coursework of Don Riley, Christ Church University College SEN INSET student, 2001.

Section 2: Practice

2:1 What programmes are in place to teach these pupils to accept, initiate and maintain relationships with others and communicate in social contexts?

2:2 What programmes are in place to teach these pupils strategies for flexible thinking?

2:3 What strategies are in place to enhance and promote non-verbal communication?

2:4 What methods are used to minimise communication difficulties on student development?

2:5 What methods are used for assessing communication skills?

2:6 What are the *different* ways in which teachers communicate with pupils with language and communication difficulties? (e.g. using exaggerated intonation or rhythm, making use of child's name to start a sentence, using eye-level contact, gesturing and pointing, using shorter sentences, avoiding complex sentences etc.)

2:7 How do staff recognise the overlap of language difficulties with cognitive development and sensory deficit?

2:8 What visual and auditory approaches are used? (e.g. cue cards, visual timetables etc.)

2:9 How is general and technical vocabulary adapted to suit the needs of the pupil?

2:10 How have the staff analysed and modified their own language, communication and behaviour when dealing with these pupils?

2:11 How is the language and communication of the pupil assessed and then used to develop appropriate teaching programmes?

2:12 How is the assessment information of other professionals incorporated into the teaching programmes?

2:13 How do staff respond appropriately to the pupils' level of language?

2:14 Are appropriate methods, such as visual, auditory or tactile, used to match and develop the pupils' communication abilities?

2:15 How are pupils taught to accept, initiate and maintain relationships with others?

2:16 In what ways does the SENCO work with parents and other professionals?

2:17 How does the SENCO provide direction through demonstration and/or specific training?

2:18 Is the pupil given time to respond?

2:19 How is the implicit made explicit?

2:20 How is commentary used to encourage joint attention e.g. commenting on what the pupil is doing?

2:21 Do the staff assess language in context, looking for consistencies and inconsistencies?

2:22 Do staff use vocabulary that is meaningful to the pupil, often using visual cues?

2:23 How is the pupil's understanding monitored and instructions/speech adjusted accordingly?

2:24 Are the aspects of language most vital in each subject considered?

2:25 How do those involved with the pupil assist his or her use of language?

2:26 Is there any evidence of consistency in the observed/recorded language behaviour? (As a guide, these can be recorded as strengths or difficulties.)

Section 3: Policy

3:1 Do the distribution and type of targets on the IEPs currently in place suggest that provision for individual pupils could be improved by the development of language teaching at whole-school level?

3:2 What are the roles and responsibilities of agencies such as the Speech and Language Therapist, Communication & Interaction team etc. in this school?

3:3 Does the SENCO advise on specialist techniques/equipment?

3:4 Does the SENCO advise on assessments to identify strengths and weaknesses?

3:5 Does the SENCO provide advice for integrating various specialist contributions?

3:6 Does the SENCO analyse and advise others' teaching and provide sensitive feedback, support and training to help them become more effective?

3:7 Is discussion and visual planning used to support the production of written work?

3:8 Are there opportunities to develop communication skills into classroom activities?

3:9 How is the development of the pupil's use of language integrated with teaching in all subjects?

3:10 How do specific subject plans include provision for language development, and what new opportunities might be developed?

3:11 Is active processing encouraged? (e.g. use of discussion, review, appropriate questioning style, problem-solving, reflection etc.)

3:12 How are the priorities in the School Improvement Plan translated into policies and strategies to ensure access to the relevant curriculum and National Curriculum?

3:13 How are progress and specialist resources monitored?

Chapter 10

Subject Leader

Kit Field and Phil Holden

Introduction

The introduction of the National Standards for Subject Leaders (NSFSL) (TTA 1998) was the first time that recognition at national level had been given to the role performed by many middle managers in schools. Indeed, the draft standards, published one year before, gave greater credence to the concept of distributed leadership (Gunther 2001) in education. Until that point in time, the majority of studies in education leadership had focused on the role of Headteachers following the introduction of the National Professional Qualification for Headteachers (NPQH), the Leadership Programme for Serving Headteachers (LPSH) and the Head-teachers' Leadership and Management Programme (HEADLAMP). The notion of distributed leadership throughout an organisation was not new, but for many schools it provided a novel solution to emerging problems and difficulties. Ofsted inspection reports (Ofsted 1993) were required to include comments on the quality of middle management and note the positive or negative impact of subject leadership. There was then a need for new solutions to new problems, which, we propose, were an inevitable outcome of educational reforms throughout the late 1980s and 1990s.

Such an analysis demands a very close examination of the NSFSL. The concept of National Standards for Subject Leaders can be broken down into four obvious components.

1   *National.* The 1990s were, for many, an age of monitoring and accountability. The need to measure performance levels against a national benchmark extends beyond the publication of assessment league tables. For teachers, in equal measure to learners, there was a perceived need to standardise procedures and criteria against which judgements of quality could be made. New pay structures, appraisal procedures and, more recently, a common performance management system needed to be seen to be fair, and also to be encouraging

enough to attract, retain and provide career progression for teachers.

2 *Standards*. Standards developed from a competence-based approach to education and training. A competence-based approach to Initial Teacher Training (ITT) was firmly established in 1992 (DES 1992). 'Raising standards' became a popular chant, even a mantra contained within the works of right wing educationalists following the Great Debate which was initiated by James Callaghan's famous Ruskin Speech of 1976. At the same time, the insistence that professional judgments should be based on hard evidence and that teaching should be an 'evidence-based profession' (Hargreaves 1996) prompted the need for a common basis and understanding. The shift towards 'standards' was the outcome of a logical progression. The imposition of standards would, it could be argued, lead to higher quality provision and outcomes, and the development of standards common to all would provide a justification for professional decisions and actions.

3 *Subject*. The key feature of the 1988 Education Reform Act (ERA) was the introduction of the National Curriculum. Although Kenneth Baker's original model has been amended twice and 'slimmed down', the National Curriculum is essentially subject based. The emphasis on subject knowledge and associated modes of thinking (Woodhead 1993) demands an input from specialists in subject-related pedagogies, as well as experts in generic approaches to teaching and learning. This balance is most evident in the latest version of the National Curriculum (QCA/DfEE 1999), which contains separate subject orders and guidance on cross-curricular learning. Many would argue that the emphasis on a subject-based approach emanated from the heavy criticism of learners' performance in relation to particular subjects – most notably in mathematics at primary school level.

4 *Leaders*. Leadership has been cited in Government-sponsored research as the key factor in effective schooling (Sammons *et al.* 1995). Prior to the introduction of the NSFSL, 'Subject Leader' was not a standard term for those with middle management responsibilities linked to the teaching and learning of academic subjects. In primary schools 'Subject Co-ordinator' was and still often is the commonly used term; and in secondary schools 'Head of Department' is usually at the top of job advertisements and job descriptions. The term 'leader' carries with it connotations. It implies vision, direction and inspiration. It is more exciting than the word 'manager', which suggests concepts of maintenance and the implementation of policies devised by others (Gunther 2001). School leaders, West (1995) points out, could not have the time, energy or expertise necessary to take responsibility for ten discrete curriculum areas. The empowerment of specialist teachers, with

management responsibility to the whole school, was seen to be a solution.

The introduction of the new term 'Subject Leader' in 1998 has enabled the establishment of a new concept. The abandonment of old language means that the new role need not be associated with baggage from the past. Indeed, a close examination of the language and its use reveals that what is now referred to as 'leadership' was once labelled 'management', and what is now understood by 'management' was once termed 'administration'. The implication is that the NSFSL, and their introduction in 1998, were intended to serve several purposes, including:

* to drive levels of pupil performance up by empowering subject specialists;
* to provide a basis for performance management and career progression for teachers;
* to generate a model of distributed leadership within the education profession

The above are not accidental consequences of the introduction and use of the National Standards, but rather part of the historical process of transforming compulsory education throughout the 1990s. It is, however, interesting to note the emphasis the Government has placed on Subject Leaders. The original intention to attach a National Professional Qualification to the fulfilment of the standards, and a national centralised training programme (as was the case with the National Professional Qualification for Headteachers), was postponed. Only now, as the National College for School Leadership becomes established itself and the profession itself begins to accept the validity of NSFSL, is middle management, or 'Leading from the Middle' (NCSL 2002), at the top of the agenda. Indeed, the new Leadership Framework (NCSL 2002) places a high priority on 'emerging leaders'. The development of a national training programme has been the first contract to be put out to tender by the National College.

Subject Leaders are not, of course, the only middle managers in schools. Special Educational Needs Co-ordinators (SENCOs), pastoral leaders (Key Stage Managers and Heads of Year) and 'Heads' of cross-curricular provision (Literacy, Numeracy, ICT) also occupy middle management positions. These posts, with the exception of SENCOs, are not supported by a set of National Standards. The NSFSL can, however, be adapted. The absence of a national training programme to date has enabled flexible and creative use of the Standards to accommodate a wide range of middle managers in schools.

From competence to Standards

It is essential to place the development of NSFSL into an historical context. The issue of Circular 9/92 (DES 1992) firmly established a competence-based approach for secondary ITT. The approach emerged as the critics of a theoretical approach to teacher training became more powerful. Lawlor (1990) asserted that teachers themselves had been mis-taught, and O'Hear's (1988) view was that teaching was best learnt by 'doing' rather than by theorising. These philosophies followed on natu-rally from the right wing 'Black Papers' of the previous decade. What emerged as an alternative was a behavioural approach, one which led to the preparation and assessment of teachers 'on the job'. Competences and subsequent performance indicators defined the way teachers should work. The education profession, however, continued to resist a prescriptive and reductionist model of 'ticking off' competences, apparently recommended by the National Vocational Qualification (NVQ) movement. Burke (1990), for example, proposed that competences were best designed and defined by the profession itself, as opposed to conforming to an externally imposed model.

Hargreaves' inaugural speech to the TTA in 1996 recommended that teaching should be an 'evidence-based profession', akin to the model adopted by the medical profession. Decision-making, he proposed, should be based upon clear and unambiguous evidence. The chief source of evid-ence in the late 1990s was, of course, the outcomes of Ofsted inspections (nationally benchmarked data), and also the results of a supposedly valid and reliable external examination system.

Running parallel to this movement – one of apparently objective data and evidence-informed educational decisions – was the 'school improve-ment' movement. As opposed to respecting only externally generated, quantitative data associated with 'school effectiveness', school 'improvers' encouraged teachers to take ownership of development and change through action research (Elliott 1991; McNiff et al. 1996) and other forms of qualitative research. For action researchers, an 'evidence-based profes-sion' meant taking ownership of the data-generating process, as well as making use of inspection and research evidence to improve practice.

The combined outcome of 'school effectiveness' and 'school improve-ment' was one where teacher professionalism can be characterised as leading change and development yet also one being accountable to others, including the public as a whole. Stenhouse's (1975) recommendation that educational research should be 'enquiry made public' took on a new meaning in the political and professional climate of the 1990s. The devel-opment of National Standards, which contain repeated reference to practi-tioner research and the productive use of valid and reliable data (see Field 2002) was almost inevitable. In the context of a national curriculum and public accountability, Subject Leaders are *the* key force for change (Harris *et al.* 2001).

On the other hand, many teachers argue that a prescribed national curriculum constrains creativity, and that the opportunities for 'leadership' as implied by the term 'Subject Leaders' are extremely limited. For this school of thought, the NSFSL are more concerned with curriculum management as Subject Leaders are expected to implement rather than innovate. The NSFSL are, following this line of argument, in short, a product of the process of centralising curriculum control since 1988.

Implementing the Education Reform Act

Prior to 1988, Religious Education was the only compulsory school subject. School curricula had to demonstrate how provision supported pupils' development by addressing the following aspects (Fowler 1990):

- aesthetic and creative;
- human and social;
- linguistic and literary;
- mathematical;
- physical;
- scientific;
- technological;
- moral;
- spiritual.

Following 1988, this single curriculum was, to all intents and purposes, replaced by ten separate subject orders (DES 1988). No single person has the expertise to lead and manage such a vast range of subject provision. Particularly in primary schools, headteachers were in danger of being over-stretched.

The Education Reform Act (DES 1988) had implications for headteachers which extended beyond curriculum management. The Local Management of Schools (LMS) initiative led to greater autonomy for the school in terms of enrolment and budgetary control. Financial responsibility and the increased power devolved to schools' governing bodies placed headteachers in the role of 'chief executives'. Open enrolment linked the recruitment of pupils to the allocation of finances. Marketing, human resource management and site management all fell under the responsibility of the headteacher.

At the same time, headteachers faced the challenge of leading 'learning organisations' (Senge 1990). It is no surprise that most turned to expert classroom practitioners for support in terms of managing the curriculum. Subject Co-ordinators and Heads of Department found themselves empowered by default – often without formal leadership and management training – for the planning, organisation, monitoring and evaluation of subject teaching and learning.

Ofsted inspections in the mid- to late 1990s identified the leadership and management of subject provision as a general weakness. Independent research (e.g. Harris 1995) concluded that successful learning was in no small way dependent upon effective and strong subject leadership.

With a need for effective Subject Leaders, and a recognition of the impact of good subject leadership, the development of a set of generic standards for all Subject Leaders came as no surprise. In this sense the NSFSL represent a set of professional expectations, as well as a means of appraising the current level of performance of curriculum managers.

A growing need for specialist subject leadership

The need for specialist Subject Leaders is not simply the outcome of a deficit model. There are also positive reasons for establishing the NSFSL.

At the heart of the NSFSL lie 'teaching and learning'. Subject Leaders are, and should be, the school experts on how their subject should be taught and learnt. Recent research into multiple intelligences (e.g. Gardner 1983), preferred learning styles (e.g. Kolb 1983) and accelerated learning (Smith 1998) has led to the need for sharing and disseminating good practice in order to build useful, subject-based teaching and learning repertoires. The 'Inclusion' movement (see, for example, Booth *et al.* 2000) recognises the necessity of addressing individual pupil needs, not least by providing a variety of teaching and learning approaches and an understanding of barriers to learning.

Pupils' motivation for and enjoyment of particular subjects is partially dependent upon the ethos and image of the subject, both in school and beyond (see Blundell and Field 2000). It behoves Subject Leaders to set the tone, and to establish an identity and integrity for any given subject. Creating a vision for the subject through teaching, learning and support activities is essential at a time when young people may not immediately recognise and respond to the perceived value of traditional academic approaches.

Research into pupils' preferred learning styles has placed additional burdens in terms of workload on teachers, as well as helping to identify new, exciting learning opportunities. There is a need to assist in the development of pupils' study skills, as well as to present pre-determined knowledge and content. The identification and presentation of appropriate learning strategies to learners, which provide access to the culture and processes associated with a particular subject discipline, is demanding of specialist subject knowledge and also of generic management skills.

Williams (1995) argues that leaders 'emerge', and the force of their beliefs and values influences others' behaviour. Managers, on the other hand, are appointed to a position and are able to wield the power that their position authorises. For many secondary and primary Subject Leaders, a position in the school's hierarchy does not reward them with the power of rank within the organisation. The NSFSL provide an official authority to back up the role they must perform. A classification of what 'subject leadership' actually means for the full range of stakeholders illustrates this point. The inclusion of such a section in the NSFSL serves to give recognition and authority to Subject Leaders as a balance for the responsibility they have. The NSFSL, to some extent, provide a status and profile commensurate with the level of responsibility of Subject Leaders.

NSFSL provide a pragmatic solution to theoretical concerns

Subject Leaders spend the majority of their working day teaching. Unlike in many other professions, middle managers in education have little time to dedicate to leadership and management tasks, and indeed 'non-contact time' often does not coincide with periods when they can plan, monitor and supervise colleagues for whom they have some responsibility. To complicate matters further, many Subject Leaders, most notably those in the primary sector (Key Stages 1 and 2), do not have responsibility 'points' to place them higher in the school hierarchy than those they 'lead'.

Leadership and management theory often separates the roles of leaders and managers. The day-to-day practices of a Subject Leader require the exercise of an amalgam of leadership and management responsibilities. Adair's (1988) concept of 'Action Centred Leadership' recommends the consideration of three key factors: the individual, the organisational culture, and the nature of the task. Sergiovanni (1995) acknowledges the power of forces which serve to determine the most appropriate leadership style. These theoretical concepts can be used to illustrate the complexity of leading in specific contexts and therefore of the Subject Leader's role. This only adds to the difficulty of coping with the inherent tensions of middle management. Subject Leaders have a responsibility to implement, through the organisation of a subject curriculum, whole-school aims and objectives. Indeed, Everard and Morris (1996) point out the impact of such forces and other external factors on the design and delivery of the curriculum. On the other hand, as Blundell and Field (2000) point out, the Subject Leader is also the public face of his or her subject. The ethos and integrity of the subject, and the need to inspire and motivate learners and teachers, rests in no small way with the Subject Leader.

The challenge of Subject *Leaders* as middle *managers* is, then, to establish a balance between leadership and management roles – to provide a vision and direction, yet also to ensure the implementation and monitoring of pre-determined policies and procedures. Over-emphasis in one direction can lead to misunderstanding. Focusing too much on the implementation role can lead to a perception of the Subject Leader as simply a teacher with additional administrative tasks, and neglect of the management functions can result in the Subject Leader being perceived as a maverick.

The NSFSL provide a structure for this balance. The inclusion of standards related to strategic planning, leading other teachers and decision-making provide clear guidance for the extent to which Subject Leaders can and should *lead*. On the other hand, responsibility for subject related management functions and clear levels of accountability are contained within the standards, including the need to contribute to and monitor whole-school aims, objectives and policies.

The NSFSL also define the bounds of the Subject Leader's responsibility. By listing the intended outcomes of effective subject leadership (in terms of its impact on other stakeholders), the scope for innovation is clarified. An interpretation of the influence of the NSFSL can therefore be made in two contrasting ways. First, for some the NSFSL can be empowering – providing the individual Subject Leader with ammunition for power and authority. Secondly, and for others, the NSFSL can be seen to be restrictive and constraining – the means by which school management teams can define the purpose and range of activities which should fall to the Subject Leader.

Part of a bigger picture

The NSFSL are not the only set of standards for those in the teaching profession. The first complete 'set' was presented as the 'Rainbow Pack' in 1998 (see Chapter 1). These have been added to, providing a raft of standards for:

- those seeking Qualified Teacher Status;
- induction for Newly Qualified Teachers;
- those 'crossing the threshold';
- those applying for the Fast Track into teaching;
- Advanced Skills Teachers;
- SEN Specialists and SENCOs;
- Subject Leaders;
- Headteachers.

Each set was not written in isolation from the others; indeed the DfEE (now DfES) has developed a National Standards Framework, containing common headings in the standards for teachers at different stages of their career. For further details, see the DfES website at www.teachernet.gov.uk/professionaldevelopment/standardsframework.

This Framework enables teachers to identify professional development needs and activities which may assist in the achievement of the higher standards to which they aspire.

For Subject Leaders, the next 'level' of National Standards in this ladder is those relevant to aspiring headteachers. In fact, many of the Standards for Headteachers relate very closely to the NSFSL. The key difference is one of scale. A Subject Leader has responsibility, through the National Standards, for teaching and learning within a specified subject. Head-teacher Standards demand similar understanding, application of skills and attributes at whole-school level, thereby incorporating a greater breadth of understanding.

In some ways, successful achievement of the NSFSL can be seen as an effective and identifiable preparation for school leadership. Application for the NPQH is judged in terms of evidence of experience and readiness to proceed to this level. The concept of exemption from some stages/courses and 'fast-tracking' is based on evidence of prior learning and competence. Evidence of effective subject leadership can therefore serve this purpose.

The new performance management procedure includes aspects of the role beyond classroom practice. The NSFSL provide useful descriptions and performance indicators to support what can be seen as judgements on an individual's effectiveness. As criteria for a broad appraisal of performance, in relation to tightly specified job descriptions and expectations, the NSFSL are helpful. They can also assist in developing job descriptions and negotiating targets for future professional development.

Once again, the NSFSL can be viewed in two ways: as a means of acknowledging and rewarding good practice, or as a set of prescriptive, expected outcomes to shape the performance of those aspiring to the role of Subject Leader. Whether empowering or constraining, the Standards do represent a basis for job descriptions, professional development and enhancement, performance management and career progression.

Making positive use of the NSFSL

The issue is, then, how the NSFSL can be used in a productive, positive way. The following case study exemplifies how issues emerging in previous sections have been used to structure a Continuing Professional Development provision for Subject Leaders. The programme also draws on Busher et al.'s (2001: 91) research findings on what constitutes an effective training programme for Subject Leaders:

- an emphasis upon collaboration;
- involvement and support of senior management;
- flexible and intermittent training points;
- external agency;
- context-related planning and development;
- necessity of enquiry and reflection;
- use of research to inform practice;
- evaluation and data analysis.

Underpinning the proposals are several essential concepts, values and beliefs. These are that:

- teaching and learning are intellectual and creative activities which demand theoretical and pragmatic understandings;
- teaching and leading teaching and learning are not best learnt only by 'doing';
- that in a practical sense leading and managing cannot be separated, and that effective practice depends on their mutual interdependence;
- leadership and management involve a focus on human relationships as well as final outcomes and results;
- Subject Leaders are accountable to pupils, parents, colleagues and the senior management team of the school in which they work.

The authors of this chapter applied these principles successfully to the design and delivery of professional development programmes that are currently being delivered in Kent, the Channel Islands, Walsall, Bradford and Liverpool.

Using the National Standards for Subject Leaders to guide Professional Development

The development of a Diploma/MA in Subject Leadership

As soon as the NSFSL were published, the authors of this chapter, members of the management team of the Centre for Education Leadership and School Improvement (CELSI) at Canterbury Christ Church University College (CCCUC), decided to create an award-bearing programme based on the standards (i.e. Diploma/MA in Subject Leadership). The impetus for this came from three assumptions:

1   That the TTA would, in due course, be introducing a National Professional Qualification for Subject Leaders (NPQSL) to act as a stepping stone towards the NPQH that was already being developed (NB: The TTA subsequently dropped plans to introduce this award)

2   That the NSFSL provided, for the first time, a nationally recognised framework to enable a comprehensive programme to be developed to meet the needs of Subject Leaders
3   That Subject Leaders would value gaining an academic award that demonstrated their knowledge and understanding of the role of the Subject Leader in supporting school improvement.

The prospective tutor team quickly realised that if a programme was to be developed it would need to relate the NSFSL to current knowledge and understanding, models and processes that underpin the leadership and co-ordination of subjects in the context of school improvement. At that time no textbook based upon the NSFSL existed, and it was therefore agreed that a book would be written to coincide with the creation of the programme that could act as a basic course text. Accordingly, in January 2000 Routledge published the tutor team's text *Effective Subject Leadership*, by Kit Field, Phil Holden and Hugh Lawlor. The nature of the book was indicative of the nature of the programmes that were subsequently designed and delivered:

- recognisable and accessible models were used to guide the reader/participant through the book/programme;
- relevant 'theory' was introduced and described in practical terms to promote understanding and analysis of current practice; and
- tasks and activities were prescribed that would enable readers/participants to apply the outcomes of their learning.

The Diploma/MA in Subject Leadership was validated and successfully launched for Kent LEA in conjunction with the Kent Advisory Service, which initially provided associate tutors to support the CELSI team. Several groups of Subject Leaders have successfully completed the programme, and many have since moved on to become more senior managers in schools. The outputs of the programme that related to school improvement have been evaluated, and there is now positive evidence that demonstrates the impact of the programme.

Serco QAA Programme for Subject Leaders

In April 2000, the senior education officers with responsibility for staff development on Jersey and Guernsey met with Phil Holden, from Serco QAA (now Serco Learning), and outlined their need for a well-structured programme to support the professional development of Subject Leaders in the Channel Islands. Serco Learning has now developed strongly as a private sector company providing services for schools and local education authorities. The officers from the Channel Islands had identified a number of key areas of the Subject Leaders' role that schools' own internal evaluation and the LEA's version of school inspection had identified as needing support:

- clarification of the role of Subject Leaders in primary and secondary schools;
- the explicit and increasingly important role in improving standards of teaching and learning and thereby improving pupils' attainment;
- up-to-date understanding of the research on teaching and learning styles and its impact on planning and classroom management;
- the ability accurately and objectively to monitor and evaluate the quality of teaching and the setting and supporting of teachers' targets for improvement; (Jersey and Guernsey were to introduce Performance Management one year after England);
- giving difficult feedback and handling conflict;
- the recruitment, deployment and development of subject staff.

The areas of knowledge and understanding that were not seen as a necessary part of the programme were those related to managing (non-human) resources. The planning group's experience of Subject Leaders' day-to-day activities showed that, for many Subject Leaders, the time that they had available outside of their own teaching was often spent on procuring, organising, checking or distributing subject-related resources. Time-management analysis had revealed that some Subject Leaders spent four or five times the amount of time on these activities than they did talking to or observing staff. In some cases, Subject Leaders did not conduct any observation of lessons in a year.

IDENTIFICATION OF STRATEGIC DEVELOPMENT AS THE KEY WEAKNESS

Phil Holden's experience of being NPQH Centre Manager for the South East had shown that many Subject Leaders in England also lacked another key area of the NSFSL: 'the strategic direction and development of the subject'. Indeed, analysis of the NPQH applications to participate in NPQH in England and from Jersey and Guernsey teachers had shown that Channel Islands teachers were generally even weaker in this area than their English counterparts. This is partly explained by some difference in the governance of Jersey and Guernsey schools: they do not have the same delegated powers and budgets, or even governors in primary schools.

However, even accounting for these differences, it was agreed that strategic thinking related to school improvement was essential to the future improvement of schools, irrespective of issues of delegation. In addition, succession planning related to the appointment of headteachers in the medium and longer term would be dramatically enhanced by the development of more effective 'middle managers'.

A SIX-DAY MODEL

Having decided that subject leadership would be a key strategic target for staff development on Jersey and Guernsey, the Directors of Education had agreed that substantial funding would be made available over a three-year period so that all the Subject Leaders who wanted to could attend a programme.

The concern of the officers and the programme designers was that any programme should have a direct impact on improving the quality of subject co-ordination, teaching, learning and attainment. It was recognised that a 'quick-fix' programme would not achieve this. A more sustained approach was required that enabled:

- tutors to introduce an appropriate amount of 'theory', models of good practice, and to engage participants intellectually and practically via discussion and activities;
- participants to absorb and reflect on new theory, ideas and models, and to discuss their reactions and practical applications with the tutors and colleagues from other schools;
- participants to take their learning back into schools so that they could share it with their headteachers and colleagues and then plan and implement change;
- tutors to offer ongoing support via e-mail;
- participants to develop and implement a subject improvement plan based around improving the quality of teaching and learning;
- participants to collect evidence of the impact of the leadership;
- tutors to organise the presentation and celebration of the Subject Leaders' development and impact to their headteachers and senior education officers.

Clearly, besides the benefits there are costs to be taken into account. In this case there were direct costs (e.g. tutor fees, materials, travel, rooms, refreshments and supply). There was also the cost to the school of the potentially disruptive amount of time that people would be away from their teaching and leadership duties.

The programme that was eventually designed and delivered took these benefits and costs into account and involved a pattern of attendance spread over one school year, usually commencing in September, January or May (see Table 10.1).

The first programme was piloted in Jersey in September 2000, and subsequent programmes were delivered from January 2001 in Jersey and Guernsey. By the end of 2002 over 300 subject leaders will have been on the programme in the Channel Islands and another 100 in England, with more planned for 2003.

Table 10.1 Programme for Subject Leaders: pattern of attendance

Day 1	Core purpose of the Subject Leader (followed up by Link Activities during a 4-week break)
Day 2	Leading and managing effective learning and teaching
Day 3	Strategic direction and development of the subject (followed up by Link Activities during a 4-week break)
Day 4	Leading and managing change
Day 5	Raising standards through effective leadership (followed up by devising and implementing a Subject Improvement Plan during the 16–20 weeks' break)
Day 6	Celebrating subject improvement (involving presentations and review of learning)

SENCO and Pastoral Tutor versions

Since its piloting in September 2000, the programme has been subject to thorough ongoing evaluation and review resulting in continuous improvement. In addition, using the same pattern, the programme was amended using the National Standards for SENCOs to support the development of those in SENCO and similar roles in schools. A further adaption was made to provide a programme for those with pastoral responsibility, although, without having their own national standards, the programme's participants were unable to gain as much from the self-analysis that is such an important feature of the Subject Leader and SENCO versions.

Key features and benefits of the Serco QAA Programme for Subject Leaders

SELF-DIRECTED PROFESSIONAL DEVELOPMENT

A crucial part of the programme is the self-analysis that starts on Day 1 of the programme and is revisited at regular intervals and reviewed on the last day. Inherent in the NSFSL is the need for self-evaluation (knowing oneself), now also recognised as a key part of having the emotional intelligence needed for leadership. In the Subject Leaders' programme, a major part of this is done using a 'MIC' analysis against the NSFSL. Participants are given a form on which are listed all the itemised skills, knowledge, understanding, attributes and elements of the four key areas that appear in the Standards. They have three columns in which to indicate a self-judgement:

- *M – maintain.* A tick in this column indicates that the participant is confident that he or she has knowledge and understanding, or skill or experience in this aspect of the Standards. However, this level must be at least maintained and kept up to date.

- *I – improve.* A tick in this column indicates that the participant thinks that he or she has not yet gained the required amount or level of knowledge, skill or experience but also thinks that with just a small amount of effort or opportunity it would be possible to reach the required standard.
- *C – change.* A tick in this column indicates that the participant thinks that he or she has not yet gained the required amount of knowledge, skill or experience, and realises that it will take a fairly substantial change in the participant, his or her opportunity to learn, or the job to access the development required to reach the required standard. The participant also recognises that it will not be possible to do this without external support.

Using this kind of analysis it is possible for the participant to gain a clear understanding of those areas of the standards that they need to prioritise for their development. These forms are taken in by the tutors and produce a computer-aided analysis of the data that shows the level that participants have judged themselves to be at compared with other colleagues. This analysis can be used by the participants to discuss changes of role with their headteacher or to choose subject improvement projects that will require the acquisition of items ticked in the 'I' and 'C' columns. The tutor team also uses them to aid the planning of future sessions and to target support to individuals.

The NSFSL have proved invaluable in benchmarking across groups and across a whole LEA. If there were ever to be a national award this process would provide a good starting point, although it would need to be backed up with the production of evidence to substantiate the claim of competence.

Other self-analysis undertaken on the programme includes looking at preferred learning modes, preferred leadership styles and ways of dealing with conflict.

TEACHING AND LEARNING AT THE CORE

The emphasis of the whole programme is improving what teachers do in the classroom that will improve learning. This requires Subject Leaders to understand fully and be able assess the quality of teaching and learning. On the programme these areas of the NSFSL are picked out, and emphasis is placed on deepening participants' knowledge of what should be in a good lesson and how to judge standards using Ofsted criteria and methodology. In this way the programme is also supporting the introduction of performance management and its requirement to assess the quality of teaching.

The programme also gives participants practice and support in feeding back and setting targets for improvement.

APPLICATION OF NEW SKILLS AND KNOWLEDGE IN SCHOOL (LINK
ACTIVITIES)

Another key feature of the programme is the setting of link activities to be
completed between sessions 1 and 2, 3 and 4, and 5 and 6. The activities
require participants to undertake actions and tasks in their school and
bring the outcomes to the next session. For instance, before Day 2,
participants are asked to look at aspects of the quality of teaching and
learning in their subject in their school. They are invited to do this by, for
example, having one of their colleagues observe and give feedback on their
own teaching before they go and observe their colleagues' lessons. Another
suggested approach is to conduct a survey of what pupils think of the
subject lessons they receive. Participants may also wish to have a frank discussion with their subject team about what they believe are the priorities
for improvement in that subject.

The outcomes of the link activities are used on the next day of the programme, and help to build towards the creation of a subject improvement
plan focused on improving the quality of lessons (i.e. the quality of planning, content delivery, interaction with pupils, work done by pupils and its
assessment). The improvement plan is reviewed and revised according to
the programme's strategic planning model, and is then implemented
between Days 5 and 6.

One of the key benefits of using link activities is that this usually promotes valuable discussion between the Subject Leader and his or her headteacher. This can be started quite early on, following the MIC analysis,
and enables the headteacher to become more familiar with the NSFSL. As
the discussions progress, many participants find that they are having much
more focused and meaningful exchanges with their headteacher. One
benefit is that because the headteacher is more aware of what the Subject
Leader is planning, he or she is in a better position to help.

GATHERING EVIDENCE AND CELEBRATING SUCCESS

On Day 6, the participants are asked to present to other participants,
headteachers (and in Jersey the Director of Education) a description of
their plan, the actions taken and an evaluation of the impact on improving
teaching and learning in their school.

To be able to do this well, participants must systematically gather and
analyse evidence of how the actions they have taken have added value.
This is more difficult for some participants because, as they realise later,
they did not set appropriate success criteria at the beginning. Participants
are thoroughly debriefed following the presentations, by peer and tutor
review. Having listened to several presentations, headteachers attending
these Day 6 events are always impressed by the scope and depth of the

participants' achievements, and normally go back to their schools energised and with a number of new ideas and insights.

PREPARATION FOR NPQH

The evidence of successful improvement does not simply serve to illustrate and celebrate the accomplishments of the Subject Leader; it is also a vital source of evidence that can be used when completing an application for NPQH or even used within that programme to demonstrate some of the National Standards for Headteachers. As mentioned earlier, one of the weak areas in applicants for NPQH is across-the-school strategic planning and action. The Serco QAA Programme for Subject Leaders offers participants insights, opportunities and support to prove a higher degree of competence in this key area than would normally be the case.

In addition, those participants who fully embrace the objectives and complete the tasks set within the Subject Leaders' programme find that they are able to enter NPQH much further into the programme, often well beyond the access stages.

QUALITY ASSURANCE

The programme is monitored from the beginning by receiving formative feedback from participants, their headteachers and officers from the sponsoring Governments and LEAs. Early feedback on the pilot programme enabled its designers to change its balance so as to enable more time for reflection during rather than between days.

A feature of the Serco QAA programme is that it is designed to be delivered to cross-phase groups. This key issue was evaluated early in the programme, and the majority of participants were very positive about this aspect. They reported that working across the phases enabled them to realise that many issues concerning subject leadership were generic, that colleagues' experiences in the different phases were helpful to all, and that group work and discussion was better informed and more creative because of the wider experiences and talents of the group.

Summative feedback from participants enables the programme to be constantly updated and improved. Information from the first groups indicated that more pre-programme information needed to be sent to prospective participants, particularly in relation to the amount of time needed to complete link activities and the Subject Improvement Project. It was also clear that participants needed to involve their headteachers throughout the programme so that they could gain support and guidance to make their project worthwhile and to ensure it made an impact. Participants who reported the greatest benefit from the programme were those who also reported that they had received the greatest amount of co-operation and support.

At the time of writing this chapter, it is not possible to present detailed outcomes from the longitudinal evaluation that is being conducted. However, early indications are that schools have benefited most where several Subject Leaders have attended the programme over a two-year period.

Conclusion – the positive influence of the NSFSL

The NSFSL have provided a much-needed framework for those responsible for managing, providing and participating in staff development related to subject leadership and other middle leader roles. The comprehensive framework also facilitates self-analysis and enables Subject Leaders to discuss their professional development using a common national framework. The Serco QAA Programme developed with Jersey and Guernsey is one example of a wider range of programmes that have emerged in England over the past few years for middle leaders. These have been developed by local education authorities, university education departments, colleges of education and private sector providers of training and development.

The latest national initiative has been the launch of 'Leading from the Middle' (LftM) by the National College for School Leadership in September 2003. In designing LftM, it is stated that:

> The National Standards for Subject Leaders have provided a valuable starting point for the Leading from the Middle Programme but NCSL also consulted over 100 teachers throughout the development of the programme [and] has taken advice from professional Associations, government agencies, LEAs and key subject associations.
>
> (NCSL Leaflet on LftM, 2003)

Further details of this programme may be found on the NCSL website at www.ncsl.org.uk

References and further reading

Adair, J. (1988) *Effective Leadership*, 2nd edn, London: Pan Books.

Blundell, S. and Field, K. (2000) 'Integrity of the subject,' in Field, K. (ed.) *Subject Leadership: A Key Reference File*, London: The Stationery Office.

Booth, T., Ainscow, M., Black-Hawkins, K. and Shaw, L. (2000) *Index for Inclusion*, Bristol: Centre for Studies on Inclusive Education (CSIE).

Burke, J. (ed.) (1990) *Competence Based Education and Training*, London: Paul Chapman Press.

Busher, H., Harris A. and Wise, C. (2000) *Subject Leadership and School Improvement*, London: Paul Chapman Press.

DES (1988) *The Education Reform Act*, London: HMSO.

DES (1992) Circular 9/92, London: HMSO.

DfEE/QCA (1999) *The National Curriculum: Handbook for Teachers*, DfEE/QCA.

Elliott, J. (1991) *Action Research for Educational Change*, Milton Keynes: Open University Press.

Everard, B. and Morris, G. (1996) *Effective School Management*, 3rd edn, London: Harper Row.

Field, K. (2002) 'Evidence-based subject leadership,' *Journal of In-Service Education* 28(3): 459–475.

Field, K., Holden, P. and Lawlor, H. (2000) *Effective Subject Leadership*, London: RoutledgeFalmer.

Fowler, W.S. (1990) *Implementing the National Curriculum: The Policy and Practice of the 1988 Education Reform Act*, London: Kogan Page.

Gardner, H. (1983) *Frames of Mind: the Theory of Multiple Intelligences*, London: Harper Row.

Gunther, H. (2001) *Leaders and Leadership in Education*, London: Paul Chapman Press.

Hargreaves, D. (1996) *Teaching as a Research Based Profession*, Teacher Training Agency Annual Lecture.

Harris, A. (1995) *Effective Subject Departments*, University of Bath.

Harris, A., Busher, H. and Wise, C. (2001) 'Effective training for subject leaders,' in *Journal of In-Service Education* 27(1): 83–94.

Kolb, D. (1983) *Experiential Learning: Experience as the Source of Learning and Development*, New York: Prentice Hall.

Lawlor, S. (1990) *Teachers Mistaught*, London: Centre for Policy Studies.

McNiff, J., Lomax, P. and Whitehead, J. (1996) *You and Your Action Research Project*, London: Routledge.

NCSL (2002) *Leadership Framework*, available at www.ncsl.org.uk/index.cfm?pageid=ldev_emergent_leading.

Ofsted (1993) *Handbook for the Inspection of Schools*, London: HMSO.

O'Hear, A. (1988) Green Paper 'Who teaches the teachers: a contribution to public debate of the DES,' London: Social Affairs Unit.

Sammons, P., Hillman, J. and Mortimore, P. (1995) *Key Characteristics of Effective Schools: A Review of School Effectiveness Research*, London: Ofsted.

Senge, P. (1990) *The Fifth Discipline*, New York: Doubleday.

Sergiovanni, T. (1995) *The Principalship: A Reflective Practice Perspective*, London: Allyn and Bacon.

Smith, A. (1998) *Accelerated Learning: Brain Based Methods for Accelerating Motivation and Achievement*, Stafford: Network Education Press.

Stenhouse, L. (1975) *An Introduction to Curriculum Research and Development*, London: Heinemann.

TTA (1998) *National Standards for Subject Leaders*, London: Teacher Training Agency.

West, N. (1995) *Middle Management in the Primary School: A Development Guide for Curriculum Leaders, Subject Managers and Senior Staff*, London: David Fulton.

Williams, V. (1995) 'Towards 2000 – organisation and relationships,' in Williams, V. (ed.) *Towards Self-Managing Schools*, Cambridge: Cambridge University Press, pp. 137–165.

Woodhead, C. (1993) 'Do we need a new National Curriculum?' in O'Hear, P. and White, J. (eds) *Assessing the National Curriculum*, London: Paul Chapman Press.

Chapter 11

Headteacher

Harry Tomlinson

Introduction of the National Standards for Headteachers, and revisions

The early consultations on the proposed National Standards for Headteachers were based on a model which was already centrally determined. The five parts for this model were: core purpose of the headteacher; key outcomes of headship; professional knowledge and understanding; skills and attributes; and key areas of headship. Though there was a full consultation, the proposals for amendment largely accepted this predetermined framework, which remains in place. This five-part structure has been sustained throughout the further development and use of the headteacher Standards for five years, and has been subsequently extended and used for the other standards developed for serving teachers. These National Standards for Headteachers are now widely used not only for the training of aspirant headteachers, National Professional Qualification for Headship (NPQH) and for the training and development programme for newly appointed headteachers (HEADLAMP), but also to provide essentially a job description for the selection of headteachers. There is some question, however, about the centrality of their significance in the Leadership Programme for Serving Headteachers (LPSH).

Training, development and assessment using the National Standards

For the purposes of professional development and training in the NPQH, the focus initially was on the practical application of the five key areas of headship, which were assessed through a continuous assessment process with tasks for each of the key areas. The final assessment concentrated on the skills and attributes part of the Standards, for which there had been little training. This problem was clearly recognised when the NPQH was revised after the review in 2000 (see below), since when the six days of face-to-face training through the NPQH process have all focused on skills and attributes, and these have been assessed not only in the final assessment but also in the school-based assessment. The use of skills and attributes within the standards is problematic. The skills – leadership, decision-making, communication and self-management – are important, but may be diminished by being conceptualised as skills. The assessment, of, for example, self-management within a one-day final assessment centre, may not allow aspirant heads to demonstrate the ability to sustain long term the capacity to manage time effectively, to work under pressure and to deadlines, to achieve challenging professional goals, and to take responsibility for their own lifelong professional development. These are assessed, and Ofsted has said that the final assessment process is rigorous and valid, but the limited one-day process cannot be fully assured to represent the very long term. The attributes are arguably the most difficult to develop and to assess. The importance of commitment, enthusiasm and self-confidence are widely accepted, but measuring them has been more problematic, and the use of the diagnostic instruments that would measure these might require a sophisticated psychological expertise.

In all the TTA and DfES development programmes and the associated assessment procedures there has been little emphasis on the professional knowledge and understanding in the National Standards, the wider political, legislative, theoretical and research context, which includes the characteristics of effective schools; how to use comparative data to set benchmarks; management, including employment law and equal opportunities legislation; the statutory framework for education; and governance at national, local and school levels. This has been an issue in discussions within the wider international community and for some of the universities which were seeking to find an appropriate means for accrediting the NPQH. The academic credibility of the NPQH has been problematic because of the focus on competency and because the professional knowledge and understanding incorporated in the Standards has largely been ignored in practice.

Use of Standards for the delivery of the NPQH and HEADLAMP

The learning process for achieving the National Professional Qualification for Headship has changed very significantly since 1997, when it first moved from trial phase to full implementation. It has always been firmly based on parts of the National Standards for Headteachers, which have remained substantially the same. The Standards have also provided a basis for structuring the HEADLAMP (Headteachers' Leadership and Management Programme) provision. HEADLAMP is a process for providing funding for professional development for newly appointed headteachers, and focuses on personal professional needs as defined by the headteacher, though subject to governor approval. It may partially be an issue associated with the Standards, as well as the formal processes for seeking the appropriate training required, that has resulted in only 80 per cent of the heads accessing HEADLAMP funding at all, and these heads in turn only accessed 80 per cent of the funding to which they were entitled. Much of the provision was from LEAs, building on their headteachers' induction programmes and knowledge gained from supporting the headteacher appraisal processes from the early 1990s.

The NPQH was consciously building on five principles in 1997 (TTA 1997). These were:

1   Rooted in school improvement and draws on the best leadership and management practice inside and outside education
2   Based on National Standards for Headteachers
3   Signals readiness for headship, but does not replace the selection process
4   Rigorous enough to ensure that those ready for headship gain the qualification, while being sufficiently flexible to take account of candidates' previous achievements and proven skills and the range of context in which they have been applied
5   Provides a baseline from which newly appointed headteachers can subsequently, in the context of their schools, continue to develop their leadership and management abilities.

Training and development, and the assessment tasks

The attempt to ensure that there was a link between training and development and the work in schools was initially of limited success. The assessment tasks for the early cohorts were not directly linked to practice in schools partly because of the attempt to ensure that all candidates worked through the same tasks, the responses to which could be then compared. In an attempt to ensure equity the setting of an activity to manage a 7 per cent cut in the school budget was problematic when schools had very different budget issues. This was more so since this remained an assessment task when school budgets were increasing. Initially, and until 2001, the selection process for starting the NPQH was carried out by LEAs with a focus on the key areas of headship, not on the other elements of the Standards.

From 1997, the ten regions in England each had a Regional Assessment Centre and a Regional Training and Development Centre. This was to ensure there was no contamination of the assessment process, strengthened by a clear separation of the two centres. This sustaining of professional integrity resulted in candidates not receiving high-quality feedback to assist their further professional growth. It also meant that LEAs were largely excluded from the process of continuously informing the determination of the learning needs of particular candidates. Now that the merged centres manage the selection process also, the focus for learning remains strongly on experience and expertise in the five key areas. The other two aspects now used for selection purposes are written evidence of why the applicants want to be a headteacher, and of their continuing professional development and learning. These do not necessarily relate directly to the National Standards.

Time demands for the NPQH

In 1997 there was an overambitious expectation of the time candidates would be willing (or indeed able) to commit. The compulsory module, based on key areas A and E, was to require 60 hours of contact time and a minimum of 120 hours on school-based projects, individual study and preparing for assessment. Since the three further modules each required half this time, this added up in total to 75 days over the three years for those who were judged by the Regional Assessment Centres to require training on the further modules. Candidates who needed to commit this considerable time were often in less senior positions, and had very little or no time within the school day for these activities. The time expectation was very quickly reduced, illustrating how the NPQH was introduced with insufficient detailed planning, preparation and research. For the first cohort there was a requirement to train, for the compulsory module, on ten Saturdays over a year. The training materials for the trial candidates were prepared by the different regions, and only after this were they made national. The richness of these materials helped ensure an eventual breadth of approach. However, it was not until the fourth cohort (in 1999) that there were very high-quality materials and consistent training programmes across the country.

The training and professional development originally focused very strongly on the key areas which were the basis of assessment. The core module, originally called the compulsory module, covered key areas A and E (Strategic direction and development of the school, and Accountability). The argument was that these two modules were in some sense at a higher and more strategic level than the other three, in that they more fully concentrated on leadership rather than management. Management was more of the focus in the modules Teaching and learning, Leading and managing staff, and Efficient and effective deployment of staff and resources. There were analogies to the more strategic leadership role of the Chair of the board of a company with the wider responsibilities for strategy and accountability, and the Production Director (curriculum and learning), Human Resources Director (leading and managing people) and Finance

Director (resource management) with more subordinate but complementary roles. Initially all candidates had to study the 'compulsory' module, though it soon became evident that there was a need for an accelerated route for those with considerable senior leadership experience, in particular acting headteachers. The implication of this was that the NPQH might be perceived as a deficit model with the need to ensure everyone had sufficient training and development to ensure they reached the minimum level. It was more important to overcome weaknesses than to develop strengths further.

The NPQH in the wider context

Initially there was widespread concern about how appropriate the NPQH was for training headteachers. Brundrett (1999) focused on the inherent tension between NPQH and the higher degree programmes in education management which had developed over the previous decade in England. In a later article (Brundrett 2001) explores this issue for the NPQH in a wider international context. The TTA's strong focus on a competency-based approach caused some disquiet with those already involved in headteacher professional development. The TTA was determined not to link the NPQH to higher education, because these degrees were perceived to be insufficiently related to practice. The NPQH did have some impact on the later redesign of higher education courses which took account of the National Standards. The analyses, Brundrett suggests, criticised the Standards in two ways. The first was that the National Standards represented a thinly disguised competence-based approach. The TTA was determined that the professional qualification would be strongly focused on practice rather than theory. There was the complementary problem of a lack of access to the knowledge base for educational leadership for candidates and, in particular, the failure to take sufficient account of the more cognitive approaches in the USA. For the first cohorts this excessive focus on the practical and professional activities was to some extent rectified by the encouragement – in some regions an expectation – of the effective use for learning of the course readers from the Education Leadership and Management in Education course, part of the Open University MA programme. The encouragement to explore the complementary educational literature provided some academic rigour. This approach was later discouraged by the TTA, and the proposal to prepare and present a collection of complementary readings to provide some access to appropriate literature was also not accepted. The professional approach, as conceptualised by the TTA, appeared to imply an anti-academic approach. This was partially a consequence of the 'professional knowledge and understanding' section of the National Standards being the one part which was not emphasised in the NPQH and HEADLAMP. Male (2001) did discover that headteachers who had achieved the NPQH felt better prepared than other newly appointed colleagues in putting their vision into words, applying educational law to specific situations, assuming responsibility for school management, and organising school administration. He could not demonstrate that this was due to the NPQH training, however.

There was initially a significant concern about the danger of political and bureaucratic control by the TTA. The failure to open the development process to accessible research enhanced the problem, an issue since the NPQH started. The research that has been completed has not been presented in the public domain, which may be why the National Standards have not been subject to public review. 'Inward-lookingness' may become an issue for the NCSL if it is insufficiently independent of Government and not significantly responsive to those elements in the profession and higher education that challenge the received orthodoxy. The linkage between theory and practice was at the heart of this discussion. Three strands to this issue are recognised by Brundrett. These refer first to the cognitive and problem-based approaches to professional education which are the focus of research and practice in the USA (see below). Secondly, there is emerging evidence about the ways in which school leaders learn which was being re-analysed in the light of theories of professional socialisation. This issue is being explored more fully now by the NCSL through online learning, and in particular on the site for currently serving headteachers 'Talking Heads'. Thirdly, there was the increased focus on professional values in professional development, which has been more central in Scottish and the USA leadership development than is evident in England.

Major review of the NPQH

Dame Patricia Collarbone, then at the London Leadership Centre, carried out a major review of the NPQH, which was running out of energy by 2000. Recruitment was falling away, and though there had been significant improvements from what was provided for the first cohort (including the accelerated route for those with considerable senior management experience and some improvement in the assessment model), it was time for a radical overhaul. There was evidence from the LPSH and the associated Headship Model (Figure 11.1) that supports the changes.

The new NPQH learning model is more competency-based, and also much more focused in schools. There were discussions about changing the format of the National Standards to reflect this, but in the end the National Standards model, which used skills and attributes, remained essentially unchanged. The potential change to using competencies and a wider restructuring and reconsideration of the Standards has not been achieved, and

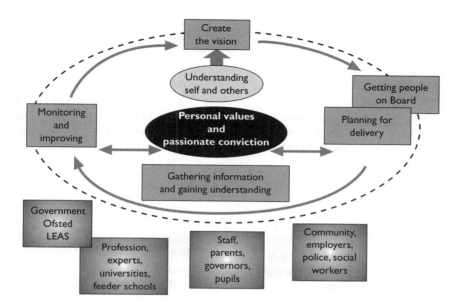

Figure 11.1 Headship Model.
Source: Hay Group.

appears not to be on the NCSL agenda. The review of the NPQH was carried out for the Department for Education and Skills (DfES), to which the leadership programmes had been transferred from the Teacher Training Agency, en route to the National College for School Leadership (NCSL), established in 2000. The changes to the NPQH transformed the programme, and made it genuinely and internationally-cutting edge. The impact on recruitment was so profound and positive that the DfES has decided, following consultation, to make the NPQH mandatory from 2004. The new school-based assessment process, much more challenging, individualised and focused on school improvement, has been particularly important.

Adult learning on-line

There is now a much clearer focus and understanding of adult learning (Collarbone 2001a) with clearly articulated links to double-loop learning and a recognition of the significance of the relationship between intelligence, emotional intelligence and spiritual intelligence in the adult learner. Tutors have become facilitators, though initially without sufficient training about the learning theory behind the new model. Facilitated self-directed learning recognises that participation in learning is voluntary. Effective practice is characterised by a respect among participants for each other's self-worth. Not only is facilitation collaborative, but also action and reflection are placed at the heart of facilitation. This aims to foster in adults a spirit of critical reflection and the nurturing of self-directed, empowered adults. The approach presented by Collarbone made a profound change to the learning process by treating senior professionals with respect. The application of this approach within the Virtual Heads environment is developing quickly, although the nature of the link with the National Standards is less clear. The technical guidance on how to use the on-line learning environment is somewhat authoritarian, and does not always respect this empowerment. There is pressure for candidates on the NPQH to make large numbers of short contributions which, if they were made, could overwhelm the regional and tutor on-line environments.

The new learning opportunities, particularly those made possible through ICT, were to help learners achieve self-direction, capitalising on the learning experience accessed through collaboration with other candidates, to develop critical reflective thinking. The Virtual Heads NPQH site provides group and tutor support within the tutor group, and direct links to up-to-date resources and access to experts. This sophisticated but practical learning process based on Vygotskian ZPD (zone of proximal development) theory, and developed by Ultralab, might be more fully shared with participants and tutors. The tutor's role has changed even during the eighteen months of implementation of this new model, with an enhanced focus on learning within the tutor group rather than supporting the individual learner. To make the learning as profound and effective as possible, tutors and learners need to understand the theory behind the on-line learning approach being used. That this has not been done may be another manifestation of the anxiety about excessive theory getting in the way of practice, which characterised the early model of the NPQH. The role of the tutor on-line is distinctive; it is to encourage learners to define their own goals and purposes and explore these with other learners. The Salmon (2000: 26) model represents a developmental model for ICT learning which might be explored to enhance e-learning (Figure 11.2).

Participation in on-line learning

The NPQH Virtual Heads website has essentially four levels of participation. There is a national level, the 'hotseats', where participants engage in discussion with leading national figures. This tends to be a more dependent relationship. At regional level participation is facilitated by lead tutors who manage the learning on the four modules covering the key areas, the sixteen units, all of which can be accessed throughout the study period. This means that candidates can manage their own learning programme. The attempts to provide a time-constrained framework for

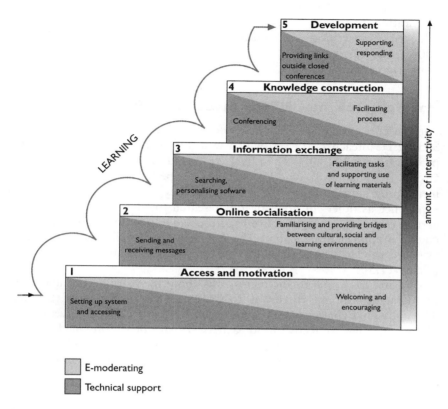

Figure 11.2 E-moderating model.

the first intake for the new NPQH and to create regional subgroups of 50 for these activities were unsuccessful. The regional site very much focuses on the key areas of headship for which candidates have received high-quality hard copy, though on-line these are continuously updated. The quality of these materials, the most traditional part of the new NPQH, is excellent, and encourages but does not require access to a broader literature. However, there is an issue, particularly for the Access Route, about the depth and quality of the learning when there is no formal assessment.

In this environment – Virtual Heads, where the views of all learners are to be valued and explored – the development of self-esteem is important. It is within the tutor group that a learner's own views are challenged in the context of critical reflection within a supportive environment. Learners may not understand how they learn if their understanding is not challenged. The processes used – for example, the recommended limitation on the length of contributions on-line – may not allow the elaboration necessary to make the learning as effective as might be achieved. Research on on-line learning, which was commissioned in mid-2002 to be carried out by the University of Bristol, should give additional rigour to the process.

Hay Research, new NPQH model and LPSH

The Teacher Training Agency developed a Leadership Programme for Serving Headteachers (LPSH) which went through a significantly different process from the NPQH. The LPSH was based on the research of the Hay Group (see Chapter 3), who had significant expertise in leadership development programmes in business, though they did not have as much experience as others of applying this research to education. Research was carried out using highly effective headteachers to determine how the model could be applied to education The first stage of this research resulted in evidence to clarify the application of the four circles model to education (Figure 11.3).

The first circle, job requirements, was about the National Standards for Headteachers, though there was no significant use of this in the training. The individual characteristics were derived from behavioural event interviews with highly effective headteachers. This evidence provided a model of combinations of characteristics against which the headteachers taking part in the LPSH could be evaluated (Figure 11.4). These characteristics

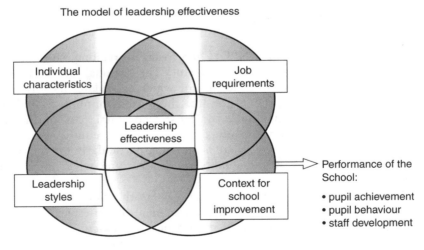

Figure 11.3 Leadership effectiveness model.

Source: Hay Group.

Models of Excellence: The Key Characteristics

PERSONAL VALUES AND PASSIONATE CONVICTION

Respect for others
Challenge and support
Personal conviction

PLANNING FOR DELIVERY AND MONITORING AND IMPROVING

Analytical thinking
Initiative
Transformational leadership
Team-working
Understanding others
Developing potential

GETTING PEOPLE ON BOARD

Impact and influence
Holding people accountable

GATHERING INFORMATION AND GAINING UNDERSTANDING

Understanding the environment
Information seeking

Figure 11.4 Models of excellence; characteristics.
Source: Hay Group.

related to both the Headship Effectiveness Model (Figure 11.1) and the Leadership Effectiveness Model (Figure 11.3) building new forms of rigour into explorations of headteacher performance.

This is a very different model from the National Standards, and concentrates on effectiveness and performance. Similarly, the measured capacity for accessing the six leadership styles which have an impact on performance – the coercive, authoritative, affiliative, democratic, pace-setting, and coaching with precise definitions as applied in the context presented by Hay – is a different approach from assessing leadership skills in the final assessment of the NPQH. In the National Standards the definition asserts that headteachers should be able to use appropriate leadership styles in different situations, but the emphasis is on what should be achieved through this leadership. The second subheading in the leadership section in the National Standards concerns professional competence and expertise. This concentrates on using inspection and research findings, and applying good practice from other sectors and organisations. This is not assessed, and is therefore not directly related to evaluating professional competence. The final circle of the Leadership Effectiveness Model presents the dimensions in the school climate, or context for school improvement, which impact on performance. These are flexibility, responsibility, standards, rewards, clarity and team commitment.

The LPSH programme was determined after piloting and further negotiations between the TTA and the Hay Group. The programme was largely coherent though with some additions inserted by the TTA such as the ICT element, which was largely unrelated to the programme, and the Partners in Leadership, which has unfortunately never produced sufficient business partners for the headteachers going through the LPSH. A few problems with the programme have emerged since it was made available, but most have been clear from the early days. These have been fully explored in the review of the LPSH for the NCSL (Collarbone 2001b). What is of concern is that what is clearly a highly developmental programme has not recruited larger numbers, possibly because of insensitive and unresponsive marketing.

Hay has subsequently carried out much fuller research and further behavioural event interviews on the characteristics of a much larger group of highly effective headteachers and deputy headteachers in a number of different schools. They were able to use the diagnostics from participants in the early LPSH programmes as well as new heads. This revealed that there were different combinations of behaviours appropriate for leaders in different kinds of schools, but also that some of the highly successful were newly appointed.

Reviews by the National College for School Leadership

The NCSL has had a full review of its provision for headteachers, and presented for consultation a package of documents to plan the way forward. This Leadership Development Framework Pack (NCSL 2002) included the review of the LPSH, which successfully addressed the issues and proposed that the programme be available for all headteachers in their fourth year of headship. This would follow the Headteachers' Induction Programme (HIP), following the review of HEADLAMP. The latter review was much less imaginative, not so much in its analysis but in its somewhat deterministic and inflexible proposals. Both the Hay-based approach to leadership development and the new HIP proposals have elements of a deficit model – that is, focusing on what an individual cannot do, rather than building on what he or she can do. A Think Tank Report to the Governing Council provided an evidence base for ten propositions for transforming learning, and the five stages of school leadership. The NCSL is providing programmes for headteachers after the NPQH, HIP and LPSH, but at present sees the emergent roles restricted to developing skills in inspection or consultancy supporting others rather than greatly improving performance in their own schools. With these documents now available from the NCSL and the evidence derived from international experience of leadership development, now may be the time for reconsideration of wider concerns about the restricted nature of the National Standards for Headteachers and their use in the NPQH, and an over-reliance on Hay-based models. This should be a broadly-based and open debate.

Scotland

In Scotland, the Scottish Qualification for Headship is based on The Standard for Headship in Scotland. This has some similarities to the English model. However, a very different accord with higher education was agreed with the universities, which validated Postgraduate Diplomas in Educational Leadership and Management or Professional Development and provided the training and development which leads also to the Scottish Qualification for Headship. Though in England there has been determination to insist that the NPQH is practical and professional, this has appeared to imply an anti-academic and anti-higher education approach that has not characterised other professions in England which have worked successfully with the universities. The NCSL is seeking to explore accreditation of the NPQH more vigorously now, but the most experienced candidates are those who work through the route which involves little professional development and can therefore provide least evidence.

The Key Purpose of Headship in Scotland is essentially the same as in England, though in Scotland the focus is on giving every pupil high quality education which promotes the highest possible standards of achievement rather than the less ambitious improved standards of learning and achievement in England. Such language distinctions are important, since the Standards were developed at the same time.

The central elements of the Scottish Standard refer directly to competence, which has been another issue in England. There is a coherent link between values, management functions and professional leadership abilities. Under 'Competence in School Leadership and Management', the Standard defines the Key Purpose of Headship and the three elements which underpin the professional practice of school leadership and management:

- professional values;
- management functions;
- professional abilities.

The three elements of practice for headship relate to three fundamental points.

1   WHY *a headteacher takes certain courses of action.* This element is concerned with the individual's professional values, commitment to learning and development, and knowledge and understanding of schools and Scottish education.

2 *WHAT the main functions of a headteacher are.* This element comprises the key functions in leading and managing schools: managing learning and teaching; managing people; managing policy and planning; and managing resources and finance.

3 *HOW a headteacher carries out these functions successfully.* This element comprises the intellectual and interpersonal abilities on which school leaders draw to carry out the key functions effectively.

Competence in relation to the Standard for Headship is defined as the ability to combine these three elements appropriately in practice. The relationship between the elements is illustrated in Figure 11.5. Thus, in order to be judged competent, an aspiring headteacher must show that he or she is capable of achieving the key purpose by carrying out the key functions of headship, drawing on appropriate professional values and abilities (Scottish Qualification for Headship, 1998).

The Scottish Qualification for Headship (SQH) was never simply seen as a qualification for aspiring headteachers; it was from the first designed to support a holistic approach to school improvement, as the Quality Initiative in Scotland's schools. As a result of this intention, the SQH is built in as part of the school improvement system. The revised version in England used this approach much more fully – in particular when, in the development phase, the tutor visits the school, and the candidate, headteacher and tutor agree a school improvement project which will form a central part of the school-based assessment. In Scotland, there was always this clear rationale and partnership:

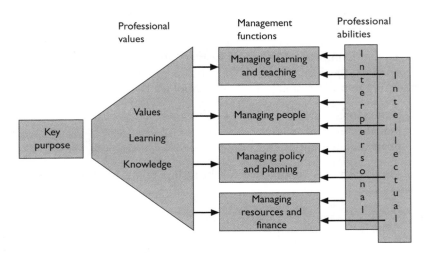

Figure 11.5 Standard for Headship.

- Candidates learn through taking deliberate action for improvement based on agreed priorities for development in their schools and through reflecting on their experience and practice during and after the intervention
- Candidates must justify their actions on the basis of professional values and show why what they are doing is of long-term benefit to pupils
- Candidates must work publicly in schools with the backing of their headteachers and the involvement of others to improve provision for pupils
- Schools and authorities are partners in the provision of the course together with approved higher education institutions. The delivery of the programme is a joint responsibility centred on improving practice in the workplace.

The competence framework on which the course is based also reflects the commitment to the professional development of practitioners, since it uses self-assessment and reflection on a model for action, values, management functions and interpersonal and intellectual abilities as the basis for the candidate's learning.

The current research process in Scotland, in the public domain, will result in the exploration of the cognitive development of candidates, and will further work on the linkage between their learning and social processes. There is now a bid for funding to explore the links between the social processes engendered by the SQH, organisational learning and the impact on schools.

In England, the research about the NPQH and LPSH which has been completed by Ofsted has not been presented in the public domain. There has never been a strong emphasis on external research throughout the NPQH development process which might have informed practice. However, the review in 2000 was very thorough and based on a full consultation. Throughout the five years' development of the NPQH there have been continuing discussions about the academic credibility of the NPQH and how it can and should count towards a Master's degree. In Scotland the academic credibility was built into the design process, so that there are more profound links with international developments which have focused on accreditation using academic qualifications. The practical and the professional were successfully aligned with this.

USA

The Interstate School Leaders Licensure Consortium Standards (ISLLC), adopted by the full consortium of 24 states in 1996 (Council of Chief State School Officers 1 1996, see http://www.ccsso/standards-assessments.html)

are the most widely recognised Standards in the USA, equivalent to the National Standards for Headteachers. That 24 states were involved in this development ensured that there was intellectual and academic challenge to the emergent proposals. The Standards were based on research about the linkages between educational leadership and productive schools, and significant trends in society and education and their implications for emerging views of leadership. They were deliberately designed to be compatible with the National Council for the Accreditation of Teacher Education (NCATE) *Curriculum Guidelines* for school administration, as well as major national reports on reinventing leadership for tomorrow's schools. The Standards recognise that leadership is a complex task, and acknowledge that effective leaders have unique and different beliefs and act differently from the norm. However, all focus fully but distinctively on learning and teaching and school improvement.

The principal preparation programmes in the USA have benefited from the academic critique which has not been evident in England. This is partly because, in the USA, school leadership training developed in the late nineteenth century. By 1947 the National Conference of Professors of Educational Administration (NCPEA) was formed as the first major organisation which attempted to influence national policy for school leadership training. By 1956 the University Council for Educational Administration (UCEA), the dominant force for the next 20 years, was established. Brundrett (2001) explores 'the tumult in attitudes to school leadership preparation programmes' in England and the USA. He notes that in the USA every element of principal training has been subjected to 'devastating attacks' with 'harsh critiques' of recruitment procedures, content, instructional techniques, the quality of the university faculty and standards of performance. These problems may have influenced the TTA in England in establishing the centralised process described above. However, this process in England has lost the benefits from the intricate interrelationships between state and national governments, university academics and industrial organisations which has resulted in the USA in the creation of new forums for discussion and varied responses to developments.

It would seem that in developing the National Standards for Headteachers and the NPQH in England it was positively determined not to include the universities and the research community in the process. Southworth, who explored primary school leadership in England (Southworth 1999), has now moved to the NCSL with responsibility for research. It may well be that a more intellectual and academic challenge might be forthcoming to inform headteacher professional growth in future. However, though there is still considerable criticism of many of the programmes in the USA because they are insufficiently related to practice, there is research evidence which can inform the debate. This is not yet the case in England.

In the USA, the shift to the post-industrial society, the advance of the global marketplace, the increased reliance on technology and market-based solutions to social needs posed new challenges for school leaders. Schooling was perceived to be changing in three ways (CCSSO 1 1996). There was a renewed struggle to refine learning and teaching to challenge and engage all youngsters more successfully. Educators were rethinking and challenging long-prevailing views about knowledge, intelligence, assessment and instruction. Secondly, community-focused and caring-centred conceptions of schooling were competing for legitimacy with more established notions of schools as hierarchies and bureaucracies. Thirdly, external stakeholders – parents, community leaders and, because this is the USA, the corporate sector – were playing increasingly enhanced roles in education. The ISLLC Standards, focusing on students and their success, emerged from a much more challenging and wider debate than occurred in England because the Chief State School Officers and universities had been interacting for many years before the ISLLC Standards were defined. The emphases are also different, in part, because of the different assessment process.

The ISLLC Standards

The ISLLC Standards are shown in Table 11.1.

For each of these standards there are associated knowledge, dispositions and performances.

The assessment is through a six-hour examination organised into two two-hour modules and two one-hour modules. All the exercises require the candidate to write responses.

Module I – Evaluation of Actions I (I hour)

Twelve short vignettes are presented of situations a principal might encounter and be required to respond to. A focused question on each asks what the principal might do next, what factors should be considered in responding, how the principal might handle the situation or dilemma, and what the potential consequences are. The answers required specific detail and a rationale.

Module II – Synthesis of Information and Problem-Solving (2 hours)

The assessment consists of two one-hour case studies anchored in issues of teaching and learning. Candidates are presented with two sets of several documents and given a short scenario describing a school and its community. Candidates are required to examine all documents and select from

Table 11.1 The ISLLC Standards

Standard 1 A school administrator is an educational leader who promotes the success of all students by facilitating the development, articulation, implementation, and stewardship of a vision of learning that is shared and supported by the school community

Standard 2 A school administrator is an educational leader who promotes the success of all students by advocating, nurturing, and sustaining a school culture and instructional programme conducive to student learning and staff professional growth

Standard 3 A school administrator is an educational leader who promotes the success of all students by ensuring management of the organisation, operations, and resources for a safe, efficient, and effective learning environment

Standard 4 A school administrator is an educational leader who promotes the success of all students by collaborating with families and community members, responding to diverse community interests and needs, and mobilising community resources

Standard 5 A school administrator is an educational leader who promotes the success of all students by acting with integrity, fairness, and in an ethical manner

Standard 6 A school administrator is an educational leader who promotes the success of all students by understanding, responding to, and influencing the larger political, social, economic, legal and cultural context

these documents relevant information to answer questions that pose complex problems and require the candidate to propose courses of action to address the problems.

Module III – Analysis of Information and Decision-Making (2 hours)

Candidates are presented with eight documents encountered by principals. At least six of the eight refer to issues involving teaching and learning. Candidates respond to a series of questions. Documents may include assessment data, parts of the school improvement plan, budget information, schedules (timetable), resource allocation documents, staff evaluations and curriculum information. Questions might include:

- What is the important issue in the data in this document?
- What other information would you need to assess the information presented in the documents?
- What steps would you take with your staff to address the issues raised by the data presented in the document?

Module IV – Evaluation of Actions 2 (1 hour)

Here there are six longer vignettes. Each presents a dilemma based on learning and teaching issues. The candidate is asked a focused analytical question, or two such questions. The response requires the candidate to balance competing claims for resources, prioritise actions, articulate the instructional issues raised by the situation, explain instructional and curricular strategies appropriate in responding to the situation, and discuss the instructional implications of a situation.

Summary

The ISLLC Standards have been subjected to a much more rigorous intellectual challenge, research and public debate because they are used, in at least 40 states, for licensure, assessment, induction, preparation, programme approval and continuing professional development (Murphy, *et al.* 1999). Arguably the National Standards for Headteachers remain essentially in the original format as presented for consultation by the Teacher Training Agency. The final assessment of NPQM in England, however, is not so heavily focused on written responses which presents challenges for ensuring equity through moderation. This just could not be achieved across such a large country as the USA. However the school-based and final assessments in England do not assess against all parts of the National Standards.

Issues for the future

The National Standards for Headteachers in England have met the needs of the NPQH, HEADLAMP and the selection of headteachers reasonably well over the last five years. Now that the NPQH has been re-developed so successfully and a new Headteachers' Induction Programme (HIP) launched (in September 2003), it is time to re-examine the National Standards for Headteachers to align them with LPSH and developments in other countries. There is increasing research evidence about leadership which could inform this debate, though the NCSL will need particularly to consider approaches which challenge their current orthodoxies if the Standards are to have wider acceptability. The six ISLLC Standards, for example, provide a more rational model for assessment. It will be important to engage with those who challenge the current format and models associated with the leadership framework and indeed the understanding of leaders and leadership which the College espouses. It will be important not to incorporate these, but to sustain the creativity that comes from encouraging alternative approaches. This process will be much more complex than the early consultation process, but it is important, as the NCSL develops a wider suite of programmes to meet the needs of leaders in schools of the future, to explore more widely the relationship between NPQH, HIP and LPSH and not to make this too rigid. The new National Standards will need to encourage different approaches, for example the capacity publicly to challenge and interrogate government priorities.

Working on behalf of the Department for Education and Skills (DfES), the NCSL began the consultation process for the revised National Standards for Headteachers during 2003. It is expected that the revised Standards will take effect from September 2004.

References and further reading

Bollington, R. (1997) 'The NPQH explained in depth,' *Professional Development Today* 1(1): 81–87.

Brundrett, M. (1999) 'The National Professional Qualification for Headship: perceptions of the providers of taught higher degrees in educational management in England and Wales,' *School Leadership & Management* 19(4): 497–510.

Brundrett, M. (2001) 'The development of school leadership programmes in England and the USA: a comparative analysis,' *Educational Management and Administration* 29(2): 229–245.

Collarbone, P. (2000a) 'Developing a model for the NPQH,' *Professional Development Today* 3(3): 83–90.

Collarbone, P. (2000b) *Aspirant Heads, Managing Schools Today*, 9(9), June/July, pp. 28–32.

Collarbone, P. (2001a) The National Professional Qualification for Headship – Presentation to Centre Managers, Nottingham (unpublished).

Collarbone, P. (2001b) *Leadership Programme for Serving Headteachers: a Review*, London: National College for School Leadership.

Council of Chief State School Officers (1) (1996) *Interstate School Leaders' Licensure Consortium: Standards for School Leaders*, Washington, D.C.: State Education Assessment Center.

Council of Chief State School Officers (2) (1996) *Principals' Licensure Assessment*, Washington, D.C.: Education Testing Service.

Garrett, V. and McGeachie, B. (1999) 'Preparation for headship? The role of the deputy head in the primary school,' *School Leadership & Management* 19(1): February, 67–81.

Johnson, H. and Castelli, M. (1998) The NPQH and Catholic Heads, *Management in Education* 12(2): 10–11.

Male, T. (2000) 'Is the National Professional Qualification for Headship making a difference?', *School Leadership & Management* 21(4): November, pp. 463–477.

Murphy, J., Yff, J. and Shipman, N. (1999) 'Implementation of the Interstate School Leaders Licensure Consortium Standards,' Paper presented at the AERA Annual Meeting, Montreal, April.

National College for School Leadership (2002) Leadership Development Framework Pack, London: NCSL.

Salmon, G. (2000) *E-Moderating: The Key to Teaching and Learning Online*, London: Kogan Page.

Scottish Qualification for Headship (1998) The Standard for Headship in Scotland. Available at www.scotland.gov.uk/education/sqh.

Shipton, J. and Male, T. (1998) 'Deputy headteachers and the NPQH,' *Management in Education* 12(3): 16–17.

Southworth, G. (1999) 'Primary school leadership in England: policy, practice and theory,' *School Leadership & Management* 19(1): February, 49–66.

Teacher Training Agency (1997) National Professional Qualification for Headship, Information for applicants, London: TTA.

Part 4

Looking to the future

Chapter 12

Towards a genuine professional standards framework for teachers

Emma Westcott

Introduction

One of my first jobs after graduation involved me in the validation and review of programmes of study in a university. I learned a great deal about what new entrants to fields as diverse as architecture and nursing had to know and be able to do in order to gain entry to their chosen profession. I was struck by the complex and subtle processes by which the requirements of initial professional education were agreed.

The process generally involved negotiation and debate between the higher education institution (HEI) and the professional body. Professional bodies recognised that the HEI was an autonomous entity responsible for specifying a course of higher study that was coherent, and of an appropriate level for the academic award it attracted. The professional bodies respected the involvement of higher education, which safeguarded standards of attainment and confirmed the complexity of a profession that required graduate entrants. HEIs understood that while they were best placed to assure academic coherence and standards, they may not have an up-to-date insight into the changing needs of new entrants in the professional field. They also understood that the professional body had a particular and distinctive stake in the professional competence of new entrants, because they would through registration be granted a licence to practise in their field. The professional body has an ongoing interest in registrants' professionalism through regulation and, in many cases, assessment against further professional standards and expectations.

The discourse of the two parties was based on mutual respect, although it was characterised by occasional frustrations about how to accommodate each other's differing needs within the confines of a time- and resource-limited programme. Some professional bodies would take a formal role in the accreditation of the HEI or the programme – the British Psychological Society, for example, participated in validation panels for psychology programmes. Others would set out criteria that must be addressed by the programme if it was to incorporate or count towards a professional entry qualification.

The very first validation event I experienced concerned an undergraduate education programme. (This preceded the establishment of the Teacher Training Agency, the government body which would later accredit providers of programmes bearing teaching qualifications, on behalf of the Secretary of State.) I was struck by the teaching profession's absence from the process, in stark contrast with other professions. When I became aware of and involved in the campaign for a professional body that might assume this role – the General Teaching Council for England – I learned that such a body had existed in Scotland since 1966 and accredited programmes leading to the award of Qualified Teacher Status (QTS). In other words, Scottish teachers were trusted to set and uphold appropriate professional standards where their colleagues south of the border were not. The English GTC has to date been given the responsibilities of a profession but not the rights – it regulates the profession by upholding professional standards, but it does not set those standards. The Secretary of State sets standards for the award of Qualified Teacher Status. The Scottish GTC is now exploring its potential role in the professional standards framework beyond entry standards, through the notion of the chartered teacher.

My contention is that we do not have a professional standards framework for teachers in England. The teaching profession has not had the opportunity to set out the knowledge, understanding, skills and commitments required of new teachers, or of experienced teachers at various critical stages of their professional development. In the space available I will delineate some of the limitations of what we currently have by way of teaching standards, and consider what might be viewed as the attributes of a genuine and robust professional standards framework for teaching.

The Secretary of State for Education and Skills has asked the General Teaching Council for its advice on the future development of professional standards, but at the time of writing this work was at a very early stage. What follows is therefore necessarily speculative, although it does draw on some of the related views already expressed by the Council.

The Teachers' Standards Framework

The Department for Education and Skills issued a fold-out document in 2001 with the title 'Teachers' Standards Framework' (DfES 2001a). A working group had been established by the DfES to inform a project to bring together all of the existing standards in a user-friendly format.

This was a valuable exercise in its own right, as the existing Standards are a confused and confusing bunch. Some are very familiar to teachers, others would barely have registered with them. Some relate to professional roles; others relate to professional phases. Some have questioned the coherence of the phase standards – whether, for example, enough progression is implied between sequential phase standards. Some are mandatory;

others are voluntary. Some are prerequisites for progression to a new role, or linked to access to better rewards; others are not.

This diversity is not *necessarily* problematic, but it does reflect the mixed provenance and purpose of standards created at different times, and even at the behest of different governments.

The GTC was involved in the working group that oversaw the development of the TSF, and its particular stake in its evolution over time is recognised in the text:

> The General Teaching Council, as the self-regulating professional body, will have an advisory role on the future development of professional standards.

> (DfES 2001a)

There are some inevitable limitations to the TSF, and these are detailed below.

Limitations of the existing framework

Whose standards?

From the perspective of the professional body for teaching, a severe limitation of the framework is that it has not been developed by teachers, for teachers. When teachers become collectively engaged in analysing their professional practice in order to distil fine judgements about levels and spheres of expertise, they are engaged in professional learning. They are also demonstrating their ownership of professional standards of teaching – as the Government has exhorted the profession in the Green Paper 'Teachers: Meeting the Challenge of Change' (1998: 1) and in the White Paper 'Schools: Building on Success' (2001b: 65). The process of reviewing one's own and colleagues' practice against standards is also a rich source of professional learning.

The professional definition and application of standards are activities that contribute to teachers' capacity and opportunity to develop ways of articulating and sharing perceptions of professional practice. It is increasingly important that members of the profession are effective teachers, *and* able to describe, and interrogate accounts of, teaching practice. This ability is needed for performance management, peer mentoring, and contributing to the development of new and experienced colleagues.

Michael Eraut (1994: 14) has suggested that teachers' professional status and standing would be enhanced by the development of a more effective language of pedagogy. He suggests that other recognised professions are more accomplished at articulating the complexity of their spheres of expertise to lay audiences, thus enhancing their professional standing.

That teachers do not set their own professional standards cannot but imply a lack of trust in the professionalism of teachers. That the Secretary of State presides over standards for teaching is also compromising. It means that professional standards can be subject to fairly frequent change. The new QTS Standards, introduced in Autumn 1998, were changed in Autumn 2002. The first National Induction Standards were introduced in 1999 and were revised in 2003. Our notions of what makes an effective new teacher will, of course, change over time, but it is difficult to believe that they change substantially every three or four years.

What does change is the political climate within which teaching takes place. One administration is squeamish about addressing race equality explicitly, and Standards make scant reference to the knowledge and awareness teachers need to raise ethnic minority pupil achievement. The next government wants to demonstrate its commitment to race equality in the wake of a high-profile racist murder, and the Standards make a number of references to ethnic minority pupils. As a result, the Standards can have a modish feel to them. For example, the QTS Standards do not capture the enduring characteristics of effective new primary teachers, such as competence in developing pupils' literacy and numeracy, but refer instead to familiarity with the 'frameworks, methods and expectations set out in the National Literacy and Numeracy Strategies' (DfES/TTA 2002). Standards that are so 'of the moment' are liable to have a limited shelf-life. These strategies have now been rebranded as the National Primary Strategy. The consequence of constant changes is that most teachers could not describe with confidence the prevailing entry standards for their own profession.

The political context of the Standards can have an adverse impact on teachers' perceptions of their credibility and worth. The Threshold Standard is regarded by many teachers as a political 'quick fix' relating to pay: even its name refers to a pay scale rather than a professional milestone. It is associated with government pronouncements that public sector reform (or 'modernisation') will be predicated on the principle of 'something for something' – increases in pay are linked explicitly to new professional undertakings and implicitly to cultural change. Headteachers' recommendations regarding threshold have been subject to scrutiny by DfES appointed advisers. Many schools will have found a way of managing the threshold assessment so that it does provide an opportunity to celebrate and affirm professional attainment, but many teachers also feel resentful of it.

Contrast this model with work underway in Australia to identify professionally derived Standards relating to the practice of the experienced and expert teacher. One subset of the profession, science teachers, has identified what it has termed 'National Professional Standards for Highly Accomplished Teachers of Science' – even the nomenclature helps to reinforce professional esteem. The Australian Science Teachers Association and the National Science Standards Committee have enabled many teachers to be involved in the formulation of Standards relating to professional knowledge, practice and attributes over a sustained period of time. Further professional learning occurs when the Standards are implemented by teachers themselves.

The Standards are contextualised in a manner likely to answer teachers' legitimate questions about their use and ultimate purpose. The publication includes a vision for the teaching of science in Australian schools. The document is also clear and authoritative about the values underpinning the creation of professional standards for teaching. Standards are variously described as:

> a means by which the profession can provide professional leadership concerning issues of quality in teaching and learning
>
> [a means by which] the profession can assume greater responsibility for the purpose and nature of professional development of its members
>
> a bridge between research and practice
>
> [giving] the profession a stronger role in the definition of teachers' work.
>
> (ASTA/NSSC 2002: 7)

This example demonstrates that there are effective alternatives to government-generated Standards that are no less rigorous and attract greater support from the profession, having greater resonance. The use of such Standards is not only a means of identifying effective professional practice; it is a source of professional learning in its own right – an important facet of self-regulation alongside the task of taking action when standards of practice are breached.

A genuine Framework of Standards?

Leaving aside the provenance of the existing Standards for teaching, let us consider the conceptual basis of the DfES' Teachers' Standards Framework. It is more of a ladder than a framework, as 'framework' implies a structure that facilitates horizontal as well as vertical movement. The careers of most teachers do not follow the path mapped out by the TSF. Significant professional roles, such as head of year or head of phase, are absent. Teachers derive professional sustenance from pursuing areas of particular expertise – for example, in working with pupils for whom English is an additional language, or through involvement in an

Education Business Partnership. When working within an area of specialism, teachers are often functioning at a higher level than their formal position – for example, classroom teacher or head of department – might suggest. A professional standards framework should provide a means of recognising and, potentially, accrediting this higher level of work on the basis of evidence.

The TSF does not provide a framework within which teachers might broaden or deepen their knowledge and skill in an area of practice. Ten areas of practice are identified and references to those areas are mapped where they occur in each of the existing Standards. One of these areas relates to professional development. Teachers are exhorted to take responsibility for their own professional development as NQTs, new teachers, teachers at threshold, Subject Leaders, SENCOs and Headteachers – although inexplicably not as Advanced Skills Teachers. Virtually the same words are used to express this Standard throughout, and there is no sense in which this competence might look different as one moves from being a trained but inexperienced teacher to one having experience and expertise. The same is true of references to keeping up to date with relevant research.

Arguably, a framework of professional standards needs to relate to roles and functions as much as phases and posts in order to capture the hybrid nature of many teachers' careers and responsibilities. It needs to capture what effective teaching looks like in relation to an aspect of professional practice – such as working with parents – at different levels of experience and proficiency.

These are important considerations for teachers, who will want to know the tangible benefits of such a framework for their professional and career development. I suspect that despite the subtitle 'helping you develop', many teachers would be unclear about the value added by the TSF in its current form.

Teaching or teachers?

The Teachers' Standards Framework issued by the DfES begins with qualified teacher status and ends with headship. It has come into being at a time when a growing proportion of those directly involved in teaching and learning do not possess QTS, with the increase in the use of teaching assistants and unqualified teachers, and the proliferation of other learning-related roles such as that of the learning mentor. There is also a substantial professional cadre of people with QTS in jobs related to teaching and learning beyond the school.

Thought might usefully be given to the development of a standards framework for *teaching*, with QTS at its core but offering opportunities for others to work towards QTS, or to demonstrate effectiveness in aspects of teaching practice at a level 'below' QTS. Many of the other adults in schools directly involved in teaching will, like teachers themselves, be functioning at different levels depending on their roles. One might expect an experienced learning support assistant to know less about curriculum and assessment than an NQT but more about different types of special needs, for example. A standards framework for teaching should be able to capture the varied nature of teaching work and provide practitioners with ideas for 'next steps' in terms of development at a number of levels.

At the moment most of the traffic in the QTS labour market is one way – out of teaching and into what might be called 'professions allied to teaching'. These might be defined as those that draw members from the teaching profession and contribute to standards of teaching, such as teacher educators, advisers and inspectors, and some roles associated with examining and curriculum development. Some of those 'allied professions' are independently developing ideas about their own professional standards – advisers are one such group. If a future standards framework for teaching could integrate Standards for Teaching with relevant Standards for Professions allied to teaching, it might facilitate two-way traffic between the two, thus improving standards, retention and motivation across the sector.

Professional expectations and entitlements

The Teachers' Standards Framework as it stands is concerned with the expectations placed upon teachers at various stages in their careers. It does not address how they might be met. One of the early products of the General Teaching Council has been a Teacher's Professional *Learning* Framework (PLF) designed to complement a standards framework, such that teachers can put together the standards expected of them with the means of enhancing their practice and meeting those standards.

There may be merit in conceiving a professional standards framework that sets out expectations of teaching practice *and* gives an indication of means by which teachers can meet those expectations.

Conclusions

The DfES is to be commended for recognising the need for a professional standards framework for teaching, and acknowledging that its Teachers' Standards Framework is a 'first step' in an evolving process. If such a framework is to make a contribution to developing effective practice, rather than merely describing it, teachers need to own and shape the standards by which they will interrogate and evaluate their own practice, and that of colleagues. The standards themselves need to resonate with teachers' own sense of what good teaching looks and feels like, and using the standards must bring tangible benefits to teachers, in terms of professional and career development.

Teachers need to experience a better balance of rights and responsibilities in their professional lives. With the establishment of the General Teaching Council, teachers have accepted responsibility for safeguarding standards of practice in the public interest. The GTC's composition reflects the community of interest in teaching standards, including parents, governors, employers and teacher educators – a robust safeguard against 'producer capure'. They should now have the right to set the professional standards they uphold when they act on breaches of conduct and competence on the part of their peers. Teachers have high professional expectations, and will set standards for teaching no less challenging than anything that might be derived in Whitehall. The Secretary of State could demonstrate faith in the professionalism of teachers by entrusting them with this important task.

References and further reading

Australian Science Teachers Association/National Science Standards Committee (2002) *National Professional Standards for Highly Accomplished Teachers of Science*, Canberra: ASTA.

DfEE (1998) Green Paper, 'Teachers: Meeting the Challenge of Change', London: DfEE.

DfES (2001a) *Teachers' Standards Framework*, London: DfES.

DfES (2001b) White Paper, 'Schools: Building on Success', London: DfES.

DfES/TTA (2002) *Qualifying to Teach*, London: TTA.

Eraut, M. (1994) *Developing Professional Knowledge and Competence*, London: Falmer Press.

General Teaching Council for England (2003) *Professional Learning Framework*, London: GTCE.

Chapter 13

Meeting future needs

Howard Green

Introduction

The development of the National Standards for teachers and school leaders in England has been an essential component of the drive for educational reform and system-wide improvement. It has made a key contribution to the framework of standards and accountability within which teachers and school leaders are now being encouraged to demonstrate 'informed professionalism' and be innovative in their schools to help secure the next stage of reform. However, will the National Standards be fit for this purpose? In this final chapter, important issues will be drawn from the previous chapters to provide responses to five questions:

1   What have been the benefits of having National Standards?
2   Do the National Standards say it all?
3   Are the National Standards sufficiently 'futures-orientated'?
4   What are the priorities for the review of existing National Standards?
5   What are the priorities for new sets of National Standards?

What have been the benefits of having National Standards?

The National Standards in England have had several positive effects, not least in providing practical, school-based benefits for busy teachers and school leaders. The application of the Standards described in the previous chapters illustrates some of these benefits:

*   It has helped teachers and school leaders to manage change and answer the question, 'what do I need to be able to do to be more effective in my role?'
*   It has provided evidence for teachers and school leaders to celebrate their achievements, i.e. 'I am doing that well or very well'
*   It has contributed to job satisfaction, i.e. 'This is what I should be doing and I am!'

- It has helped school leaders to identify the support teachers need, i.e. 'I should be doing this, I want to do it, but I need training and support to develop'
- It has focused professional development on the real needs of individuals and specific groups, i.e. if the individual teacher, the line-manager and/or the team undertake a review against Standards prior to a programme of professional development, the programme itself can be targeted specifically at the needs of the individual or the group
- It has enabled participants (of professional development) and head-teachers to evaluate the impact of training and development activities using Standards as a more precise criterion for evaluation and subsequent action
- It has allowed for a growing sense of progression in teaching, i.e. entry to the profession and induction, followed by opportunities to move on past the pay threshold or to Advanced Skills Teacher status and then to various formal leadership roles
- It has created in many teachers a more reflective way of working and an increased commitment to further adult learning
- It has helped with recruitment and retention by signalling that, within the teaching profession, there is progression and scope for challenge and support, i.e. this is a profession that knows what it is doing and what it is aiming for.

The benefit of the Standards being 'National Standards' has been the availability of a common language for discourse about teaching and school leadership and associated training and development, even if the language is not yet as consistent or coherent as it might be. This has resulted in greater clarity about the tasks of teaching, the relationship between teaching and learning, and the differences between less effective, effective and highly effective teaching. There has been a parallel development in the understanding of school leadership and management. The impact of the Standards in these areas has been complemented by the growing evidence base from Ofsted inspections. This has been described in Chapter 2, and is available from the wide range of Ofsted publications, including the annual report of the Chief Inspector of Schools and the recent report on leadership and management (Ofsted 2003).

Do the National Standards say it all?

Joseph Whitworth contributed to the nineteenth century efforts to set standards for the manufacturing industry by attempting to define the 'standard flat surface' – a fascinating challenge, but considerably less daunting than trying to define the qualities of an 'effective' or 'highly effective' teacher or school leader. No set of standards can finally sum up the training and development needs of human beings undertaking complex tasks like teaching or school leadership.

Although this may seem obvious, it does help to explain some of the tensions behind any attempt to analyse and describe human activities. Hugh Lawlor makes reference to the challenges to 'competency-based' models in the early days of the National Standards for teachers and school leaders (Chapter 2). David Brunton provides an interesting analysis of the differences between competencies, personal characteristics and professional capabilities: all attempts to describe aspects of a teacher's work. He also identifies the contrast between standards designed for a basic 'entry level' of performance, e.g. QTS and Headteacher, and those designed for high performance, e.g. Threshold, AST and Fast Track (Chapter 8).

Progress has been made in at least acknowledging, if not dealing with, the difficulties described in the previous paragraphs. For example, the work by the Hay Group, the focus of Chapter 3, has provided deeper insights into the processes of effective and highly effective teaching and school leadership. This has extended earlier work that focused mainly on the knowledge, understanding and skills required for these roles.

Hay's studies have been given further impetus by widespread interest in the work of people like Daniel Goleman (1998) on emotional intelligence and Danah Zohar and Ian Marshall (2000) on spiritual intelligence. The specific training and development needs of teachers and school leaders in faith-based schools has still not been addressed through National Standards. Michael Fullan (2001) has also been writing persuasively about the understanding and the qualities required for the leadership of effective schools in times of rapid change. The context within which teachers and school leaders now work demands an ability to cope with change, and must inform the processes of devising, applying and reviewing sets of National Standards. These insights into the nature of human motivation and the factors influencing behaviour confirm that National Standards, or anything like them, should never be accepted as 'saying it all'. Kenneth Leithwood and Rosanne Steinbach (2003) propose regular cycles for the review and modification of Standards, perhaps every five to seven years.

Alongside the emerging evidence described above, the DfES is now emphasising the importance of strategies for sustained improvement and the transition from good to great schools – the transformational agenda. It is within this context that some of the above studies have particular relevance, as they point to the key differences between effective and highly effective people in key roles like classroom teacher, middle leader and headteacher. However, a major task remains fully to integrate these people, process and values-based dimensions of various professional roles into the relevant sets of National Standards and then train, develop and assess them appropriately.

There has been a concern, coming mainly from higher education and expressed in this book by Harry Tomlinson (Chapter 11), that the National Standards and associated training and development programmes have not included a sufficient focus on adult learning through reflection on research about highly effective classroom practice and school leadership. For example, in England the National Standards for Headteachers, the National Professional Qualification for Headship and the Leadership Programme for Serving Headteachers were developed by the Teacher Training Agency and not within the context of higher education. It is possible that the work of the National College for School Leadership, now with responsibility for the national headship programmes and also with a commitment to research, will help to correct any imbalances that may have existed and rebuild the bridges with higher education. As evidence that this shift may be happening, the development by NCSL of the National Programme for Subject Leaders (Leading from the Middle) has been undertaken by leadership centres located at two university education departments.

It has also been suggested that the use of Standards promotes a 'deficit' model of training and development, telling us what people *cannot* do. However, Standards do not have to be viewed in this way. They can be seen as an opportunity for teachers, team leaders and school leaders to identify and affirm what has been achieved and to provide a more specific focus for further professional development.

Are the National Standards sufficiently 'futures-orientated'?

There is a danger that, in seeking to define the role expectations and benchmarks for performance for any occupational group, the scope will be limited to the experience and needs of the present (or, at worst, the past) rather than the future. One way round this problem is to design sets of National Standards to be as generic, and therefore timeless, as possible. Then 'futures-orientated' case studies can be created for training and development based on the Standards. Also, evidence that demonstrates 'futures' thinking could be expected from applicants when Standards are being used as the basis for a selection process, e.g. Threshold, Advanced Skills Teacher, NPQH assessment and Fast Track.

In addition, the strategic leadership component of relevant Standards, e.g. for Subject Leader and Headteacher, might make explicit reference to 'futures' thinking and the long-term dimension of school development planning. Currently they only do this by implication. The impact of national policy initiatives (like the Literacy, Numeracy and Key Stage 3 Strategies) on the curriculum, pedagogy and school leadership also need to be considered. They could also be used to provide appropriate material for training and development, particularly in programmes based on the leadership Standards.

More significantly, there have been several substantial shifts in the expectations of schools, teachers and headteachers emerging from recent government policies. These include, for example:

- awareness and application of the growing evidence base about effective learning and teaching, school improvement and effectiveness and leadership;
- developing the capacity within schools for self-generated and sustained improvement based on the school as a learning community (for children, young people and adults) and distributed leadership – the dawn of the era of 'informed professionalism';
- new arrangements for the inspection of schools by Ofsted, with less frequent and 'lighter touch' inspections for those that have satisfactory or better levels of performance, which will mean that schools must have effective approaches to self-evaluation in place;
- reform of the workforce so that headteachers and subject leaders have time to lead as well as manage; teachers have more time to observe each other at work, evaluate classroom practice, plan together and try new approaches to teaching and learning; and support staff, particularly teaching assistants, can take on extended roles in the classroom;
- getting the balance right between challenge and support to raise the standards of performance of individuals, teams and the whole school;
- collaborative work, rather than competitive relationships, between schools in order to create opportunities for sharing good practice, facing challenges together and learning from wider experience, e.g. NCSL's Networked Learning Communities, collaborative partnerships between schools for use of the DfES's Leadership Incentive Grant (LIG).

These changes, all of which envisage different ways of working in the future, are likely to create pressure for the review of most sets of National Standards. Each review should also be set within the context of international experience. It is interesting to note, in this context, that the proposed revisions to the National Standards for Headteachers include two new subheadings: Creating the Future and Community through Collaboration.

What are the priorities for the review of existing National Standards?

The previous sections have highlighted a significant number of issues that would justify a systematic review of all the National Standards. To these should be added the need to reconsider the status of the standards deemed to be 'advisory' rather than 'statutory', and to create greater coherence between the different sets of standards. The standards that are 'advisory' may not be taken as seriously and, although it is possible to identify common threads running through the different standards, there is ample evidence of inconsistency in the details.

The Standards for Qualified Teacher Status and Induction were both reviewed between 2001 and 2003. As a result, the new QTS Standards (now called 'Qualifying to Teach Standards') may have removed the need for separate Standards for SEN Specialist Teachers.

The National Standards for Headteachers are being reviewed by the National College for School Leadership, with new Standards likely to take effect from September 2004. This review can draw from the international experience described by Harry Tomlinson (Chapter 11) and the broader perspective provided by contributors to the recent book edited by Philip Hallinger (2003). Of particular interest are the contrasting chapters by Murphy and Shipman (2003) on developing standards for school leadership development in the USA, and by Leithwood and Steinbach (2003) on the need to create a second generation of school leadership standards.

For teachers, there is a need to look at the relationship between the Standards for Threshold and Advanced Skills Teacher. There are significant differences between them, and the potential for confusion, in the use of words like 'consistent', 'effective' and 'excellent'.

For middle leaders, the Standards for Subject Leader and Special Educational Needs Co-ordinator will also need to be reviewed, considering the changing expectations and responsibilities of these roles and also the wider range of 'middle leader' roles in schools, e.g. 'pastoral leader' and 'Key Stage leader'.

Reviewing National Standards in England is becoming an increasingly complex process as additional government agencies have a legitimate part to play in the reviews. For example, the Teacher Training Agency, the General Teaching Council (England) and the National College for School Leadership would expect to be formally involved in reviews of the National Standards, working with the Department for Education & Skills and the Office for Standards in Education. It is important to note that, in Chapter 12, Emma Westcott proposes a more fundamental teacher-led review of all the Standards. Any review process must, of course, include consultation with a wide range of other organisations, including professional bodies like the teacher unions, subject associations, local education authorities and governor associations. However, this is not the same as a teacher-led review.

The Standards are also providing the framework for a growing number of national training and development programmes, with the result that any changes to them will have implications for programme materials and trainer retraining. For all these reasons, the review of National Standards cannot be entered into lightly and is likely to proceed by gradual adaptation rather than more fundamental change. Certainly, each review process should help to reduce the overlap and duplication between different sets of Standards.

What are the priorities for new sets of National Standards?

Two new sets of National Standards are currently being developed in England for use by the education profession. As part of the arrangements for the reform of the school workforce and tackling the issue of teacher workload, the DfES is developing Standards for Higher Level Teaching Assistants. David Miliband (2003), the Minister for School Standards, has said:

> The new high level teaching assistants will have a professional standards framework and training which will be developed by the Teacher Training Agency and linked to relevant modules for Qualified Teacher Status. It will provide a foundation from which many high level teaching assistants could progress, in time, to become qualified teachers.

The Standards for Higher Level Teaching Assistants should be very helpful not only for defining their role and providing a framework for training and development, but also by raising the status of support staff in schools and creating a new pathway into teaching. These Standards are being developed for the DfES by the TTA and a pilot training programme based on them will be piloted during 2004.

The second new set of Standards is for School Improvement Professionals, who are employed by LEAs and usually work with groups of schools. These Standards are being developed by the local authorities themselves.

Is there a need for any other Standards? Gaps can be identified; for example, there are no nationally accepted standards in England for senior school administrators (or bursars), and reference has already been made to the wider roles of middle leaders in schools, beyond subject leadership. It has also been suggested that there should be formal recognition of other differences between schools by appropriate adaptation of the relevant sets of National Standards, for example, the role of headteacher in small primary, special or church schools. The best way ahead in these situations may be to retain a generic set of National Standards but to allow specific interpretations of them to support the more precisely targeted provision of training and development.

Conclusion

The development of the National Standards for teachers and school leaders in England, and now the first sets of Standards for school support staff and school improvement professionals, has occurred within the wider context of similar work in other professions and across the public and private sectors of employment. Much has been achieved, and the Standards now have many positive applications. Practical, and more fundamental, concerns about the development and application of professional standards for schools in England have been raised and are being addressed. The systematic review of the Standards has been underway since 2001 and is continuing. They are not and never will be 'tablets of stone'.

Although questions remain about the future of the Standards, particularly their degree of ownership by the teaching profession their existence helps to create the framework of discipline and accountability within which the creativity of individual teachers, leaders and schools can be encouraged to flourish for the sake of further improvement. Jim Collins (2001), in his account of the ways in which good organisations can become great, describes the 'culture of discipline' that is one of their characteristics:

> A culture of discipline involves a duality. On the one hand, it requires people who adhere to a coherent system; yet, on the other hand, it gives people freedom and responsibility within the framework of that system.

In contributing to that culture of discipline for the education service in England, the application of the National Standards must avoid the worst excesses of sterile lists of 'to do' statements and tick-boxes for assessing performance. Certainly the English Standards need much greater coherence. All sets of Standards must also actively promote the innovation and risk-taking that will be needed by autonomous schools and informed professionals to secure the next stage of school improvement. The Standards should be used increasingly as a means to an end: that is, by providing the foundations that will enable teachers, leaders and key support staff to use their own professionalism and creativity to have an enhanced impact on standards in classrooms. National Standards should exist primarily to empower, not to prescribe or constrain, and to point the way towards excellence.

References and further reading

Collins, J. (2001) *Good to Great*, London: Random House Business Books.
Fullan, M. (2001) *Leading in a Culture of Change*, San Francisco: Jossey Bass.
Goleman, D. (1998) *Working with Emotional Intelligence*, London: Bloomsbury.

Hallinger, P. (ed.) (2003) *Reshaping the Landscape of School Leadership Development*, Lisse: Swets & Zeitlinger.

Leithwood, K. and Steinbach, R. (2003) 'Toward a second generation of school leadership Standards', in Hallinger, P. (ed.) *Reshaping the Landscape of School Leadership Development*, Lisse: Swets and Zeitlinger, pp. 257–272.

Miliband, D. (2003) quoted on the Department for Education & Skills website at www.dfes.gov.uk.

Murphy, J. and Shipman, N. (2003) 'Developing Standards for school leadership development: a process and rationale', in Hallinger, P. (ed.) *Reshaping the Landscape of School Leadership Development*, Lisse: Swets and Zeitlinger, pp. 69–83.

Ofsted (2003) *Leadership and Management: What Inspection Tells Us*, London: Ofsted Publications Centre.

Zohar, D. and Marshall, I. (2000) *Spiritual Intelligence: the Ultimate Intelligence*, London: Bloomsbury.

Index